Eating Disorders Information for Teens

TEEN
HEALTH
SERIES

First Edition

Eating Disorders Information for Teens

Health Tips about Anorexia, Bulimia, Binge Eating, and Other Eating Disorders

Including Information on the Causes, Prevention, and Treatment of Eating Disorders, and Such Other Issues as Maintaining Healthy Eating and Exercise Habits

◆

Edited by Sandra Augustyn Lawton

Omnigraphics

615 Griswold Street • Detroit, MI 48226

Bibliographic Note

Because this page cannot legibly accommodate all the copyright notices, the Bibliographic Note portion of the Preface constitutes an extension of the copyright notice.

Edited by Sandra Augustyn Lawton

Teen Health Series

Karen Bellenir, *Managing Editor*
David A. Cooke, M.D., *Medical Consultant*
Elizabeth Barbour, *Research and Permissions Coordinator*
Cherry Stockdale, *Permissions Assistant*
Dawn Matthews, *Verification Assistant*
Laura Pleva Nielsen, *Index Editor*
EdIndex, Services for Publishers, *Indexers*

* * *

Omnigraphics, Inc.

Matthew P. Barbour, *Senior Vice President*
Kay Gill, *Vice President—Directories*
Kevin Hayes, *Operations Manager*
Leif Gruenberg, *Development Manager*
David P. Bianco, *Marketing Director*

* * *

Peter E. Ruffner, *Publisher*

Frederick G. Ruffner, Jr., *Chairman*

Copyright © 2005 Omnigraphics, Inc.

ISBN 0-7808-0783-9

Library of Congress Cataloging-in-Publication Data

Eating disorders information for teens : health tips about anorexia,
bulimia, binge eating, and other eating disorders including information on
the causes, prevention, and treatment of eating disorders, and such other
issues as maintaining healthy eating and exercise habits / edited by Sandra
Augustyn Lawton.
    p. cm. -- (Teen health series)
  Includes index.
  ISBN 0-7808-0783-9 (hardcover : alk. paper)
  1. Eating disorders--Juvenile literature. 2. Eating disorders in
adolescence--Juvenile literature. I. Lawton, Sandra Augustyn. II. Series.
  RC552.E18E282117 2005
  616.85'26'00835--dc22

∞

This book is printed on acid-free paper meeting the ANSI Z39.48 Standard. The infinity symbol that appears above indicates that the paper in this book meets that standard.

Printed in the United States

Table of Contents

Preface ix

Part I: Eating Disorders: An Overview

Chapter 1—Frequently Asked Questions About Eating Disorders 3

Chapter 2—Who Develops Eating Disorders? 15

Chapter 3—All Ethnic And Cultural Groups Are At Risk For
Eating Disorders 27

Chapter 4—Boys And Eating Disorders 41

Chapter 5—What Causes Eating Disorders? 45

Chapter 6—How Are Eating Disorders Diagnosed? 57

Chapter 7—Statistics On Eating Disorders 63

Part II: Specific Eating Disorders

Chapter 8—Anorexia Nervosa 69

Chapter 9—Frequently Asked Questions About Anorexia 79

Chapter 10—How Serious Is Anorexia? 85

Chapter 11—Bulimia Nervosa 91

Chapter 12—Frequently Asked Questions About Bulimia 99

Chapter 13—How Serious Is Bulimia? 103

Chapter 14—Binge Eating Disorder 107

Chapter 15—Frequently Asked Questions About Binge
         Eating Disorder 117

Chapter 16—Lesser-Known Eating Disorders 121

Part III: Athletics And Eating Disorders

Chapter 17—Athletes With Eating Disorders: An Overview............... 131

Chapter 18—Identifying Athletes At Risk For Eating Disorders 135

Chapter 19—Compulsive Exercise 143

Chapter 20—Sports And Women Athletes:
         The Female Athlete Triad 149

Part IV: Prevention And Treatment Of Eating Disorders

Chapter 21—Reducing Your Risk Of Eating Disorders 161

Chapter 22—Body Image And Self-Esteem 167

Chapter 23—How Can I Improve My Self-Esteem? 175

Chapter 24—Helping A Friend With An Eating Disorder 181

Chapter 25—Talking To Your Health Care Provider
         About Eating Disorders 187

Chapter 26—Treatment For Eating Disorders 193

Chapter 27—Psychological Therapies For Eating Disorders 207

Chapter 28—Medications For Eating Disorders 215

Part V: Other Health Issues Related To Eating Disorders

Chapter 29—Dental Problems Associated With Eating
         Disorders 219

Chapter 30—Osteoporosis Associated With Eating Disorders 223

Chapter 31—Diabetes And Eating Disorders 227

Chapter 32—Substance Abuse And Eating Disorders 233

Chapter 33—Eating Disorders And Pregnancy 239

Part VI: Maintaining Healthy Eating And Exercise Habits

Chapter 34—An Action Guide To Healthy Eating 249

Chapter 35—What You Should Know About Sports Nutrition 265

Chapter 36—What's The Right Weight For My Height? 275

Chapter 37—Body Mass Index (BMI) 279

Chapter 38—How Can I Lose Weight Safely? 283

Chapter 39—Is A Vegetarian Diet Right For Me? 287

Chapter 40—Fitness Fundamentals 293

Part VII: If You Need More Information

Chapter 41—Additional Reading About Eating Disorders 307

Chapter 42—Directory Of Eating Disorder Organizations 313

Index 325

Preface

About This Book

More than eight million Americans suffer from eating disorders such as anorexia nervosa, bulimia nervosa, and binge eating disorder. Furthermore, almost half of all Americans know someone with an eating disorder. Eating disorders affect people of all races, impact men as well as women, and can result in serious emotional and physical health consequences, including death. Although the exact causes of eating disorders are unknown, teens seem particularly vulnerable. According to the National Women's Health Information Center, anorexia nervosa ranks as the third most common chronic illness among adolescent females in the United States.

Eating Disorders Information for Teens provides information about anorexia nervosa, bulimia nervosa, and other kinds of eating disorders. It describes risk factors, symptoms, medical complications, and treatments. It offers facts about body image, self-esteem, nutrition, and exercise and includes a section that examines the relationship between athletics and eating disorders. Information about maintaining healthy eating and exercise habits is also included along with suggestions for additional reading and a directory of resources.

How To Use This Book

This book is divided into parts and chapters. Parts focus on broad areas of interest; chapters are devoted to single topics within a part.

Part I: Eating Disorders: An Overview discusses the factors that contribute to the development of eating disorders, describes how they are diagnosed, and offers related statistics. It explains the characteristics most often associated with eating disorders and explains which ethnic and cultural groups are most at risk.

Part II: Specific Eating Disorders provides details about the three most common eating disorders—anorexia nervosa, bulimia nervosa, and binge eating— and also describes several lesser-known eating disorders. It includes frequently asked questions about the disorders and supplies pertinent information regarding the serious nature of the disorders and their consequences.

Part III: Athletics And Eating Disorders takes a look at the relationship between athletes and eating disorders and talks about ways of identifying athletes at risk. It also discusses compulsive exercise and describes the unique concerns of women athletes, including a group of three traits that together form a condition called the female athlete triad.

Part IV: Prevention And Treatment Of Eating Disorders discusses ways to reduce risks associated with eating disorders. It offers suggestions for improving body image and self-esteem and describes ways to help a friend with an eating disorder. Suggestions for developing a relationship with a health care provider are included along with descriptions of various treatments, including psychological therapies and medications.

Part V: Other Health Issues Related To Eating Disorders provides information on how eating disorders can lead to or complicate the course of other conditions, including dental problems, osteoporosis, diabetes, substance abuse, and pregnancy.

Part VI: Maintaining Healthy Eating And Exercise Habits offers facts about sensible dietary choices and physical fitness. It discusses sports nutrition, the body mass index, and safe weight-loss strategies. It concludes with a chapter offering a well-rounded strategy for staying fit.

Part VII: If You Need More Information provides suggestions for additional reading about eating disorders, nutrition, fitness, and other related topics. It also provides a directory of organizations able to provide more information.

Bibliographic Note

This volume contains documents and excerpts from publications issued by the following government agencies: Centers for Disease Control and Prevention

(CDC); National Cancer Institute; National Institute of Diabetes and Digestive and Kidney Diseases (NIDDK); National Institutes of Health Osteoporosis and Related Bone Diseases—National Resource Center; National Women's Health Information Center (NWHIC); and the President's Council on Physical Fitness and Sports.

In addition, this volume contains copyrighted documents and articles produced by the following organizations and individuals: A.D.A.M., Inc.; Academy for Eating Disorders; Akron Children's Hospital; Mary Allen; Anorexia Nervosa and Related Eating Disorders, Inc.; Eating Disorders Foundation of Victoria, Inc.; David M. Edwards; Hazelden Foundation; Helpguide.org; Kathy Kater; National Center on Addiction and Substance Abuse (CASA) at Columbia University; National Eating Disorders Association; Nemours Foundation; Palo Alto Medical Foundation; Renfrew Center; Screening for Mental Health, Inc.; Roberta Trattner Sherman; South Carolina Department of Mental Health; Ron Thompson; University of Alabama at Birmingham Health System; University of Arkansas for Medical Sciences; University of Massachusetts Amherst Center for Nutrition in Sport and Human Performance; University of Minnesota; and University of Wisconsin—Eau Claire Counseling Services.

Full citation information is provided on the first page of each chapter. Every effort has been made to secure all necessary rights to reprint the copyrighted material. If any omissions have been made, please contact Omnigraphics to make corrections for future editions.

Acknowledgements

In addition to the organizations listed above, special thanks are due to research and permissions coordinator Elizabeth Barbour and to managing editor Karen Bellenir.

About the *Teen Health Series*

At the request of librarians serving today's young adults, the *Teen Health Series* was developed as a specially focused set of volumes within Omnigraphics' *Health Reference Series*. Each volume deals comprehensively with a topic selected according to the needs and interests of people in middle school and high school.

Teens seeking preventive guidance, information about disease warning signs, medical statistics, and risk factors for health problems will find answers to their questions in the *Teen Health Series*. The *Series*, however, is not intended to serve as a tool for diagnosing illness, in prescribing treatments, or as a substitute for the physician/patient relationship. All people concerned about medical symptoms or the possibility of disease are encouraged to seek professional care from an appropriate health care provider.

If there is a topic you would like to see addressed in a future volume of the *Teen Health Series*, please write to:

Editor
Teen Health Series
Omnigraphics, Inc.
615 Griswold Street
Detroit, MI 48226

Locating Information within the *Teen Health Series*

The *Teen Health Series* contains a wealth of information about a wide variety of medical topics. As the *Series* continues to grow in size and scope, locating the precise information needed by a specific student may become more challenging. To address this concern, information about books within the *Teen Health Series* is included in *A Contents Guide to the Health Reference Series*. The *Contents Guide* presents an extensive list of more than 10,000 diseases, treatments, and other topics of general interest compiled from the Tables of Contents and major index headings from the books of the *Teen Health Series* and *Health Reference Series*. To access *A Contents Guide to the Health Reference Series*, visit www.healthreferenceseries.com.

Our Advisory Board

We would like to thank the following advisory board members for providing guidance to the development of this *Series*:

Dr. Lynda Baker
Associate Professor of Library and Information Science
Wayne State University, Detroit, MI

Nancy Bulgarelli
William Beaumont Hospital Library, Royal Oak, MI

Karen Imarisio
Bloomfield Township Public Library, Bloomfield Township, MI

Karen Morgan
Mardigian Library, University of Michigan-Dearborn
Dearborn, MI

Rosemary Orlando,
St. Clair Shores Public Library, St. Clair Shores, MI

Medical Consultant

Medical consultation services are provided to the *Teen Health Series* editors by David A. Cooke, M.D. Dr. Cooke is a graduate of Brandeis University, and he received his M.D. degree from the University of Michigan. He completed residency training at the University of Wisconsin Hospital and Clinics. He is board-certified in internal medicine. Dr. Cooke currently works as part of the University of Michigan Health System and practices in Brighton, MI. In his free time, he enjoys writing, science fiction, and spending time with his family.

Part One

Eating Disorders: An Overview

Chapter 1

Frequently Asked Questions About Eating Disorders

What are eating disorders?

Eating disorders are real illnesses that can affect how we eat and how we feel about food. They can be treated to help people who have them have healthy and full lives. From time to time, we all change our eating habits. Sometimes we reduce the amount of food we eat or go on a diet to shed some pounds or we eat more to gain weight. These can be healthy ways to control or reach our ideal body weight. But, people who have eating disorders have unhealthy ways, or patterns, of eating. They may eat too much and become overweight or way too little and become very thin. Sometimes a person can eat so little, or nothing at all, they actually begin to starve (called anorexia nervosa). A person can also eat an extreme amount of food all at once and then do things like vomit to rid the body of food (called bulimia nervosa). And, a person may not be able to control the need to overeat, often keeping it a secret (called binge eating

About This Chapter: Text in this chapter is from "Frequently Asked Questions about Eating Disorders", a fact sheet produced by the National Women's Health Information Center (NWHIC), a component of the U.S. Department of Health and Human Services (DHHS), Office on Women's Health, 2002.

disorder). People can also have wrong ideas, or misperceptions, of their body weight. People with eating disorders can feel certain they weigh too much, even though they may be well under the ideal body weight for a person their size.

✤ It's A Fact!!
How Do You Get Addicted?

Question: How do you get addicted to bulimia or anorexia?

Answer: Many people compare bulimia and anorexia to alcoholism and other addictions because they have many features in common. Addictions cause an altered state of consciousness, generally begin gradually and escalate, are difficult to stop, and can be seen as coping mechanisms, even though they are self-destructive.

The altered states produced by bulimia and anorexia have been described in various ways—an exhilarating triumph over food, over nature, and over other people, as an anesthesia blocking out painful feelings or conflicts, or as a sense of security with a soothing companion who "makes everything okay".

Bulimia and anorexia express emotional pain and conflict. When bulimia or anorexia becomes like an addiction—a compulsion that interferes with other aspects of a person's life—the altered states the eating disorder provides are being used to help someone to cope with life.

However, eating disorders are not like other addictions. While it is possible to permanently swear off cigarettes, alcohol, drugs, and gambling, we need to eat in order to live. The goal of recovery is to develop a healthy relationship with food, and, as with other addictions, to develop constructive ways to cope with life and its challenges.

Source: © 2002 The Renfrew Center. All rights reserved. Reprinted with permission. For additional information, call 1-800-RENFREW or visit http://www.renfrewcenter.com.

Eating disorders affect people of all ages, race, and income levels. But, these disorders affect women much more than they do men. Women make up more than 90 percent of people with these disorders. Without treatment, an eating disorder can take over a person's life and cause serious illness and death. These disorders can increase risk for osteoporosis (thinning of the bones) and heart problems. People who have eating disorders can also have depression and anxiety, and may turn to alcohol and drugs for relief.

Who is at risk for eating disorders?

In the United States and other Western countries, women are more at risk for eating disorders than are men. These disorders affect 8 to 10 times more women than men. In the U.S., it was thought that eating disorders affected mostly white women. But, recent research has shown that black women are affected as well. One study found that black women were more likely than white women to have repeated episodes of binge eating disorder. This may put black women more at risk for obesity (being overweight).

Women may be more at risk for eating disorders because of a need to have the "ideal" figure often shown in the media (TV, magazines, and movies). The "thin is best" view can affect girls and young women in particular. They often go on strict diets to look like the girls and women they see in the media. Pressure from friends to be thin and to diet can also happen. For women, body image, or how you feel about how you look, can affect feelings about body weight. Not liking how much you weigh, feeling fat, and wanting to be thin can make you worry more about how you look than other things, such as your own ideas or what you want to do in your life. Sometimes, young women who are at a normal weight, or even underweight, may feel that they are too fat. A woman may also feel that how she looks or how much she weighs makes up a major part of her self-esteem. While young women may be most at risk for eating disorders, these disorders are affecting older women in growing numbers.

What causes eating disorders?

No one knows for sure what causes eating disorders. It is known, though, that these disorders can't be willed or wished away—treatment is needed. If you or someone you know has an eating disorder, don't wait to get help. Talk with a health care provider, the sooner the better.

Much research has been focused on how personality and environment can put a person at risk for an eating disorder. People with eating disorders are thought to share certain traits, such as low self-esteem (how you feel about who you are), feelings of helplessness, and a fear of becoming over-weight. Eating disorders seem to develop as a way of dealing with stress. These disorders appear to run in families, affecting women more than men. Research has shown that a woman's social environment, including her family and friends, can affect how she feels about body weight. For instance, fre-quent talk about being thin and dieting may put pressure on a person to be thin. Being teased about being overweight by family and friends can lead to low self-esteem and unhealthy eating in young girls and women. Also, young people who are involved in sports or activities that emphasize thinness (mod-eling, dancing, long distance running, and gymnastics) are more likely to develop eating disorders.

Research is also looking at the role genetics and a person's biological make-up and body chemistry play in eating disorders. Studies funded by the Na-tional Institute of Mental Health have focused on serotonin, a substance found in the brain that can affect appetite and a person's ability to control impulses and moods. In women, researchers are exploring how eating dis-orders may affect serotonin levels and how the brain signals the body about hunger and fullness. For example, most women feel better—in terms of full-ness and mood—after eating. But for women with anorexia, not eating can actually improve mood and feelings of well being. Knowing how serotonin affects eating disorders will help researchers to figure out which women are more at risk for these disorders and better ways to treat them.

What are the most common types of eating disorders? What ef-fects do they have on a person's health?

The three most common types of eating disorders are:

- **Anorexia Nervosa:** Starving yourself by eating very little or nothing at all. People who have this condition can have a strong fear of body fat and weight gain. To stay thin, a person may diet, fast, or exercise too much. Taking laxatives, diuretics, or enemas to rid the body of food is also common. Women with anorexia can have menstrual periods that are not regular or none at all. Girls with anorexia often get their periods later than girls who don't have this illness. People with this illness may think they are overweight, even when they are very skinny. The process of eating becomes an obsession, or something you can't stop thinking about. Eating habits develop that are not normal, such as staying away from food and meals, picking out only a few foods and eating these in small amounts, or carefully weighing out food portions to eat. People with anorexia may also check their body weight a lot.

Anorexia can cause the same types of problems that happen when a person is starving. The lack of food can cause a person to become very thin, develop brittle hair and nails, dry skin, and a low pulse rate, and become not able to stand the cold, and suffer from constipation and sometimes diarrhea. It can also affect a person's blood count, causing mild anemia, reduce muscle mass, stop a woman's menstrual period, and lead to swollen joints. Lack of calcium, due to a poor diet, places anorexics at higher risk for osteoporosis (bone thinning) later in life. Many people with this illness have depression, anxiety, and problems with alcohol or drugs. The most serious problems include death from starvation, the heart stopping, or suicide.

- **Bulimia Nervosa:** When a person binges, or eats an extreme amount of food all at once and then purges—vomits, takes laxatives or diuretics (water pills)—to rid the body of food. Exercising to excess and fasting can also occur to make sure no weight is gained after binge eating. People with this eating disorder feel no control during the times they are eating to excess. This illness most often starts in the late teenage years or early adult life. Like anorexics, people with bulimia have extreme worry about food, body weight, and body shape. Many bulimics binge and purge in secret, and still keep a normal body weight. By doing so, a person can often hide this illness for years. Feelings of disgust and shame after binge eating are common, as well as feelings of relief after purging. Eating binges can happen once or twice a week or as much as a few times a day. Depression, boredom, or anger can trigger them. The need to binge and purge can be constant or can happen once in a while, with periods of time where no bingeing occurs.

Health problems from bulimia are mostly related to electrolyte imbalance (when the amounts of sodium and potassium in the body become too much or too little) and repeated purging behaviors. Purging causes the body to lose potassium, which can damage heart muscle and increase a person's risk for heart attack. Frequent vomiting can inflame the esophagus (tube that connects the throat with the stomach) and damage tooth enamel. Other problems caused by bulimia include scarring on the back of fingers from pushing them down the throat to cause vomiting, loss of or change in menstrual periods, and no sex drive. People with this illness can have trouble dealing with and controlling impulses, stress, and anxiety. They may also have depression, obsessive-compulsive disorder (an illness where you have unwanted thoughts and behaviors you can't stop repeating), and other mental illnesses. Problems with alcohol and drugs are not uncommon. Bulimics are also likely to be anorexic.

• **Binge Eating Disorder (BED):** When a person can't control the desire to overeat and often keeps the extreme eating a secret. People with this eating disorder feel no control during the times they are eating to excess. During binge eating, a person may eat more quickly than normal, eat until feeling discomfort, eat large amounts of food when not hungry, and eat alone. Unlike bulimia and anorexia, a person doesn't try to rid the body of extra food by doing things like vomiting, fasting, or exercising to the extreme. Because of this, many people who have this illness are overweight. A person can feel disgust, shame, and guilt during a binge, which can lead to bingeing again, causing a cycle of binge eating. Like with anorexia, people with BED can fear gaining weight, want to lose weight, and dislike the way their bodies look.

BED most often starts in the late teenage years or early adult years. Some experts believe BED is the most common eating disorder. The illness often develops soon after extreme weight loss from a diet. BED can be hard to diagnose and can be mistaken for other causes of obesity (being overweight). People with BED are often overweight because they maintain a high calorie diet without exercising. Medical problems can happen, like those found with obesity, such as high cholesterol levels, high blood pressure, and diabetes. BED also increases a person's risk for gallbladder disease, heart disease, and some types of cancer. People with BED often suffer from depression.

There are two other types of eating disorders. Eating disorder not otherwise specified (EDNOS) is the name for disorders of eating that don't fit into one of the three disorders described above. With EDNOS, a person has some form of abnormal eating but not all the symptoms needed to be diagnosed with an eating disorder. For instance, a person with EDNOS may purge him or herself after eating, but do so with less frequency or intensity than someone who has bulimia.

More common than eating disorders is a condition called disordered eating. This is when a person diets, binges, or purges, but doesn't do so often or severely enough to be diagnosed with an eating disorder. A person may change how they eat after a stressful event or an illness, before an important speech or work event, or before a sports competition. Disordered eating can lead to weight loss or weight gain, but rarely requires treatment. But, if the disordered eating becomes long lasting, causes upset and stress, changes the way a person feels about themselves or how they look, or starts to get in the way of daily activities, they need to get help right away. Don't wait to see if the problem goes away by itself; talk with a health care provider about where to go for help.

How can you tell if someone has an eating disorder?

Because many people with eating disorders keep them a secret, their conditions can go unnoticed for long periods of time, even years. With anorexia, signs such as extreme weight loss are easier to see. But, bulimics who can stay at their normal body weight may be better able to hide their illness. Family members and friends may notice some of the warning signs of an eating disorder.

A person with anorexia may:

• Eat only "safe" foods low in calories and fat.

• Have odd rituals, such as cutting food into small pieces or measuring food.

- Spend more time playing with food than eating it.

- Cook meals for others without eating.

- Exercise to excess.

- Dress in layers to hide weight loss.

- Spend less time with family and friends.

- Become withdrawn and secretive.

A person with bulimia may:

- Become very secretive about food.

- Spend a lot of time thinking about and planning the next eating binge.

- Keep making trips to the bathroom after eating.

- Steal food or hoard it in strange places.

- Eat to excess.

A person with binge-eating disorder may:

- Become very secretive about food.

✔ **Quick Tip**
Obsessed With Food And Weight

Question: Just because I weigh myself all the time, weigh all of my food, avoid fat, and run every morning doesn't mean I have an eating disorder, does it? My weight is in the normal range, but my friends tell me I am obsessed with food and weight like an anorexic.

Answer: It is hard to hear friends label you with words like "obsessed" or "anorexic". It sounds as though you are wondering if there are reasons for your friends' concern.

You may want to ask yourself whether you have developed anorexic thinking and/or an eating disorder lifestyle. Do you see yourself as fat, even though others see you as thin? Do your moods depend on your weight on the scale? Do you spend much of your time thinking about food and calories? Are you spending less time in fun and social activities? Do you try to be perfect in your work, your relationships, and your health? Do you eat less or exercise more when you are upset? If you find that any of these questions relate to your situation, it might be beneficial to get professional help. A psychotherapist can help you understand whether your focus on food and exercise has become problematic and how to develop a healthy relationship with yourself and your body.

- Spend a lot of time thinking about and planning the next eating binge.

- Start eating alone most of the time.

- Steal food or hoard it in strange places.

- Eat to excess.

- Become overweight.

- Become withdrawn, not wanting to go out or see family and friends.

If you or someone you know has any of these warning signs, see a health care provider right away. There is help for people with these disorders and, with help, they can lead a healthy and full life.

What are the treatments for eating disorders?

Eating disorders can be treated and a person can return to a healthy weight. Success in treating eating disorders is greatest when they are found early and treated right away. The longer abnormal ways of eating go on, the harder it is to overcome the disorder. Plus, more damage is done to the body over time, which can result in serious health problems.

There is no one, or best, way to treat these complex disorders. Most people with eating disorders are treated by a team of health care providers and receive medical care, psychotherapy (sometimes called "talk therapy"), and nutritional counseling. Professionals who provide psychotherapy can be therapists, psychologists, psychiatrists, social workers, or counselors. Types of psychotherapy include cognitive-behavioral therapy (changes how a person thinks about, and then reacts to, a situation that makes them anxious or fearful) family therapy, and group therapy. In some cases, a person may need to go into the hospital or into an in-patient or residential program. Medication is also sometimes used to treat the disorder and prevent relapse (or keep it from coming back). Certain antidepressants, called selective serotonin reuptake inhibitors or SSRIs, have been shown to help maintain weight and reduce anxiety for people with anorexia and bulimia. Training to build self-esteem can also be helpful.

Will having an eating disorder keep me from getting pregnant or having a healthy baby?

Having an eating disorder can make it harder for a woman to get pregnant. It may cause early delivery, or premature birth, which can cause problems (sometimes life threatening) in a newborn. Women with eating disorders have higher rates of miscarriage than do women who don't have these disorders. If a woman doesn't eat lots of different healthy foods during pregnancy, she and her baby can have health problems. It is best to get treated for an eating disorder before you try to get pregnant. But, even if your eating disorder was treated and now gone, it could come back during the stress of pregnancy. Making sure you have good support from family, friends, and your health care provider is key to having a healthy pregnancy. Keep in mind you will also need plenty of support after the baby is born. Some women can feel "blue" or have depression after giving birth, which can make an eating disorder come back. Talk with your health care provider if you are thinking about getting pregnant or are pregnant.

What should you do if you or someone you know has an eating disorder?

Support is important when you or someone you know has an eating disorder. Tell someone you trust about your problem. It may be a family member, friend, counselor, religious or community leader, or doctor. Talking to a school counselor or mental health professional is a good place to start. Seeing

---

✎ What's It Mean?

Laxatives: A substance that promotes bowel movements. [1]

Miscarriage: An unplanned loss of a pregnancy. Also called a spontaneous abortion. [2]

Source: [1] "Dictionary of Cancer Terms," National Cancer Institute, available at www.nci.nih.gov; cited December 2004. [2] "NWHIC Web Site Glossary," U.S. Department of Health and Human Services, Office on Women's Health, available at www.4woman.gov, 2004.

a health care provider as soon as you can is important too. Your doctor can help you get the help you need for your eating disorder. You can also learn about healthier ways to eat. Don't put off seeing a doctor, thinking you will get better on your own. Keep in mind, an eating disorder can cause serious harm to your body and to your emotional health.

What is the latest research on eating disorders?

The National Institutes of Mental Health (NIMH) conducts and funds research on eating disorders. Researchers are looking at how well psychotherapy and medications work, either when used alone or together, to help people with these disorders. Also being studied is the role family background (genetics), appetite and exercise, and emotions and social behaviors play in eating disorders. New research is focused on whether brain serotonin (a substance that affects appetite, impulses and moods) is linked to eating disorders in women.

Chapter 2

Who Develops Eating Disorders?

Many factors contribute to the risk of developing an eating disorder.

Age

In general, eating disorders occur in adolescents and young adults, although one study reported that 5% of cases occurred in children under 12 years old.

Age Of Onset For Bulimia: A 1997 survey of high school students by the Centers for Disease Control reported that 4.5% induced vomiting after meals or used laxatives to lose weight. Estimates of the prevalence of bulimia nervosa among young women range from about 3% in adolescents to 10% in college women. Some experts claim that even these percentages grossly underestimate the problem because many people with bulimia are able to conceal their purging and do not become noticeably underweight. For example, a European study detected bulimic behavior in 14.4% of adolescents 14 to 16 years old, with full-blown bulimia observed in 1.8% of girls and 0.3% of boys.

Age Of Onset For Anorexia Nervosa: After asthma and obesity, anorexia nervosa is the third most common chronic illness in adolescent women. It is estimated to occur in 0.5% to 3% of all teenagers. Anorexia usually first occurs in adolescence with peaks at 13 to 14 years of age and at 17 to 18 years of age. Over the past 40 years, however, the incidence has been steady in teenagers, but it has increased threefold in young adult women.

Gender

Studies typically report that 90% of those with eating disorders are females. However, the prevalence in males appears to be increasing. For example, a 2000 study of teenagers in Minnesota reported that 13% of girls and 7% of boys reported disordered eating behavior.

When eating disorders occur in young adults, men are more apt to conceal them, so the incidence among males may be underreported. One study of Navy men, for example, reported a prevalence of 2.5% for anorexia, 6.8% of bulimia, and 40% for binge eating.

Studies suggest that the psychiatric and behavioral profiles of men and women with eating disorders are very similar to each other, although there are some differences. Excessive physical activity is more prevalent in males with anorexia. Anorexics tend to have very low sexual interest, although there is a higher rate of homosexuality among young men than women. Sexual preference for men may tend to differ, however, by the specific eating disorders. One study reported that 42% of male civilians with bulimia were homosexual or bisexual while 58% of the men with anorexia were asexual.

Ethnic Factors

Most studies of individuals with eating disorders have been conducted using Caucasian middle-class females. Studies are now reporting, however, that minority populations, including Hispanic-Americans and African-Americans, are significantly affected. There is some indication that African-American girls and young women may be at particular risk for eating disorders because of poor body images caused by cultural attitudes that denigrate the physical characteristics of minorities. In one study, bulimia was equally common among both Caucasian and African American women, although the latter were more likely to binge recurrently, to fast, and to use laxatives and diuretics to control weight. Binge eating may be an even more severe problem in Hispanic-Americans. A 2000 study on Asian women also reported rates of dieting and body dissatisfaction that were similar to those in other cultures, but Asian women had much lower percentages of actual eating disorders.

Socioeconomic Factors

Living in any economically developed nation on any continent appears to pose more of a risk for eating disorders than belonging to a particular population group. Symptoms remain strikingly similar across high-risk countries.

Income Levels: Oddly enough, within developed countries there appears to be no difference in risk between the rich and the poor. Some studies suggest that those in lower economic groups may be at higher risk for bulimia.

Urban Life: City living is a risk factor for bulimia but it has no effect on the risk for anorexia.

Intelligence: In one sample, people with eating disorders scored significantly higher than average on IQ tests. People with bulimia, but not anorexia, had higher nonverbal than verbal scores.

Personality Disorders

A 2000 study reported that people with eating disorders tended to share similar personality traits, including low self-esteem, dependency, and problems with self-direction. Researchers have been attempting to determine specific personality disorders or behavioral characteristics that might put people at higher risk for one or both of the eating disorders. Some studies have reported the following personality disorders linked to particular eating disorders:

- Avoidant personalities, mostly seen in anorexia. Such people are generally high functioning, persistent, and perfectionists.

- Dependent personalities, mostly seen in anorexia. This group is usually over-controlled and withdrawn.

- Borderline and histrionic personalities, mostly seen in bulimia. Such individuals are emotionally uncontrolled and impulsive.

• Narcissism is seen in both anorexia and bulimia.

It should be noted that any of these personality traits can appear in either patients with bulimia or anorexia. Some experts believe that the patient's specific personality disorder, rather than whether they are anorexic or bulimic, may be the more important factor in determining treatment choice.

Avoidant Personalities: Some studies indicate that as many as a third of anorexic restrictors have avoidant personalities. This personality disorder is characterized by the following:

✎ What's It Mean?

Anabolic Steroids: The familiar name for synthetic substances related to the male sex hormones. They promote the growth of skeletal muscle and the development of male sexual characteristics. [1]

Asexual: A lack of interest in sex. (Also can refer to organisms that reproduce by nonsexual means or reproduce without having "males" and "females" as part of the process.) [2]

Asthma: When your airways are inflamed, causing you to wheeze, feel shortness of breath, cough and feel a tightness in your chest. [3]

Bisexual: A sexual attraction to people of both sexes. [2]

Calcium: A mineral found in teeth, bones, and other body tissues. [4]

Diuretic: A drug that increases the production of urine. [4]

Histrionic Personality: When a person has a pattern of excessive emotional expression and the need for attention and approval. [2]

Homosexuality: A sexual attraction to people of the same sex. [2]

Hypochondriasis (Hypochondria): When a person believes that real or imagined physical symptoms are signs of a serious illness even though their doctor assures them there is no serious illness. [2]

- Being a perfectionist

- Being emotionally and sexually inhibited

- Having less of a fantasy life than people with bulimia or those without an eating disorder

- Not being rebellious, or being perceived as always being "good"

- Being terrified of being ridiculed or criticized or of feeling humiliated. People with anorexia are extremely sensitive to failure, and any criticism, no matter how slight, reinforces their own belief that they are "no good."

IQ (Intelligence Quotient) Tests: A series of tests used to determine the general intelligence of a person compared to other people the same age. [2]

Narcissism: When a person has an extreme sense of self-importance and a preoccupation with his or her self. [2]

Type 1 Diabetes: A condition characterized by high blood glucose levels caused by a total lack of insulin. Occurs when the body's immune system attacks the insulin-producing beta cells in the pancreas and destroys them. The pancreas then produces little or no insulin. Type 1 diabetes develops most often in young people but can appear in adults. [5]

Type 2 Diabetes: A condition characterized by high blood glucose levels caused by either a lack of insulin or the body's inability to use insulin efficiently. Type 2 diabetes develops most often in middle-aged and older adults but can appear in young people. [5]

Source: [1] "Anabolic Steroid Abuse," Research Report Series, National Institute on Drug Abuse, U.S. Department of Health and Human Services, available at www.nida.nih.gov, 2004. [2] Editor. [3] "4Girls Web Site Glossary," 4Girls Health, U.S. Department of Health and Human Services, Office on Women's Health, available at www.4girls.gov, 2004. [4] "Dictionary of Cancer Terms," National Cancer Institute, available at www.nci.nih.gov; cited December 2004. [5] "Diabetes Dictionary," National Institute of Diabetes and Digestive and Kidney Diseases, available at www.diabetes.niddk.nih.gov, 2003.

The person with both anorexia and an avoidant personality disorder may develop a behavioral and eating pattern as follows:

- For such individuals, achieving perfection, with all that that involves, is the only way they believe they can obtain love.

- Part of the drive for perfection and love is being trouble-free and attaining some ideal image of thinness. Eating is also associated with lower animal drives, so fasting has been linked historically to saintliness. The individual is driven to demand nothing, including food.

- Failure is inevitable, since being loved has nothing to do with being perfect. (In fact, people who are always seeking perfection often alienate others around them.)

- This failure to achieve love is followed by a sense of being even more imperfect (which is equivalent to being fat) and a renewed sense of striving for perfection (i.e., becoming even thinner).

In keeping with the avoidant personality, one expert described her anorexic patients as having a total lack of self, well beyond having low self-esteem. In support of this, a 2002 study reported that women with eating disorders were less likely to attend to their own needs and to care for themselves. In other words, they felt "self-less" and experienced guilt if they felt they were promoting their own self-interest.

The process of not eating may become an act of passive revenge on those whose love is always out of reach: "See? I am slowly disappearing, and you will be very sad when I am gone."

Obsessive-Compulsive Personality: Obsessive-compulsive personality defines certain character traits (e.g., being a perfectionist, morally rigid, or preoccupied with rules and order). This personality disorder has been strongly associated with a higher risk for anorexia. These traits should not be confused with the anxiety disorder called obsessive-compulsive disorder (OCD), although they may increase the risk for this disorder [see page 22].

Borderline Personalities: Studies indicate that almost 40% of people who are diagnosed with bulimic anorexia (losing weight by bingeing and purging) may have borderline personalities. Such people tend to:

• Have unstable moods, thought patterns, behavior, and self-images. People with borderline personalities have been described as causing chaos around them by using emotional weapons, such as temper tantrums, suicide threats, and hypochondriasis.

• Be frantically fearful of being abandoned.

• Be unable to be alone.

• Have difficulty controlling their anger and impulses. (In fact, between one-quarter and one-third of people with bulimia have impulsive symptoms.)

• Be prone to idealize other people. Frequently this is followed by rejection and by disappointment.

Some research has suggested that the severity of this personality disorder predicts difficulty in treating bulimia, and it might be more important than the presence of psychological problems, such as depression.

Narcissism: Studies have also found that people with bulimia or anorexia are often highly narcissistic and tend to:

• Have an inability to soothe oneself.

• Have an inability to empathize with others.

• Have a need for admiration.

• Be hypersensitive to criticism or defeat.

♣ **It's A Fact!!**

Being Overweight

A 2002 study reported that among American teenagers, 18% of overweight girls and 6% of overweight boys reported extreme eating disorder behaviors, including use of diet pills, laxatives, diuretics, and vomiting. With the increasing epidemic of obesity in America, such behaviors will only compound the health problems in obese young people.

Accompanying Emotional Disorders

Between 40% and 96% of all eating-disordered patients experience depression and anxiety disorders. Depression, anxiety, or both is also common in families of patients with eating disorders. It is not clear if emotional disorders, particularly obsessive-compulsive disorder (OCD), cause the eating disorders, increase susceptibility to them, or share common biologic cause.

Obsessive-Compulsive Disorder (OCD): Obsessive-compulsive disorder is an anxiety disorder that occurs in up to 69% of patients with anorexia and up to 33% of patients with bulimia. In fact, some experts believe that eating disorders are just variants of OCD. Obsessions are recurrent or persistent mental images, thoughts, or ideas, which may result in compulsive behaviors (repetitive, rigid, and self-prescribed routines) that are intended to prevent the manifestation of the obsession. Women with anorexia and OCD may become obsessed with exercise, dieting, and food. They often develop compulsive rituals (e.g., weighing every bit of food, cutting it into tiny pieces, or putting it into tiny containers). The presence of OCD with either anorexia or bulimia does not, however, appear to have any influence on whether a patient improves or not.

Other Anxiety Disorders: A number of other anxiety disorders have been associated with both bulimia and anorexia.

- **Phobias:** Phobias often precede the onset of the eating disorder. Social phobias, in which a person is fearful about being humiliated in public, are common in both types of eating disorders.

- **Panic Disorder:** Panic disorder often follows the onset of an eating disorder. It is characterized by periodic attacks of anxiety or terror (panic attacks).

- **Post-Traumatic Stress Disorder:** One study of 294 women with serious eating disorders reported that 74% of them recalled a traumatic event and more than half exhibited symptoms of post-traumatic stress disorder (PTSD), which is an anxiety disorder that occurs in response to life-threatening circumstances.

Depression: Depression is common in people with eating disorders, particularly anorexia. Depression and eating disorders are also linked to a similar seasonal pattern, as indicated by the following observations:

- For many people, depression is more severe in darker winter months. Similarly, a subgroup of bulimic patients suffers from a specific form of bulimia that worsens in winter and fall. Such patients are more apt to have started bingeing at an earlier age and binge more frequently than those whose bulimia is more consistent year round.

- Onset of anorexia appears to peak in May, which is also the peak month for suicide.

Major depression is unlikely to be a cause of eating disorders, however, because treating and relieving depression rarely cures an eating disorder. The severity of the eating disorder is also not correlated with the severity of any existing depression. In addition, depression often improves after anorexic patients begin to gain weight.

Body Image Disorders

Body Dysmorphic Disorder: Body dysmorphic disorder involves a distorted view of one's body that is caused by social, psychologic, or possibly biologic factors. It is often associated with anorexia or bulimia, but it can also occur without any eating disorder. People with this disorder commonly suffer from emotional disorders, including obsessive-compulsive disorder and depression. (Some evidence suggests that treatment with fluoxetine (Prozac), a common antidepressant known as an SSRI, helps reduce this problem, even in people without an eating disorder.)

Muscle Dysmorphia: Experts are also increasingly reporting a disorder in which people have distorted body images involving their muscles. It tends to occur in men who perceive themselves as being "puny," which results in excessive body building, preoccupation with diet, and social problems. Such individuals are prone to eating disorders and other unhealthy behaviors, including the use of anabolic steroids.

Excessive Physical Activity

Highly competitive athletes are often perfectionists, a trait common among people with eating disorders.

Female Athletes And Dancers: Women in "appearance" sports, including gymnastics and figure skating, and in endurance sports, such as track and cross-country, are at particular risk for anorexia. Success in ballet also depends on the development of a wiry and extremely slim body. Estimates for episodes of eating disorders among such athletes and performers range from 15% to over 60%.

Male Athletes: Male wrestlers and lightweight rowers are also at risk for excessive dieting. One-third of high school wrestlers use a method called weight cutting for rapid weight loss. This process involves food restriction and fluid depletion by using steam rooms, saunas, laxatives, and diuretics. Although male athletes are more apt to resume normal eating patterns once competition ends, studies show that the body fat levels of many wrestlers are still well below their peers during off-season, and are often as low as 3% during wrestling season. Of concern is a recently recognized body-image disorder, referred to as muscle dysmorphia, which occurs mostly in men who are preoccupied with weight lifting and who perceive themselves as puny.

Men And Women In The Military: Studies also show a higher-than-average risk for eating disorders in men and women in the military. A study of eating behavior on one Army base reported that 8% of the women had an eating disorder, compared to 1% to 3% in the civilian female population.

Vegetarianism

In general, vegetarianism, with careful planning, is a healthy practice for both adults and adolescents. Studies report, however, that vegetarianism in adolescence may be a risk factor for eating disorders in both males and females. In one study, while vegetarian teens ate more fruits and vegetables, they were also twice as likely to diet frequently, four times as likely to intensively diet, and eight times as likely to use laxatives as their non-vegetarian peers.

This study does not mean that being a vegetarian equates with having an eating disorder. It does suggest, however, that parents with children who suddenly become vegetarian, should be sure that their children are eating a balanced meal with sufficient protein, calories, and important minerals, such as calcium. Parents also might suspect anorexic behavior in their child under certain conditions:

- If the child has stopped eating meat only to avoid fat rather than from other motives, such as love of animals or to improve health

- If vegetarian diet coincides with rapid weight loss

- If the child avoids important vegetable products because of calories (such as whole grains) or because of fats and oils (such as tofu, nuts, and dairy products)

Diabetes Or Other Chronic Diseases

According to one survey, 10.3% of teenage girls and 6.9% of boys with chronic illness, such as diabetes or asthma, had an eating disorder.

Diabetes: Eating disorders are particularly serious problems for people with either type 1 or type 2 diabetes.

- Binge eating (without purging) is most common in type 2 diabetes and, in fact, the obesity it causes may even trigger this diabetes in some people.

- Both bulimia and anorexia are common in type 1 diabetes. Some experts report that one-third of insulin-dependent patients have an eating disorder, most often because diabetic women omit or underuse insulin in order to control weight. If such patients develop anorexia, their extremely low weight may appear to control the diabetes for a while. Eventually, however, if they fail to take insulin and continue to lose weight, these patients develop life-threatening complications.

Early Puberty

There is a greater risk for eating disorders and other emotional problems for girls who undergo early puberty, when the pressures experienced by all adolescents are intensified by experiencing, possibly alone, these early physical changes, including normal increased body fat. One interesting study reported the following:

- Before puberty, girls ate quantities of food appropriate to their body weight, were satisfied with their bodies, and noted their depression increased with lower food intake.

- After puberty, girls ate about three-quarters of the recommended calorie intake, had a worse body self-image, and noted their depression increased with higher food intake.

This study reported on girls without eating disorders, but it certainly suggests patterns that can lead to eating problems, particularly in girls who go through puberty early.

Chapter 3

All Ethnic And Cultural Groups Are At Risk For Eating Disorders

At Risk: All Ethnic And Cultural Groups

Boys And Girls Of All Ethnic Groups Are Susceptible To Eating Disorders

Many people believe that eating disorders commonly occur among affluent white females. Although the prevalence of these disorders elsewhere in the population is much lower, an increasing number of males and minorities are also suffering from eating disorders.

Girls and boys from all ethnic and racial groups may suffer from eating disorders and disordered eating. The specific nature of the most common eating problems, as well as risk and protective factors, may vary from group to group, but no population is exempt. Research findings regarding prevalence rates and specific types of problems among particular groups are limited, but it is evident that disturbed eating behaviors and attitudes occur across all cultures.

About This Chapter: Text in this chapter is from several fact sheets within *BodyWise Handbook*, produced by the National Women's Health Information Center (NWHIC), a component of the U.S. Department of Health and Human Services (DHHS), Office on Women's Health, revised May 2004; available online at http://www.4woman.gov/BodyImage/Bodywise.cfm.

♣ It's A Fact!!

**Cultural Norms Regarding
Body Size Can Play A Role In The
Development Of Eating Disorders**

In Western cultures, the ideal female body is thin. Membership in ethnic groups and cultures that do not value a thin body may protect girls from body dissatisfaction and weight concerns. However, young people who identify with cultures that prefer larger body sizes may be at risk for becoming overweight or obese. Research also suggests that women who think they are smaller than the body size favored by their cultural group may be at risk for binge eating.

Large percentages of African American, American Indian, and Hispanic females are overweight. Being overweight is a risk factor for engaging in disordered eating behaviors. Risk factors and incidence rates for eating disorders can vary dramatically among subgroups of a specific population.

Eating Disorders Among Ethnically And Culturally Diverse Girls May Be Underreported And Undetected

Eating disorders among ethnically and culturally diverse girls may be underreported due to the lack of population-based studies that include representatives from these groups. The perception that non-white females are at decreased risk may also contribute to the lack of detection. Stereotyped body images of ethnically diverse women (e.g., petite Asian American, heavier African American) can also deter detection. In addition, for some ethnic and cultural groups, seeking professional help for emotional problems is not a common practice.

Girls of different ethnic and cultural groups often receive treatment for the accompanying symptoms of an eating disorder, such as depression or malnutrition, rather than for the eating disorder itself. When these girls are finally diagnosed as having an eating disorder, the disorder (especially anorexia) tends to be more severe. This problem is exacerbated by the difficulty they may have in locating culturally sensitive treatment centers.

African American Girls

African American Girls Are At Risk

Many people believe that only White girls are affected by eating disorders. In reality, no ethnic or socioeconomic group is immune to the dangers of this disease. Cases of eating disorders among diverse racial ethnic groups, including African Americans, are often underreported because studies typically do not include ethnically diverse populations.

After White Americans, African Americans comprise the ethnic and cultural group about which most studies on eating disorders are available. While there are no incidence or prevalence rates for eating disorders in the African American population, recent studies are providing clinical accounts of eating disorders in African American women.

Numerous studies have documented a high rate of eating disorder behaviors and risk factors, including body dissatisfaction among African American women. More specifically, research demonstrates that binge eating and purging is at least as common among African American women as White women.

Unfortunately, little work has been undertaken regarding differences in presentation of symptoms, cultural-specific risk factors, and effective treatment methods for African Americans.

The belief that African American women do not experience eating disorders contributes to the lack of identification of eating disorder problems among this population. Since the early detection of an eating disorder is very important for its successful treatment, this misperception can result in serious health problems for African American girls.

African American Girls Are Not Immune To The Pressure To Be Thin

The African American culture is more accepting of diverse body sizes and seems to favor a broader beauty ideal. This tolerance may help protect some African American girls from body dissatisfaction and low self-image.

However, as Black girls approach adolescence, they become more concerned with thinness. Studies indicate that when African American girls experience social pressure to be thin, they express the same type of body dissatisfaction and drive for thinness as White girls.

Adolescents from middle-class African American families may be particularly vulnerable to the influence of the White beauty ideal. Essence, a magazine that caters to African American women, regularly runs stories on body size anxiety and eating disorders. A survey of its readers indicated that African American women appear to have at least equal levels of abnormal eating attitudes and behaviors as White women. Studies indicate that Blacks who identify with mainstream culture exhibit more eating problems, including dieting and fear of fat.

Media targeting African Americans and other racial and ethnic and cultural groups in this country are increasingly embracing the beauty as thinness ideal. Black female stars in the music, film, and fashion industries are just as thin as their White counterparts. The influence of these role models may contribute to body dissatisfaction and weight control behaviors among African American girls.

African American Women Experience High Rates Of Obesity, A Risk Factor For Eating Disorders

Although the preference for a larger body size may help protect African American girls from body dissatisfaction and dieting, it can encourage obesity, which is also a risk factor for eating disorders. Black women are more than three times as likely as White women to be obese. Black women and girls are also less likely to exercise than their White counterparts. African American families with low incomes are particularly at risk for obesity, due in part to a diet of food that is high in fat.

African American girls are not likely to be heavier than White girls are during childhood; but after adolescence their body mass index (BMI) surpasses that of White adolescent girls. This increase may be partially due to metabolic differences, since Black women and girls tend to have lower resting expenditures than their White counterparts. Weight gain during adolescence may contribute to body dissatisfaction, disordered eating, and eating disorders.

✎ What's It Mean?

Body Mass Index (BMI): A measure used to evaluate body weight relative to a person's height. BMI is used to find out if a person is underweight, normal weight, overweight, or obese. [1]

Diuretic: A drug that increases the production of urine. [2]

Laxatives: A substance that promotes bowel movements. [2]

Metabolism: The total of all chemical changes that take place in a cell or an organism. These changes produce energy and basic materials needed for important life processes. [2]

Source: [1] "Diabetes Dictionary," National Institute of Diabetes and Digestive and Kidney Diseases, available at www.diabetes.niddk.nih.gov, 2003. [2] "Dictionary of Cancer Terms," National Cancer Institute, available at www.nci.nih.gov; cited December 2004.

Black women who consider themselves heavier than the body ideal preferred by their culture, particularly those who are obese, may experience weight dissatisfaction and a desire to be thinner. Overweight women are more likely than women of normal weight to experience teasing, criticism, or discrimination. These pressures may contribute to binge eating, a disorder that is more common among people who have a history of obesity than others. People with this disorder eat a large amount of food in a short period of time and feel a lack of control over their eating.

Women who consider themselves thinner than the ideal may also be at risk for binge eating. These women may experience body dissatisfaction along with a desire to gain weight in order to approximate their cultural ideal.

African American Women Engage In Binge Eating In High Rates

The first large-scale study of recurrent binge eating in Black women indicated that Black women were as likely as White women to report that they had engaged in binge eating and self-induced vomiting. More specifically, a greater number of Black women than White women reported that they had used laxatives, diuretics, or fasting to control their weight. Almost twice as many Black women as White women were identified as probable eating disorder cases. Recurrent binge eaters, regardless of race, are overweight and report a greater number of psychiatric symptoms than those who do not binge eat frequently. In addition, some researchers believe that racial prejudice and discrimination toward African Americans result in a sense of isolation that may contribute to binge eating.

American Indian And Alaska Native Girls

American Indian Girls Are At Risk

Many people believe that only White girls are affected by eating disorders. In reality, no ethnic or socioeconomic group is immune to the dangers of this disease. Cases of eating disorders among diverse racial and ethnic groups, including American Indians and Alaska Natives, are often under-reported because studies typically do not include ethnically diverse populations.

Studies indicate that American Indian and Alaska Native adolescents are increasingly exhibiting disturbed eating behaviors and using unhealthy practices to control their weight. Disordered eating has been shown to occur more often among this group than among White, Hispanic, African American, or Asian girls.

In a large study involving 545 Hispanic, American Indian, and White high school students, American Indians consistently scored the highest on each of seven items representing disturbed eating behaviors and attitudes. This study, which included 129 American Indians, also found very high rates of self-induced vomiting and binge eating among this group. Other small studies of American Indian adolescents also indicate high rates of disordered eating, including dieting and purging.

American Indian Youth Express High Levels Of Body Dissatisfaction

The largest and most comprehensive survey undertaken to date on the health status of Native American youths living on or near reservations involved 13,454 American Indians and Alaska Natives in grades 7 through 12. Approximately 41% of the adolescents reported feeling overweight, 50% were dissatisfied with their weight, and 44% worried about being overweight.

Among American Indian youth, body dissatisfaction is associated with unhealthy weight control behaviors. In the Indian Adolescent Health Study mentioned above, almost half of the girls and one-third of the boys had been on weight loss diets in the past year, with 27% reporting self-induced vomiting and 11% reporting the use of diet pills. Girls who reported feeling overweight were more likely to engage in unhealthy weight control practices.

Acculturation May Increase Vulnerability

Increased contact with the mainstream culture that equates thinness with beauty seems to contribute to higher rates of disordered eating among American Indian girls. In one study, anorexic Navajo girls from Arizona were more likely to come from upwardly mobile families who moved off the reservation. In a second study, child and adolescent members of a tribe were much more likely to prefer thinner body sizes than elder tribe members.

Eating disturbances have also been associated with racism, social isolation, low self-worth, and pressure to look a certain way, which may increase vulnerability to developing eating disorders.

Obesity Is Also A Risk Factor

American Indians have a high prevalence of obesity in all age groups and both sexes. Children who are obese are at risk for developing eating disorders and for becoming obese adults. More specifically, being overweight is a risk factor for eating disturbances in ethnically diverse women. Attention needs to be focused, therefore, on the prevention and treatment of obesity in American Indian adolescents.

Among American Indian Youth, Disordered Eating Is Linked To Other Harmful Behaviors

The Indian Adolescent Health Study indicates that disordered eating behaviors are related to other health-compromising behaviors. Frequent dieting and purging among American Indian girls was associated with a wide range of risk factors, such as high emotional stress, binge eating, alcohol and tobacco use, thoughts and attempts of suicide, delinquent behaviors, and physical and sexual abuse.

The early identification of disordered eating behaviors may help uncover risk factors for other unhealthy and possibly more serious behaviors among these adolescents.

Asian And Pacific Islander Girls

Asian American Girls Are At Risk

Many people believe that only White girls are affected by eating disorders. In reality, no ethnic or socioeconomic group is immune to the dangers of this disease. Studies typically do not include ethnically diverse populations; therefore, cases of eating disorders among diverse racial ethnic groups, including Asian Americans, are often underreported. In addition, many Asian Americans equate psychological problems with weakness and shame; therefore, women and girls may avoid seeking treatment.

♣ It's A Fact!!

The term Asian American/Pacific Islander refers to the more than seven million people from 28 Asian countries and 25 Pacific Island cultures in the U.S. The largest subgroups are Chinese, Filipino, Japanese, Asian Indians, Koreans, and Vietnamese. Hawaiians comprise the largest subgroups of Pacific Islanders (58%), followed by residents of Samoa, Guam, and Tonga. Each subgroup has its own history, language, and culture.

Asian American Girls Express High Levels Of Body Dissatisfaction

Many Asian American girls struggle with self-esteem and identity based largely on issues of attractiveness. Research that included Asian American girls reported that often they are as concerned or more concerned than White girls about their weight and shape.

In a study of more than 900 middle school girls in northern California, Asian American girls reported greater body dissatisfaction than White girls. Among the leanest 25% of girls, Asian girls reported significantly more dissatisfaction than White girls.

Recent research on Asian Americans suggests that body dissatisfaction is increasing due to the promotion of the Western beauty ideal. One study, for example, reported that Japanese Americans desired to be taller, weigh less, and have larger busts and smaller waists and hips. Some researchers believe that racism and sexism may contribute to negative feelings among Asian American women regarding their physical features, such as eye and nose shape, skin color, straight hair, and short stature. Eyelid and nose reconstructions are the most popular types of surgery requested by Asian American women.

Perfectionism And Need For Control Can Also Contribute To Eating Disorders

Asian Americans are often perceived as the "model minorities" and are expected to be successful and high achieving. Asian American girls may try to seek power and identity through the pursuit of a physically ideal body. The drive to become the "perfect Asian woman" can lead to perfectionism, which is linked to eating disorders, particularly anorexia. In addition, the cultural value of "saving face," which promotes a facade of control, may also contribute to disordered eating or eating disorders.

Acculturation May Increase Vulnerability

Adapting to a new culture creates a set of stressors that for Asian American and immigrant girls may cause confusion about identity, including gender roles. For example, an adolescent girl raised by her family to be obedient and demure may experience emotional turmoil in a Western culture that prizes independence and individualism.

For Asian American girls, acculturation can lead to feelings of isolation, low self-esteem, and the devaluation of native cultural identity, which can increase their vulnerability to eating disorders.

Highly acculturated Chinese females are more likely to report bulimic behaviors and a drive for thinness than those who stay closer to their family values. One report found that the more acculturated Asian American girls were at greatest risk for adopting the "dysfunctional" behaviors of White American society, including poor eating habits and accepting media messages regarding standards of beauty.

Obesity Is Also A Risk Factor

Rates of obesity are very high for some Asian/Pacific Islanders, such as Hawaiians and Samoans. Overweight and obesity are risk factors for disordered eating behaviors, such as bingeing and purging. Dieting for weight loss is also associated with the development of eating disorders and other unhealthy behaviors, including skipping meals and diet-binge cycles. One study, in fact, revealed that binge eating was more prevalent in Asian American than White females.

Latina Girls

Latina Girls Are At Risk

Many people believe that only White girls are affected by eating disorders. In reality, no ethnic or socioeconomic group is immune to the dangers of this disease. Studies typically do not include ethnically diverse populations; therefore, cases of eating disorders among Hispanics are often underreported.

Research on eating disorders among Latina girls is limited. However, recent studies indicate that Latina girls are expressing the same concerns about body weight as White girls and that many are engaging in disordered eating behaviors, including dieting and purging, to lose weight.

The myth that Latinas do not experience eating disorders contributes to the lack of identification of the disease among this population. Since the early detection of an eating disorder is very important for its successful treatment, this misperception can result in serious health problems for Latina girls.

Although this information addresses eating disorders among Latinas in general, these disorders will affect each subgroup of Latinas in a different way. There is no single Latina standard regarding body size and eating patterns. In addition, within each cultural group, socioeconomic status may also affect the risks for developing eating disorders. For example, Latinas from families with low incomes may face a greater risk for obesity, while those from higher income families may be at a higher risk for dieting to try to fit in with their middle or upper middle class peers.

♣ It's A Fact!!

The terms "Hispanic" or "Latina" encompass diverse groups who immigrated to the U.S. Among the largest Hispanic populations in this country are Mexican Americans, Puerto Ricans, and Cuban Americans. The Hispanic population is growing faster than any other ethnic group in this country; it has more than doubled in the past 20 years. By the year 2020, it is estimated that Hispanics will be the single largest minority group in the U.S. Hispanics are predominantly young, with more than one in three being under the age of 18.

Hispanic Girls Express High Levels Of Body Dissatisfaction

Studies show that Latinas express the same or greater concerns about their body shape and weight as White females. In a study of more than 900 middle school girls in northern California, Hispanic girls reported higher levels of body dissatisfaction than any other group. Among the leanest 25% of girls, both Hispanic and Asian girls reported significantly more dissatisfaction than White girls.

Media targeting Latinas, including Hispanic television and magazines, are increasingly reinforcing the ideal of thinness as beauty. For example, although Mexicans have traditionally preferred a larger body size for women, many Mexican American women are idealizing and desiring a thinner figure than the one they currently have. For all racial and ethnic groups, body dissatisfaction is strongly linked with eating disorders.

Low Self-Esteem And Depression Can Contribute To Eating Disorders

Research suggests that Latina girls are at a high risk for mental health problems such as depression. Latina girls also report lower self-esteem and less body satisfaction than girls from other racial and ethnic backgrounds. Studies indicate that as Latinas move from elementary to middle school and on to high school, they may suffer a greater loss of self-esteem than White or Black girls.

Hispanic girls may lack not only the high sense of self worth demonstrated by many African American girls, but also the academic opportunities available to some White girls. In addition, some Latinas may experience prejudice and discrimination based on ethnicity, language, and social status, which can contribute to low self-esteem and depression.

Obesity Is Also A Risk Factor For Eating Disorders

Hispanics, like African Americans, experience high rates of obesity. Among girls ages 5-17, Black and Hispanic girls have been found to have the highest measures of body mass index (BMI), exceeding those of White and Asian girls. They are also less likely to exercise than their White counterparts.

Hispanic children consume the most fast food of all ethnic groups. Research has shown that thigh fat diets greatly contribute to the high rates of obesity among low-income Hispanic families.

> **☞ Remember!!**
> Girls who are influenced by more than one race or culture may experience anxiety and confusion about their identity that may also contribute to disturbed eating behaviors.

For Latinas, as well as women from other ethnic and cultural groups, obesity is linked with weight dissatisfaction and with a desire to be thinner. Overweight women are more likely than women of normal weight to experience teasing, criticism, or discrimination.

Obesity is also a risk factor for binge eating. In a recent study of 31 middle schools and high schools in Minnesota, binge eating was more prevalent among Hispanic girls than among those of other cultural backgrounds.

Dieting And Purging Are Widely Prevalent Among Hispanic Girls

Studies indicate that Latinas and White girls have similar rates of disordered eating behaviors. In fact, Latina girls seem to be particularly at risk for two types of disordered eating behaviors: dieting and purging.

Hispanic high schoolers have been found to have rates of bulimia comparable to those of Whites. Along with Black girls, Latinas have been found to use laxatives more frequently than girls from other racial groups.

Acculturation May Increase Vulnerability

For Latinas and other groups, acculturation can have an impact on body size preference and body image. Heaviness is seen as a sign of affluence and success in some traditional Hispanic cultures; but as Hispanics acculturate to the standards of beauty in this country, they may seek to achieve thinner bodies. Hispanic women born in the U.S. are more likely to prefer a smaller body size. Those who immigrate after age 17 are less likely to desire a thin body.

High levels of acculturation are associated not only with a drive for thinness but also with less healthy eating behaviors. As a result, second and third generation Hispanic adolescents are more likely to be obese than their first generation peers.

Chapter 4

Boys And Eating Disorders

Boys Can And Do Develop Eating Disorders

Eating disorders often are seen as problems affecting only girls. However, studies suggest that hundreds of thousands of boys are experiencing these disorders. Although bulimia is not common among males, 1 in 4 preadolescent cases of anorexia have been found to occur in boys. Studies also suggest that boys may be as likely as girls to develop binge eating disorder.

Males make up the majority of people identified as having muscle dysmorphia, a type of body image disorder characterized by extreme concern with becoming more muscular. People with this disorder, which has been found to occur among bodybuilders, see themselves as puny despite being very muscular, and are likely to use steroids and other drugs to gain muscle mass.

Factors Associated With Eating Disorders Are Similar For Males And Females

The characteristics of males with eating disorders are similar to those seen in females with eating disorders. These factors include low self-esteem, the need to

About This Chapter: Text in this chapter is from a fact sheet within *BodyWise Handbook*, produced by the National Women's Health Information Center (NWHIC), a component of the U.S. Department of Health and Human Services (DHHS), Office on Women's Health, May 2004; available online at http://www.4woman.gov/BodyImage/Bodywise/bp/boys.pdf

> ✎ **What's It Mean?**
>
> Osteoporosis: A condition that is characterized by a decrease in bone mass and density, causing bones to become fragile. [1]
>
> Steroids: A class of drugs that are available legally only by prescription to treat conditions that occur when the body produces abnormally low amounts of testosterone, such as delayed puberty and some types of impotence. They are also prescribed to treat body wasting in patients with AIDS and other diseases that result in loss of lean muscle mass. [2]
>
> Source: [1] "Dictionary of Cancer Terms," National Cancer Institute, available at www.nci.nih.gov; cited December 2004. [2] "Info Facts," National Institute on Drug Abuse, U.S. Department of Health and Human Services, available at www.nida.nih.gov, 2004.

be accepted, an inability to cope with emotional pressures, and family and relationship problems. Homosexuality also appears to be a risk factor for males because it may include them in a subculture that places a premium on appearance.

Both males and females with eating disorders are likely to experience depression, substance abuse, anxiety disorders, and personality disorders. However, substance abuse is more common among males than females with eating disorders. Male patients with eating disorders have been found to be more severely affected by osteoporosis than female patients.

Boys May Try To Lose Fat And Gain Muscle To Improve Body Image And/Or Athletic Performance

While the female body ideal is thin, the male ideal is lean, V-shaped, and muscular. Unlike girls, who generally want to lose weight, boys are equally divided between those who want to lose weight and those who want to gain weight. Boys who consider themselves overweight want to lose weight, while those who think they are too thin want to gain weight. All want to be more muscular.

Boys may try to lose fat and/or gain muscle for many reasons. Some of these are: to avoid being teased about being fat; to improve body image; to increase strength and/or to improve athletic performance in wrestling, track, swimming, or other sports.

Overweight boys are at a higher risk for dieting than those who are not overweight. Boys who think they are too small, on the other hand, may be at a greater risk than other boys for using steroids or taking untested nutritional supplements such as protein and creatine to increase muscle mass.

♣ It's A Fact!!

Students of all ethnic and cultural groups are vulnerable to developing eating disorders. For example, Black and Hispanic boys have been found to be more likely to binge eat than Caucasian boys.

Boys Are Less Likely To Be Diagnosed Early With An Eating Disorder

Doctors reportedly are less likely to make a diagnosis of eating disorders in males than females. Other adults who work with young people and parents also may be less likely to suspect an eating disorder in boys, thereby delaying detection and treatment. A study of 135 males hospitalized with an eating disorder noted that the males with bulimia felt ashamed of having a stereotypically "female" disorder, which might explain their delay in seeking treatment. Binge eating disorder may go unrecognized in males because a male who overeats is less likely to provoke attention than a female who overeats.

♣ It's A Fact!!
Action Figures Are Bulking Up

A recent study noted that some of the most popular male action figures have grown extremely muscular over time. Researchers compared action toys today—with their original counterparts. They found that many action figures have acquired the physiques of bodybuilders, with particularly impressive gains in the shoulder and chest areas. Some of the action toys have not only grown more muscular but have also developed increasingly sharp muscle definition, such as rippled abdominals. As noted in the study, if the GI Joe Extreme were 70 inches in size, he would sport larger biceps than any bodybuilder in history.

Chapter 5

What Causes Eating Disorders?

There is no single cause for eating disorders. Although concerns about weight and body shape underlie all eating disorders, the actual cause of these disorders appear to result from a convergence of many factors, including cultural and family pressures and emotional and personality disorders. Genetics and biologic factors may also play a role.

Negative Family Influences

Negative influences within the family play a major role in triggering and perpetuating eating disorders. Some studies have produced the following observations and theories regarding family influence.

- **Insecure Infancy:** Some experts theorize that parents who fail to provide a safe and secure foundation in infancy may foster eating disorders. In such cases, children experience so-called insecure attachments. They are more likely to have greater weight concerns and lower self-esteem than are those with secure attachments.

- **Parental Behaviors:** Poor parenting by both mothers and fathers have been implicated in eating disorders. One study found that 40% of nine- to ten-year-old girls try to lose weight generally with the urging of their mothers. Some studies have found that mothers of anorexics tend to be over-involved in their child's life, while mothers of people with bulimia are critical and detached. On the other hand, a 2002 study reported that the father's behavior also plays a very important role in a child's eating disorder. Some research, for example, strongly implicates overly critical fathers, brothers, or both in the development of anorexia in both girls and boys.

- **Family History Of Addictions Or Emotional Disorders:** Studies report that people with either eating disorder are more likely to have parents with alcoholism or substance abuse than are those in the general population. Parents of people with bulimia appear to be more likely to have psychiatric disorders than parents of patients with anorexia.

- **History Of Abuse:** Women with eating disorders, particularly bulimia, appear to have a higher incidence of sexual abuse. Studies have reported sexual abuse rates as high as 35% in women with bulimia.

- **Family History Of Obesity:** People with bulimia are more likely than average to have an obese parent or to have been overweight themselves during childhood.

At least one study has reported that the most positive way for parents to influence their children's eating habits and to prevent weight problems and eating disorders is to have healthy eating habits themselves.

Problems Surrounding Birth

In some studies, people with anorexia have reported a higher than average incidence of problems during the mother's pregnancy or after birth. These problems include the following:

- Infection
- Physical trauma
- Seizures
- Low birth weight
- Older maternal age

Some experts believe that such patients experienced an injury to the brain while in the womb that predisposed them to eating problems in infancy and to subsequent eating disorders later in life. Studies have suggested that people with anorexia often had stomach and intestinal problems in infancy.

Genetic Factors

Anorexia is eight times more common in people who have relatives with the disorder, and some experts estimate that genetic factors may influence more than half of the variances in eating disorders. For example, a 2000 study reported that twins had a tendency to share specific eating disorders (anorexia nervosa, bulimia nervosa, and obesity). Some evidence has reported an association with genetic factors responsible for serotonin, the brain chemical involved with both well being and appetite. Some inherited traits that might make someone susceptible to eating disorders include the following:

- A genetic propensity toward thinness caused by a faster metabolism and reinforced by cultural approval could predispose some people to develop anorexia.

- An inherited propensity for obesity could also trigger an eating disorder to compensate.

- Inherited personality traits also play some causal role.

Cultural Pressures

The approach to food in Western countries is extremely problematic. Enough food is produced in the U.S. to supply 3,800 calories every day to each man, woman, and child, far more than any single person needs to sustain life. Obesity is a global epidemic, and few people living in this over-fed and sedentary culture eat a meal guiltlessly. One can nearly make the sweeping generalization that everyone who lives in a developed nation is at risk for either obesity or some eating disorder.

One interesting anthropologic study reported the following observations:

- During historical periods or in cultures where women are financially dependent and marital ties are stronger, the standard is toward being curvaceous, possibly reflecting a cultural or economic need for greater reproduction.

- During periods or in cultures where female independence has been possible, the standard of female attractiveness tends toward thinness.

Whether or not the current Western cultural pressure is for fewer children, the response of the media to both the cultural drive for thinness and overproduction of food play major roles in triggering obesity and eating disorders.

- On the one hand, advertisers heavily market weight-reduction programs and present anorexic young models as the paradigm of sexual desirability. Clothes are designed and displayed for thin bodies in spite of the fact that few women could wear them successfully.

- One study reported that teenage boys and girls who made strong efforts to look like celebrities of the same sex were more likely to be constant dieters.

- On the other hand, the media floods the public with attractive ads for consuming foods. And, the emphasis is on "junk" foods.

♣ It's A Fact!!

New research suggests that there is a biological link between stress and the drive to eat. Comfort foods—high in sugar, fat, and calories—seem to calm the body's response to chronic stress. In addition, hormones produced when one is under stress encourage the formation of fat cells. In Westernized countries life tends to be competitive, fast paced, demanding, and stressful. There may be a link between so-called modern life and increasing rates of overeating, overweight, and obesity. (Study published in *Proceedings of the National Academy of Sciences*. Author is Mary Dallman, professor of physiology, University of California at San Francisco [September 30, 2003].)

In a country where obesity is epidemic, young women who achieve thinness believe they have accomplished a major cultural and personal victory. They have overcome the temptations of junk food and, at the same time, created body images idealized by the media. Weight loss brings a feeling of triumph over helplessness. This sense of accomplishment is often reinforced by the envy of heavier companions who perceive the anorexic friend as being emotionally stronger and more sexually attractive.

Excessive Athleticism And The Female Athlete Triad: The cultural attitude toward physical activity is a fitting companion to the general disordered attitude regarding eating. Americans are encouraged to admire physical activity only as an intense competitive effort that few can attain, leaving most people in their armchairs as spectators (and at risk for obesity).

In the small community of athletes, excessive exercise is associated with many cases of anorexia (and, to a lesser degree, bulimia). In young female athletes, anorexia postpones puberty, allowing them to retain a muscular boyish shape without the normal accumulation of fatty tissues in breasts and hips that may blunt their competitive edge. Many coaches and teachers compound the problem by overstressing calorie counting and loss of body fat. Some over-control the athletes' lives and are even abusive to an athlete that goes over the weight limit. (Male athletes are also vulnerable to their coaches' influence. Anorexia is also a problem among this group.)

In response, people who are vulnerable to such criticism may lose excessive weight, which has been known to be deadly even for famous athletes. The term "female athlete triad" in fact, is now a common and serious disorder facing young female athletes and dancers and describes the combined presence of the following problems:

- Eating disorders.
- Amenorrhea (absence or irregular menstruation). Evidence is mounting that overly restricting calories may be more important than low weight in causing menstrual problems. Studies suggest that amenorrhea occurs even in women with normal weight if they severely diet.
- Osteoporosis. Bone loss, on the other hand, appears to be related to low weight. The more severe the weight loss, the more bone is lost.

In one study, female athletes who consumed a high-fat diet (35% of daily calories) performed longer and with greater intensity than those with a standard athletic low-fat diet (27% of daily calories). And such a diet appeared to be more estrogen-protective.

Hormonal Abnormalities

Hormonal problems are rampant in eating disorders and include chemical abnormalities in the thyroid, the reproductive regions, and areas related to stress, well being, and appetite. Many of these chemical changes are certainly a result of malnutrition or other aspects of eating disorders, but they also may play a role in perpetuating or even creating susceptibility to the disorders.

The primary setting of many of these abnormalities originates in a small area of the brain called the limbic system. A specific system called hypothalamic-pituitary-adrenal axis (HPA) may be particularly important in eating disorders. It originates in the following regions in the brain:

- **Hypothalamus.** The hypothalamus is a small structure that plays a role in controlling our behavior, such as eating, sexual behavior, and sleeping, and regulates body temperature, emotions, secretion of hormones, and movement.

- **The Pituitary Gland.** The pituitary gland develops from an extension of the hypothalamus downwards. It is involved in controlling thyroid functions, the adrenal glands, growth, and sexual maturation.

- **Amygdala.** This small almond-like structure lies deep in the brain and is associated with regulation and control of major emotional activities, including anxiety, depression, aggression, and affection.

Stress Hormones: The HPA systems trigger the production and release of stress hormones called glucocorticoids, including the primary stress hormone cortisol. Chronically elevated levels of stress chemicals have been observed in patients with anorexia and bulimia. Cortisol is very important in marshaling systems throughout the body (including the heart, lungs, circulation, metabolism, immune systems, and skin) to deal quickly with any threat. Among the

♣ It's A Fact!!
Social Factors

Sometimes appearance-obsessed friends or romantic partners create pressure that encourages eating disorders. Ditto for sorority houses, theatre troupes, dance companies, school cliques, and other situations where peers influence one another in unhealthy ways.

People vulnerable to eating disorders also, in most cases, are experiencing relationship problems, loneliness in particular. Some may be withdrawn with only superficial or conflicted connections to other people. Others may seem to be living exciting lives filled with friends and social activities, but later they will confess that they did not feel they really fit in, that no one seemed to really understand them, and that they had no true friends or confidants with whom they could share thoughts, feelings, doubts, insecurities, fears, hopes, ambitions, and so forth. Often they desperately want healthy connections to others but fear criticism and rejection if their perceived flaws and shortcomings become known.

specific effects is inhibition of neuropeptide Y (NPY), a powerful appetite stimulant that also has anti-anxiety properties. This process may serve as a biologic link between extreme stressful conditions in a young person's life and the later development of anorexia, although some imaging studies indicate that stress-hormone-related changes occur after anorexia has developed. More work is needed to determine if changes in stress hormones are a cause or a result of eating disorders.

Release Of Neurotransmitters: The HPA system also releases certain neurotransmitters (chemical messengers) that regulate stress, mood, and appetite and are being heavily investigated for a possible role in eating disorders. Abnormalities in the activities of three of them, serotonin, norepinephrine, and dopamine, are of particular interest. Serotonin is involved with both well being and appetite (among other traits), and norepinephrine is a stress hormone. Abnormalities in both have been observed in patients who binge and in those with anorexia or bulimia. Dopamine is involved in reward-seeking behavior, so deficiencies might create a more intense need for rewards, such as carbohydrates. Studies on dopamine abnormalities have been mixed, however.

Low Leptin Levels: Leptin is a hormone that appears to trigger the hypothalamus to stimulate appetite, and low levels have been observed in people with anorexia and bulimia.

Low Reproductive Hormones: The hypothalamic-pituitary system is also responsible for the production of important reproductive hormones that are severely depleted in anorexics. Although most experts believe that these reproductive abnormalities are a result of anorexia, others have reported that in 30% to 50% of people with anorexia, menstrual disturbances occurred before severe malnutrition set in and remained a problem long after weight gain, indicating that hypothalamic-pituitary abnormalities precede the eating disorder itself.

Compensating For Mood Swings During Binge-Purging Cycles

Low levels of serotonin have been observed not only in eating disorders but also in depression. One theory for the persistence of the binge-purge cycle in bulimia involves restoring serotonin imbalances and so improving mood. It involves the following:

- Bingeing elevates tryptophan, a compound found in food, particularly carbohydrates, which is essential to the production of serotonin in the brain. People may binge in order to produce serotonin, thereby improving their mood. An initial increase in tryptophan, however, produces depression in some people. Both events are consistent with a study on young people with bulimia who reported negative moods before bingeing and even worse moods right after bingeing.

- Such depression may become associated with guilt over bingeing and the need to purge. Right before and after a purge cycle, however, studies report an improvement in mood, which might indicate the delayed increase in serotonin triggered by the tryptophan. The heightened mood after the purge cycle may be due to stimulation of natural opioids that occur during this process.

- The binge-purge cycle might then be stimulated by chemical changes and perpetuated by feelings of guilt and depression after bingeing and release from guilt and euphoria during and after purging.

✤ **It's A Fact!!**

Psychological Factors

People with eating disorders tend to be perfectionistic. They have unrealistic expectations of themselves and others. In spite of their many achievements, they feel inadequate, defective, and worthless. In addition, they see the world as black and white, no shades of gray. Everything is either good or bad, a success or a failure, fat or thin. If fat is bad and thin is good, then thinner is better, and thinnest is best—even if thinnest is sixty-eight pounds in a hospital bed on life support.

Some people with eating disorders use the behaviors to avoid sexuality. Others use them to try to take control of themselves and their lives. They are strong, usually winning the power struggles they find themselves in, but inside they feel weak, powerless, victimized, defeated, and resentful.

People with eating disorders often lack a sense of identity. They try to define themselves by manufacturing a socially approved and admired exterior. They have answered the existential question, "Who am I?" by symbolically saying "I am, or I am trying to be, thin. Therefore, I matter."

People with eating disorders often are legitimately angry, but because they seek approval and fear criticism, they do not know how to express their anger in healthy ways. They turn it against themselves by starving or stuffing.

Source: Reprinted with permission from http://www.anred.com. © 2004 Anorexia Nervosa and Related Eating Disorders, Inc. All rights reserved.

Infections

In some cases, infection has been associated with anorexia. In such cases, immune factors released to fight these infections may cause inflammation and injury in the areas of the brain that affect appetite and behavior.

Streptococcal Infection: The bacteria responsible for strep throat and rheumatic fever—called group A beta-hemolytic streptococcal (GABHS)—is now a suspect in some cases of anorexia. Some children who have been

✎ What's It Mean?

Carbohydrate: A sugar molecule. Carbohydrates can be simple, such as glucose, or complex, such as starch. [1]

Hormone: A chemical made by glands in the body. Hormones circulate in the bloodstream and control the actions of certain cells or organs. Some hormones can also be made in a laboratory. [1]

Malnutrition: A disorder caused by a lack of proper nutrition or an inability to absorb nutrients from food. [1]

Metabolism: The total of all chemical changes that take place in a cell or an organism. These changes produce energy and basic materials needed for important life processes. [1]

Mononucleosis: A viral infection, which causes a fever, sore throat, and swollen lymph glands, especially in the neck. It is often transmitted by saliva. [2]

Puberty: The process of developing from a child to sexual maturity, when a person becomes capable of having children. [3]

Thyroid: A gland located beneath the voice box (larynx) that produces thyroid hormone. The thyroid helps regulate growth and metabolism. [1]

Source: [1] "Dictionary of Cancer Terms," National Cancer Institute, available at www.nci.nih.gov; cited December 2004. [2] Editor. [3] "4Girls Web Site Glossary," 4Girls Health, U.S. Department of Health and Human Services, Office on Women's Health, available at www.4girls.gov, 2004.

infected with these bacteria develop a syndrome that includes obsessive-compulsive disorder (OCD), tics, and anorexia nervosa. The syndrome is called PANDAS (Pediatric Autoimmune Neuropsychiatric Disorders Associated with Streptococcus). More research is needed to confirm this as an actual cause of anorexia and to determine if it may be treatable with antibiotics.

Epstein Barr Virus: Epstein Barr, the virus that causes mononucleosis, has also been associated with the development of anorexia.

Chapter 6

How Are Eating Disorders Diagnosed?

What Are The Symptoms Of Eating Disorders?

Possibly the most bewildering symptom of eating disorders is the distorted body image (body dysmorphia). Although people typically associate distorted body image with severe anorexia, one study indicated that distortion might be more prevalent in people with bulimia. People with bulimia were more likely than those with anorexia to overestimate their size. There was also a greater disparity between what they wanted to look like and what they believed they looked like. In another study, people with anorexia tended to have an accurate perception of their upper body, but overestimated the size of their abdominal and pelvic area.

Symptoms Specific To Bulimia Without Anorexia

People with bulimia nearly always practice it in secret, and, although they may be underweight, they are not always anorexic. Symptoms or signs of bulimia may, therefore, be very subtle and go unnoticed. They may include the following:

- Evidence of discarded packaging for laxatives, diet pills, emetics (drugs that induce vomiting), or diuretics (medications that reduce fluids).

About This Chapter: Information in this chapter is excerpted from "Eating Disorders: Anorexia and Bulimia," © 2003 A.D.A.M., Inc. Reprinted with permission.

- Regularly going to the bathroom right after meals.

- Suddenly eating large amounts of food or buying large quantities that disappear right away.

- Compulsive exercising.

- Broken blood vessels in the eyes (from the strain of vomiting).

- Swollen salivary glands. These occur, within days of vomiting, in about 8% of people with bulimia. They often give a pouch-like appearance to areas below the corners of the mouth.

♣ It's A Fact!!

Interview Tests

It is recommended that a supportive companion be present during part of the initial medical interview to offer additional information on the patient's eating history and to help offset any resistance or denial the patient may express.

Various questionnaires are available for assessing patients. Of note is a brief British test called the SCOFF questionnaire. It is proving to be very reliable in accurately identifying both very young and adult patients who meet the full criteria for anorexia or bulimia nervosa. (It may not be as accurate in people who do not meet the full criteria.)

SCOFF Questionnaire

1. Do you feel **Sick** because you feel full?

2. Do you lose **Control** over how much you eat?

3. Have you lost more than **One** stone (about 13 pounds) recently?

4. Do you believe yourself to be **Fat** when others say you are thin?

5. Does **Food** dominate your life?

Answering yes to two of these questions is a strong indicator of an eating disorder.

- Dry mouth.

- Teeth develop cavities, diseased gums, and irreversible enamel erosion from excessive acid. (Gargling with baking soda after purging rather than using toothpaste may help neutralize the acid.)

- Rashes and pimples.

- Small cuts and calluses across the tops of finger joints. (These cuts can occur from repeated self-induced vomiting, in which a person thrusts the hand down the throat past the front teeth.)

Symptoms Specific To Anorexia

The primary symptom of anorexia is major weight loss from excessive and continuous dieting, which may either be restrictive dieting or binge-eating and purging.(Note: Young women who have both diabetes and eating disorders may have normal weight or even be overweight from the effects of insulin. However, they still are at high risk from the medical consequences of anorexia.)

Other symptoms may include the following:

- Menstruation may be infrequent or absent.

- Often, compulsive exercising coupled with emaciation leads to orthopedic problems, particularly in dancers and athletes. Such problems, in fact, may be the first sign of trouble that force these patients to seek medical help.

- Refusal to eat in front of others.

- Ritualistic eating, including cutting food into small pieces.

- Hypersensitivity to cold. (In fact, some women wear several layers of clothing to both keep warm and hide their thinness.)

- Yellowish skin, especially on the palms of the hands and soles of the feet. (This occurs in people eating too many vitamin A-rich vegetables, such as carrots.)

- The skin may be dry and covered with fine hair.

- Normal scalp hair may be thin.

- The feet and hands may be cold or sometimes swollen.

- The stomach is often distressed and bloated after eating.

Thinking may be confused or slowed, and an anorexic patient may have poor memory and lack judgment.

What Will Confirm A Diagnosis Of Eating Disorders?

The first step towards a diagnosis is to admit the existence of an eating disorder. Often, the patient needs to be compelled by a parent or others to see a doctor because the patient may deny and resist the problem. Some patients may even self-diagnose their condition as an allergy to carbohydrates, because after being on a restricted diet, eating carbohydrates can produce gastrointestinal problems, dizziness, weakness, and palpitations. This may lead such people to restrict carbohydrates even more severely.

✎ What's It Mean?

Electrocardiogram: An external, noninvasive test that records the electrical activity of the heart. [1]

Electrolytes: A substance that breaks up into ions (electrically charged particles) when it is dissolved in body fluids or water. Some examples of electrolytes are sodium, potassium, chloride, and calcium. Electrolytes are primarily responsible for the movement of nutrients into cells and the movement of wastes out of cells. [2]

Menstrual: The blood flow from the uterus that happens about every 4 weeks in a woman. [1]

Protein: A molecule made up of amino acids that are needed for the body to function properly. Proteins are the basis of body structures such as skin and hair and of substances such as enzymes and antibodies. [2]

Source: [1] "NWHIC Web Site Glossary," U.S. Department of Health and Human Services, Office on Women's Health, available at www.4woman.gov, 2004. [2] "Dictionary of Cancer Terms," National Cancer Institute, available at www.nci.nih.gov; cited December 2004.

It is often extremely difficult for parents as well as the patient to admit that a problem is present. For example, because food is such an intrinsic part of the mother/child relationship, a child's eating disorder might seem like a terrible parental failure. Parents may have their own emotional issues with weight gain and loss and perceive no problem with having a "thin" child.

Diagnosing Bulimia Nervosa

In spite of the prevalence of bulimia, in one study only 30% of Midwest family physicians had ever diagnosed bulimia in a patient. Younger and female physicians are more likely to detect bulimia. A physician should make a diagnosis of bulimia if there are at least two bulimic episodes per week for three months. Because people with bulimia tend to have complications with their teeth and gums, dentists could play a crucial role in identifying and diagnosing bulimia.

Diagnosing Anorexia Nervosa

Generally, an observation of physical symptoms and a personal history will quickly confirm the diagnosis of anorexia. The standard criteria for diagnosing anorexia nervosa are:

- The patient's refusal to maintain a body weight normal for age and height.
- Intense fear of becoming fat even though underweight.
- A distorted self-image that results in diminished self-confidence.
- Denial of the seriousness of emaciation and starvation.
- The loss of menstrual functions for at least three months.

The physician then categorizes the anorexia further:

- Restricting (severe dieting only).
- Anorexia bulimia (binge-purge behavior).

Because the disorder rarely shows up in men, physicians may not be on the lookout for it in male patients, even if they show classic symptoms of anorexia. Physicians should be very aware of these symptoms in anyone, particularly in athletes and dancers.

Diagnosing Complications Of Eating Disorders

Once a diagnosis is made, physicians should immediately check for any serious complications of starvation. They should also rule out other medical disorders that might be causing the anorexia. Tests should include the following:

- A complete blood count.

- Tests for electrolyte imbalances. Low potassium levels indicate that the disorder is more likely to be accompanied by the binge-purge syndrome.

- Test for protein levels.

- An electrocardiogram and a chest x-ray.

- Tests for liver, kidney, and thyroid problems.

- A bone density test.

Chapter 7

Statistics On Eating Disorders

Prevalence

- It is estimated that 8 million Americans have an eating disorder—seven million women and one million men.

- One in 200 American women suffer from anorexia.

- Two to three in 100 American women suffer from bulimia.

- Nearly half of all Americans personally know someone with an eating disorder. (Note: One in five Americans suffers from mental illnesses.)

- An estimated 10–15% of people with anorexia or bulimia are males.

Mortality Rates

- Eating disorders have the highest mortality rate of any mental illness.

- A study by the National Association of Anorexia Nervosa and Associated Disorders reported that 5–10% of anorexics die within 10 years after contracting the disease; 18–20% of anorexics will be dead after 20 years and only 30–40% ever fully recover.

About This Chapter: "Eating Disorders," reprinted with permission from the South Carolina Department of Mental Health.

- The mortality rate associated with anorexia nervosa is 12 times higher than the death rate of all causes of death for females 15–24 years old.

- 20% of people suffering from anorexia will prematurely die from complications related to their eating disorder, including suicide and heart problems.

Access To Treatment

- Only 1 in 10 people with eating disorders receive treatment.

- About 80% of the girls/women who have accessed care for their eating disorders do not get the intensity of treatment they need to stay in recovery—they are often sent home weeks earlier than the recommended stay.

- Treatment of an eating disorder in the U.S. ranges from $500 per day to $2,000 per day. The average cost for a month of inpatient treatment is $30,000. It is estimated that individuals with eating disorders need anywhere from 3–6 months of inpatient care. Health insurance companies, for several reasons, do not typically cover the cost of treating eating disorders.

- The cost of outpatient treatment, including therapy and medical monitoring, can extend to $100,000 or more.

Adolescents

- Anorexia is the 3rd most common chronic illness among adolescents.

- 95% of those who have eating disorders are between the ages of 12 and 25.

- 50% of girls between the ages of 11 and 13 see themselves as overweight.

- 80% of 13-year-olds have attempted to lose weight.

Racial And Ethnic Minorities

- Rates of minorities with eating disorders are similar to those of white women.

- 74% of American Indian girls reported dieting and purging with diet pills.

- Essence magazine, in 1994, reported that 53.5% of their respondents, African-American females, were at risk of an eating disorder.

- Eating disorders are one of the most common psychological problems facing young women in Japan.

♣ It's A Fact!!
Celebrities Who Have Suffered With Eating Disorders

- Jane Fonda
- Susan Dey
- Alexandra Paul
- Princess Di
- Karen Carpenter
- Cathy Rigby
- Cherry Boone O'Neill
- Lynn Redgrave
- Jeannine Turner

- Jamie Lynn-Sigler
- Justine Batemen
- Tracey Gold
- Nadia Comaneci
- Elton John
- Joan Rivers
- Barbara Niven
- Paula Abdul

Part Two

Specific Eating Disorders

Chapter 8

Anorexia Nervosa

Anorexia (or anorexia nervosa) is an eating disorder centered on an obsessive fear of weight gain. Anorexia involves self-starvation and excessive weight loss. Although anorexia is a mental disorder, the physical consequences are serious and sometimes life threatening.

What are the signs and symptoms of anorexia?

The behavioral warning signs and symptoms of anorexia nervosa are:

- Avoidance of eating
    - Denies feeling hungry
    - Avoids social gatherings where food is involved
    - Develops food rituals that allow for eating very little, eats in secrecy, eats foods in a certain order, excessive chewing, rearranges food on the plate, eats unnaturally small amounts of food
- Dramatic weight loss
    - Refuses to maintain the minimal normal body weight for age and height

- Denies the serious consequences of low body weight

- Obsession with dieting and weight loss

  - Weighs self several times a day and focuses on the smallest fluctuation in weight

  - Terrified of gaining weight or being fat

  - Even when thin, sees self as overweight

  - Bases self-worth on body weight and body image

- Excessive focus on an exercise regimen

How is anorexia different from bulimia?

The classic form of anorexia (restricting type) involves weight loss through self-starvation and excessive exercise. In another form of anorexia, the individual not only cuts calories, but also behaves similarly to the bulimic: bingeing on foods, and then purging. With the symptoms of both anorexia and bulimia, an individual is considered to have anorexia of the binge-eating/purging type.

Who is likely to suffer from anorexia?

Anorexia nervosa is more common in females and usually begins in adolescence. Between 1% and 2% of all females develop anorexia. Less than 1% of males develops anorexia nervosa. The disorder is more common in industrialized countries where thinness is a positive cultural trait. A person with a family member who has anorexia is more likely to develop anorexia.

What are the effects of anorexia?

Anorexia nervosa can have severe medical consequences. Because the anorexic individual does not consume enough calories or nutrients to support the maintenance and growth of the body, all body processes slow down to conserve energy. This slowing down has serious physical, emotional, and behavioral effects.

Physical Effects

- Loss of menstrual periods

- Dry, brittle bones due to significant bone density loss (osteoporosis)

- Dry, brittle nails and hair, or hair loss

- Lowered resistance to illness

- Hypersensitivity to heat and cold

- Bruises easily

- Appears to need less sleep than normal eaters

- Digestive problems such as bloating or constipation

- Muscle loss and weakness

- Severe dehydration, which can result in kidney failure

- Fainting, fatigue, and overall weaknes.

- Eventual growth of a downy layer of hair (lanugo) all over the body, including the face (the body is trying to stay warm)

- In severe cases, heart trouble, low blood pressure, low heart rate, low body temperature, poor circulation, anemia, stunted growth, and even death

♣ It's A Fact!!
Did You Know?

- 90 to 95% of those with anorexia nervosa are girls and women.

- Left untreated, some of the physical effects of anorexia are irreversible.

- Anorexia nervosa has one of the highest death rates of any mental disorder. 5 to 20% of those with anorexia nervosa will die. The period of time of self-starvation is the critical factor for survival.

Emotional And Behavioral Effects

- Difficulty in concentrating on anything else except weight

- Isolation from family and friends

- Emotional regression to a child-like state

- Irritability

- Feelings of guilt and depression
- Dependence upon alcohol or drugs to handle the negative outlook

✎ What's It Mean?

Anemia: A condition in which the number of red blood cells is below normal. [1]

Constipation: A condition in which the stool becomes hard and dry. A person who is constipated usually has fewer than three bowel movements in a week. Bowel movements may be painful. [2]

Endocrine Disorder: A disorder of the endocrine glands. These are glands that secrete substances which are released directly into the circulation and which influence metabolism and other body functions. [3]

Heart Arrhythmia: A change in the regular beat of the heart. [4]

Low Blood Pressure: When a person's blood pressure is too low, there is not enough blood flow to the heart, brain, and other vital organs. Symptoms include dizziness and lightheadedness. [5]

Metabolic Disorder: A condition in which normal metabolic processes are disrupted, usually because of a missing enzyme. [1]

Nutrients: chemical compounds (such as protein, fat, carbohydrate, vitamins, or minerals) that make up foods. These compounds are used by the body to function and grow. [1]

Source: [1] "Dictionary of Cancer Terms," National Cancer Institute, available at www.nci.nih.gov; cited December 2004. [2] "Digestive Diseases Dictionary," National Institute of Diabetes and Digestive and Kidney Diseases, available at www.digestive.niddk.nih.gov, 2000. [3] "Genetics Home Reference Glossary," a service of the U.S. National Library of Medicine, available at www.ghr.nlm.nih.gov, 2004. [4] "Heart and Cardiovascular Disease," U.S. Department of Health and Human Services, Office on Women's Health, available at www.4woman.gov, 2002. [5] Editor.

What causes anorexia?

Research about the causes of anorexia is not definitive, and no one yet knows the exact cause. A combination of biological, social, and psychological factors may cause anorexia.

Biological Causes

Some research indicates that higher levels of the neurotransmitter serotonin (a brain chemical) make the individual withdraw socially and have less desire for food. However, the higher level of serotonin may be a result of the anorexia, rather than a cause.

Individuals may have a genetic predisposition for anorexia. Individuals with anorexia often have family members with the disorder.

Social Causes

The cultural or social environment may cause or reinforce a propensity toward anorexia. Particular professions (fashion model, horse jockey) and sports (ballet, gymnastics) emphasize thinness and low body weight. Female athletes are particularly prone to being anorexic. Coaches may encourage them to lose weight, and they may notice improved performance with some weight loss. However, the anorexic does not know when to stop losing weight, and, ultimately, hinders performance by not consuming enough calories or nutrients to fuel the body.

Some cultures value thinness as a key element of attractiveness, especially for women. Thus, social pressure is a cause of anorexia.

Families that are overprotective or emphasize overachievement or physical fitness often produce anorexic family members.

Psychological And Emotional Causes

Some personality traits are associated with anorexia: perfectionism, obsessiveness, approval seeking, low self-esteem, withdrawal, irritability, and black-or-white (all-or-nothing) thinking.

Major life events may trigger anorexia: life transitions, emotional upsets, or sexual or physical abuse.

Anorexia Nervosa In Males

Anorexia nervosa is a severe, life-threatening disorder in which the individual refuses to maintain a minimally normal body weight, is intensely afraid of gaining weight, and exhibits a significant distortion in the perception of the shape or size of his body, as well as dissatisfaction with his body shape and size.

Behavioral Characteristics

- Excessive dieting, fasting, restricted diet

- Food rituals

- Preoccupation with bodybuilding, weight lifting, or muscle toning

- Compulsive exercise

- Difficulty eating with others, lying about eating

- Frequently weighing self

- Preoccupation with food

- Focus on certain body parts; e.g., buttocks, thighs, and stomach

- Disgust with body size or shape

- Distortion of body size; i.e., feels fat even though others tell him he is already very thin

Emotional And Mental Characteristics

- Intense fear of becoming fat or gaining weight

- Depression

- Social isolation

- Strong need to be in control

- Rigid, inflexible thinking, "all or nothing"

- Decreased interest in sex or fears around sex

- Possible conflict over gender identity or sexual orientation

- Low sense of self worth—uses weight as a measure of worth

- Difficulty expressing feelings

- Perfectionistic—strives to be the neatest, thinnest, smartest, etc.

- Difficulty thinking clearly or concentrating

- Irritability, denial—believes others are overreacting to his low weight or caloric restriction

- Insomnia

Physical Characteristics

- Low body weight (15% or more below what is expected for age, height, and activity level)

- Lack of energy, fatigue

- Muscular weakness

- Decreased balance, unsteady gait

- Lowered body temperature, blood pressure, pulse rate

- Tingling in hands and feet

- Thinning hair or hair loss

- Lanugo (downy growth of body hair)

- Heart arrhythmia

- Lowered testosterone levels

Mental health experts think that the feelings of being overwhelmed and powerless in adolescence can bring about a desire to maintain control in some realm of life, such as control of body weight. Being in total control of what enters the mouth can give the adolescent a feeling of powerfulness. Thus, the period of adolescence may cause anorexia to manifest itself.

Other (Combination) Causes

Relational or early life trauma (sometimes called developmental trauma) affects the brain, which in turn can impact both biology and psychology. Symptoms can include obsessive, compulsive eating disorders like anorexia.

What should you do if you suspect anorexia in yourself or others?

Because anorexia nervosa can result in death, and because so many sufferers deny that they have a problem, it is incumbent upon others to take action. The sooner that someone takes action, the better, because the length of time that a person continues with the disorder is related to the chance of death. The body slowly quits functioning. Early treatment is essential.

What is the treatment for anorexia?

Treatment for anorexia involves both the body and the mind. Early treatment for anorexia involves behavioral techniques, psychotherapy for improved self-esteem, and a variety of approaches including nutritional therapy, massage, and relaxation exercises.

Treatment of anorexics is especially difficult because these individuals are resistant to getting help. More than 95% of anorexics deny that they have a problem and view treatment as an attempt to "make them fat." They believe that their low body weight is the solution, not the problem. This means that those who are close to the anorexic individual must take an active role in getting help. They may need to accompany the anorexic to appointments to make sure that the anorexic's behaviors are adequately described.

When a person with suspected anorexia consults a doctor for diagnosis and treatment, the doctor first makes sure that endocrine, metabolic, and central nervous system disorders do not explain the apparent weight loss.

They do a physical exam and take a physical history. In an anorexic individual, the physical problems are usually the result of not eating.

Early treatment is essential. The effects of anorexia on the mind and body are severe. Not only does the anorexic look and feel awful, but also the disorder can be life threatening. Treatment works best before too much weight is lost. Weight held at a low level for a long time gives a poor prognosis for recovery.

First Treatment: Restoration Of Body Weight And Eating Patterns

The first order of treatment is to restore normal body weight and eating patterns. Along with weight gain comes improved body functioning. After the body weight is stabilized, treatment can progress to dealing with the psychological and physical problems that are a result of not eating.

A dietitian can be instrumental in guiding the anorexic individual to better eating habits. Sound nutrition can repair the weakened body.

Therapeutic Treatment

Therapy can address the need for increased self-esteem. Therapy helps the individual to see that they are not really overweight.

Support groups are helpful, but because anorexics deny their problem, they may be unwilling to attend support groups.

Sometimes family therapy is the best approach.

Medications As Treatment

Medications do not cure anorexia, but anti-depressant drugs may be prescribed for the depression and anxiety that often accompany anorexia.

Timing Of Treatment Is Critical

Left untreated, anorexia can cause irreversible physical damage. In addition, anorexia nervosa has one of the highest death rates of any mental disorder: 5 to 20% of those with anorexia nervosa will die. The period of time of self-starvation is the critical factor for survival. Anorexia is a lifelong illness and relapses are common: 40% of anorexics recover, 30% improve, and 30% have significant problems with anorexia throughout their lives.

Chapter 9

Frequently Asked Questions About Anorexia

What is anorexia?

Anorexia (a-neh-RECK-see ah) nervosa, typically called anorexia, is a type of eating disorder that mainly affects girls and young women. A person with this disorder has an intense fear of gaining weight and limits the food she eats. She

- Has a low body weight.
- Refuses to keep a normal body weight.
- Is extremely afraid of becoming fat.
- Believes she is fat even when she's very thin.
- Misses three (menstrual) periods in a row—for girls/women who have started having their periods.

What causes it?

Anorexia is more than just a problem with food. It's a way of using food or starving oneself to feel more in control of her life and to ease tension,

About This Chapter: Text in this chapter is from "Frequently asked Questions about Anorexia Nervosa," a fact sheet produced by the National Women's Health Information Center (NWHIC), a component of the U.S. Department of Health and Human Services (DHHS), Office on Women's Health, August 2004; available online at http://www.4woman.gov/faq/Easyread/anorexia-etr.htm.

anger, and anxiety. While there is no single known cause of anorexia, several things may contribute to the development of the disorder:

- **Biology:** Several biological factors, including genetics and other re-lated hormones, may contribute to the onset of the disorder.

- **Culture:** Some cultures in the U.S. have an ideal of extreme thinness. Women may define themselves on how beautiful they are.

- **Personal feelings:** Someone with anorexia may feel badly about her-self, feel helpless, and hate the way she looks. She has unrealistic ex-pectations of herself and strives for perfection. She feels worthless, despite achievements and perceives a social pressure to be thin.

- **Stressful events or life changes:** Things like starting a new school or job or being teased, to traumatic events like rape, can lead to the onset of anorexia.

- **Families:** People with a mother or sister with anorexia are more likely to develop the disorder. Parents who think appearance is very impor-tant, diet themselves, and criticize their children's bodies are more likely to have a child with anorexia.

What are signs of anorexia?

A person with anorexia will have many of these signs:

- Looks a lot thinner
- Uses extreme measures to lose weight
- Makes herself throw up
- Takes pills to urinate or have a bowel movement (BM)
- Takes diet pills
- Doesn't eat or follows a strict diet
- Exercises a lot
- Weighs food and counts calories
- Moves food around the plate; doesn't eat it

- Has a distorted body image

- Thinks she's fat when she's too thin

- Wears baggy clothes to hide appearance

- Fears gaining weight

- Weighs herself many times a day

- Acts differently

- Talks about weight and food all the time

- Won't eat in front of others

- Acts moody or depressed

- Doesn't socialize

✎ What's It Mean?

C-section (Cesarean): Procedure where the baby is delivered through an abdominal incision. [1]

Hormone: A chemical made by glands in the body. Hormones circulate in the bloodstream and control the actions of certain cells or organs. Some hormones can also be made in a laboratory. [2]

Menstrual: The blood flow from the uterus that happens about every 4 weeks in a woman. [1]

Miscarriage: An unplanned loss of a pregnancy. Also called a spontaneous abortion. [1]

Ovulate: The release of a single egg from a follicle that developed in the ovary. It usually occurs regularly, around day 14 of a 28-day menstrual cycle. [1]

Source: [1] "NWHIC Web Site Glossary," U.S. Department of Health and Human Services, Office on Women's Health, available at www .4woman.gov, 2004. [2] "Dictionary of Cancer Terms," National Cancer Institute, available at www.nci.nih.gov; cited December 2004.

What happens to your body with anorexia?

The body doesn't get the energy from foods that it needs, so it slows down. Look at the picture to find out how anorexia affects your health.

Can someone with anorexia get better?

Yes. People with this disorder can get better. The treatment depends on what the person needs. The person must get back to a healthy weight. Many times, eating disorders happen with other problems, like depression and anxiety problems. These problems are treated along with the anorexia and may involve medicines that help reduce feelings of depression and anxiety. With outpatient care, the patient goes to the hospital during the day for treatment, but lives at home.

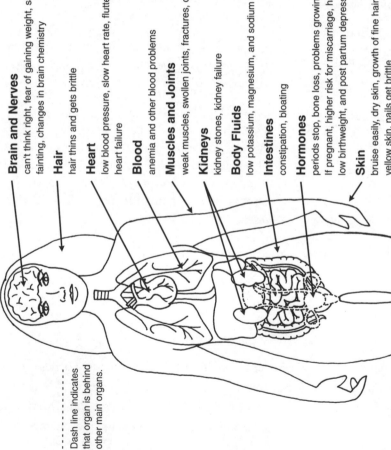

Brain and Nerves
can't think right, fear of gaining weight, sad, moody, irritable, bad memory, fainting, changes in brain chemistry

Hair
hair thins and gets brittle

Heart
low blood pressure, slow heart rate, fluttering of the heart (palpitations), heart failure

Blood
anemia and other blood problems

Muscles and Joints
weak muscles, swollen joints, fractures, osteoporosis

Kidneys
kidney stones, kidney failure

Body Fluids
low potassium, magnesium, and sodium

Intestines
constipation, bloating

Hormones
periods stop, bone loss, problems growing, trouble getting pregnant. If pregnant, higher risk for miscarriage, having a C-section, baby with low birthweight, and post partum depression

Skin
bruise easily, dry skin, growth of fine hair all over body, get cold easily, yellow skin, nails get brittle

- - - - - - - - -
Dash line indicates that organ is behind other main organs.

Figure 9.1. Anorexia Affects Your Whole Body

Sometimes, the patient goes to a hospital and stays there for treatment. Different types of health care providers, like doctors, nutritionists, and therapists, will help the patient get better. These providers will help the patient regain the weight, improve physical health and nutrition, learn healthy eating patterns, and cope with thoughts and feelings related to the disorder. After leaving the hospital, the patient continues to get help from her providers. Individual counseling can also

---

✔ Quick Tip

I'm Afraid Of Losing My Muscle Tone

Question: I have been in recovery from anorexia for the past five years. It has been a long, up and down process. During this time, I have been unable to exercise due to physical concerns. While I understand the reasons behind this— fear of organ failure, heart attack, major injuries, I find myself in a rather difficult and challenging situation now. Before getting into recovery, I was very active and engaged in a number of athletic pursuits. Working on recovery required me to give these things up so that my body could heal. So now I find myself facing another challenge. I have learned that suffering with muscle atrophy feels very different on your body when you are at a dangerously low weight than it does at a healthy weight range. I am feeling very afraid that I will not be able to get back the muscle tone I had before I became so sick. I am experiencing an increased amount of body shame and distorted body image problems. Do you have any suggestions for developing healthy exercise patterns after a long period of recovery? I am so afraid that this current place I am in will lead to a relapse back into my anorexia if I cannot find a solution.

Answer: You absolutely do not have to be afraid that you will never regain your muscle tone, but you must eat healthfully and exercise appropriately to help yourself get back to where you want to be. If you aren't in treatment now, you need to see someone right away to support you as you struggle with your doubts, and also refer you to other professionals who can help you medically and with your exercise patterns. If you have a therapist, make sure to bring up your worries in your next session.

Source: © 2002 The Renfrew Center. All rights reserved. Reprinted with permission. For additional information, call 1-800-RENFREW or visit http://www.renfrewcenter.com.

help someone with anorexia. Counseling may involve the whole family too, especially if the patient is young. Support groups may also be a part of treatment. Support groups help patients and families talk about their experiences and help each other get better.

Can women who had anorexia in the past still get pregnant?

It depends. Women who have fully recovered from anorexia have a better chance of getting pregnant. While a woman has active anorexia, she does not get her usual periods and doesn't normally ovulate, so it would be harder to get pregnant. However, she may get pregnant as she regains weight because her reproductive system is getting back to normal. After they gain back some weight, some women may skip or miss their periods, which can cause problems getting pregnant. If this happens, a woman should see her doctor.

Can anorexia hurt a baby when the mother is pregnant?

If a woman with active anorexia gets pregnant, the baby and mother can be affected. The baby is more likely to be born at a low weight and born early. The mother is more likely to have a miscarriage, deliver by C-section, and have depression after the baby is born.

Chapter 10

How Serious Is Anorexia?

Anorexia nervosa is a very serious illness that has a wide range of effects on the body and mind. It is also associated with other problems ranging from frequent flus and general poor health to life-threatening conditions. Some experts believe that it should not be approached as a simple eating disorder but as a serious condition requiring staging according to severity.

At this time no treatment program for anorexia nervosa is completely effective. Recovery rates vary between 23% and 50%, and relapses range from 4% to 27%. Even for those who recover, one study indicated that recovery took between four and nearly seven years. Depending on the duration of the study, anorexic patients have reported death rates ranging from 4% to 25%. Even after treatment and weight gain, many patients continue to display characteristics of the disorder, including perfectionism and a drive for thinness that could keep them at risk for recurrence. In spite of these very serious findings, this condition has received very little research attention.

Hormonal Changes

One of the most serious effects of anorexia is hormonal change, which can have severe health consequences:

- Reproductive hormones, including estrogen and dehydroepiandrosterone (DHEA), are lower. Estrogen is important for healthy hearts and bones. DHEA, a weak male hormone, may also be important for bone health and for other functions.

- Thyroid hormones are lower.

- Stress hormones are higher.

- Growth hormones are lower. Children and adolescents with anorexia may experience retarded growth.

The result of many of these hormonal abnormalities in women is long-term, irregular or absent menstruation (amenorrhea). This can occur early on in anorexia, even before severe weight loss. Over time this causes infertility, bone loss, and other problems. Low weight alone may not be sufficient to cause amenorrhea. Extreme fasting and purging behaviors may play an even stronger role in hormonal disturbance.

> ♣ It's A Fact!!
> According to different studies, the risk for early death is higher for people with the following conditions or characteristics:
>
> - Being younger
>
> - Having bulimia anorexia. (The mortality rate is twice as high in this group than in the anorexic-restrictor types.)
>
> - Being severely low in weight at the time of treatment
>
> - Being sick for more than six years
>
> - Having been previously obese
>
> - Having personality disorders
>
> - Having an accompanying severe psychological disorder
>
> - Having a dysfunctional marriage
>
> - Being male. (The higher risk for life-threatening medical problems in males may be due to their tendency to be diagnosed with anorexia later than women.)

Psychologic Effects And Suicide

Adolescents with eating behaviors associated with anorexia (fasting, frequent exercise to lose weight, and self-induced vomiting) are at high risk for anxiety and depression in young adulthood. Some studies estimate that between 12% and 18% of people who are anorexic also abuse alcohol or drugs. Even worse, suicide has been estimated to account for as many as half the deaths in anorexia. In one study, suicide rates occurred in 1.4% of women with anorexia. The study, however, only looked at female death records. Such records may not have always recorded anorexia as an accompanying condition, so the incidence of suicide in anorexia may be much higher.

Heart Disease

Heart disease is the most common medical cause of death in people with severe anorexia. The effects of anorexia on the heart are as follows:

- Dangerous heart rhythms, including slow rhythms known as bradycardia, may develop. Such abnormalities can show up even in teenagers with anorexia.

- Blood flow is reduced

- Blood pressure may drop

- The heart muscles starve, losing size

- Cholesterol levels tend to rise

A primary danger to the heart is from abnormalities in the balance of minerals, such as potassium, calcium, magnesium, and phosphate, which are normally dissolved in the body's fluid. The dehydration and starvation that occurs with anorexia can reduce fluid and mineral levels and produce a condition known as electrolyte imbalance. Electrolytes (e.g., calcium and potassium) are critical for maintaining the electric currents necessary for a normal heartbeat. An imbalance in these electrolytes can be very serious and even life threatening unless fluids and minerals are replaced. Heart problems are a particular risk when anorexia is compounded by bulimia and the use of ipecac, a drug that causes vomiting.

Long-Term Outlook On Fertility

After treatment and an increase in weight, estrogen levels are usually restored and periods resume. In severe anorexia, however, even after treatment, normal menstruation never returns in 25% of such patients.

✎ What's It Mean?

Anemia: A condition in which the number of red blood cells is below normal. [1]

Bone Marrow: The soft, sponge-like tissue in the center of most large bones. It produces white blood cells, red blood cells, and platelets. [1]

Calcium: A mineral found in teeth, bones, and other body tissues. [1]

Cholesterol: A fat-like substance in the body. The body makes and needs some cholesterol, which also comes from foods such as butter and egg yolks. Too much cholesterol may cause gallstones. It also may cause fat to build up in the arteries. This may cause a disease that slows or stops blood flow. [2]

Constipation: A condition in which the stool becomes hard and dry. A person who is constipated usually has fewer than three bowel movements in a week. Bowel movements may be painful. [2]

Enzyme: A protein that speeds up chemical reactions in the body. [1]

Estrogen: A hormone that promotes the development and maintenance of female sex characteristics. [1]

Infertility: The inability to produce children. [1]

Testosterone: A hormone that promotes the development and maintenance of male sex characteristics. [1]

Thyroid: A gland located beneath the voice box (larynx) that produces thyroid hormone. The thyroid helps regulate growth and metabolism. [1]

Type 1 Diabetes: A condition characterized by high blood glucose levels caused by a total lack of insulin. Occurs when the body's immune system attacks the insulin-producing beta cells in the pancreas and destroys them. The pancreas then produces little or no insulin. Type 1 diabetes develops most often in young people but can appear in adults. [3]

Source: [1] "Dictionary of Cancer Terms," National Cancer Institute, available at www.nci.nih.gov; cited December 2004. [2] "Digestive Diseases Dictionary," National Institute of Diabetes and Digestive and Kidney Diseases, available at www.digestive.niddk.nih.gov, 2000. [3] "Diabetes Dictionary," National Institute of Diabetes and Digestive and Kidney Diseases, available at www.diabetes.niddk.nih.gov, 2003.

- If a woman with anorexia becomes pregnant before regaining normal weight, she faces a higher risk for miscarriage, cesarean section, and for having an infant with low birth weight or birth defects. She is also at higher risk for postpartum depression.

- Women with anorexia who seek fertility treatments have lower chances for success.

Long-Term Effect On Bones And Growth

Almost 90% of women with anorexia experience osteopenia (loss of bone minerals) and 40% have osteoporosis (more advanced loss of bone density). Up to two-thirds of children and adolescent girls with anorexia fail to develop strong bones during their critical growing period. Boys with anorexia also suffer from stunted growth. The less the patient weighs, the more severe the bone loss. Women with anorexia who also binge-purge face an even higher risk for bone loss.

Bone loss in women is mainly due to low estrogen levels that occur with anorexia. Other biologic factors in anorexia also may contribute to bone loss, including high levels of stress hormones (which impair bone growth) and low levels of calcium, certain growth factors, and DHEA (a weak male hormone). Weight gain, unfortunately, does not completely restore bone. Only achieving regular menstruation as soon as possible can protect against permanent bone loss. The longer the eating disorder persists the more likely the bone loss will be permanent.

Testosterone levels decline in boys as they lose weight, which also can affect their bone density. In young boys with anorexia, weight restoration produces some catch-up growth, but it may not produce full growth.

Neurological Problems

People with severe anorexia may suffer nerve damage that affects the brain and other parts of the body. The following nerve-related conditions have been reported:

- Seizures
- Disordered thinking

• Numbness or odd nerve sensations in the hands or feet (a condition
  called peripheral neuropathy)

Brains scans indicate that parts of the brain undergo structural changes
and abnormal activity during anorexic states. Some of these changes return
to normal after weight gain, but there is evidence that some damage may be
permanent. Still, the extent of the neurologic problems is unclear, and some
studies have been unable to determine specific mental problems associated
with anorexia.

Blood Problems

Anemia is a common result of anorexia and starvation. A particularly
serious blood problem is pernicious anemia, which can be caused by severely
low levels of vitamin B_{12}. If anorexia becomes extreme, the bone marrow
dramatically reduces its production of blood cells—a life-threatening condition called pancytopenia.

Gastrointestinal Problems

Bloating and constipation are both very common problems in people with
anorexia.

Multiorgan Failure

In very late anorexia, the organs simply fail. The main signal for this is
elevated levels of liver enzymes, which require immediate administration of
calories.

Complications In Diabetic Adolescents

Eating disorders are very serious for young people with type 1 diabetes.
The complications of anorexia that affect all patients are even more dangerous in this group of patients. Hypoglycemia, or low blood sugar, for example,
is a danger for anyone with anorexia, but it is a particularly dangerous risk
for those with diabetes. One study found that 85% of young women with
diabetes and eating disorders had retinopathy, damage to the retina in the
eye, which can lead to blindness.

Chapter 11

Bulimia Nervosa

Bulimia often starts when a young woman hears others at school talking about this "easy" method of weight control: you can eat anything you want, as much as you want, but never gain a pound! It sounds too good to be true and, unfortunately, it is.

Bulimia nervosa is a serious, potentially life-threatening eating disorder characterized by unhealthy methods of getting rid of food to avoid gaining weight (such as vomiting, abusive use of laxatives or water pills, fasting and extreme exercise). Bulimics usually resort to these methods after compulsively eating large amounts of food in a short period of time, a behavior known as binge eating. The syndrome is called "binging and purging." However, some bulimics will engage in purging simply if they eat more food than they feel they should.

How is bulimia different from anorexia?

Unlike anorexics, bulimics do not avoid eating. People with bulimia can be hard to pick out because their weight may be average or above average. Bulimics and anorexics do share an obsessive concern with body size, fear of weight gain, guilt, poor self-image and eating in secrecy. Some people can have both anorexia and bulimia. About 50% of anorexics develop bulimia.

Who are the most common sufferers of bulimia?

Like anorexia, bulimia is most often found in young women ages 11 to 17, but has been seen in women even into their 60s. Although once considered a white, affluent disorder, bulimia has become common among all races and income levels. Although not as common, males can also become bulimic.

What are some signs and symptoms of bulimia?

Bulimia is usually well concealed from family or friends and can remain undetected for many years. Bulimia is diagnosed when several of the following symptoms exist simultaneously:

Behavioral Signs

- Eating unusually large amounts of food with no apparent change in weight

- Disappearance of large amounts of food in short periods of time

- The presence of wrappers and containers indicating the consumption of large amounts of food

- Frequent trips to the bathroom after meals, signs and/or smells of vomiting, evidence of laxatives or diuretics

- Going to the kitchen after everyone else has gone to bed; going for unexpected walks or drives at night (bulimics try to binge when other people are not around)

- Excessive, rigid exercise regimen

- Creation of complex lifestyle schedules or rituals to make time for binge-and-purge sessions

> ✤ **It's A Fact!!**
> **Did You Know?**
>
> - Approximately 80% of bulimia nervosa patients are female.
>
> - Bulimia rarely works well for weight loss.
>
> - When someone says, "I'd rather die than be fat," she might die. The loss of potassium and other minerals from bulimia can lead to heart problems and even death.

Physical Signs

- Unusual swelling of the cheeks or jaw area

- Calluses on the back of the hands and knuckles (from self-induced vomiting)

- Discoloration, staining, or deterioration of tooth enamel (caused by stomach acid)

- Broken blood vessels in the eyes

- Brittle hair or nails; dry or sallow skin

- Stomach pain

Emotional Signs

- Withdrawal from usual friends and activities

- Preoccupation with body weight, weight loss, dieting, and control of food

- Depression and mood swings

- Extreme or impulsive behavior, such as excessive spending sprees or substance abuse

✎ What's It Mean?

Cardiac Arrhythmia: Any variation from the normal rhythm or rate of the heartbeat. [1]

Constipation: A condition in which the stool becomes hard and dry. A person who is constipated usually has fewer than three bowel movements in a week. Bowel movements may be painful. [2]

Diuretic: A drug that increases the production of urine. [3]

Electrolytes: A substance that breaks up into ions (electrically charged particles) when it is dissolved in body fluids or water. Some examples of electrolytes are sodium, potassium, chloride, and calcium. Electrolytes are primarily responsible for the movement of nutrients into cells and the movement of wastes out of cells. [3]

Esophagus: The muscular tube through which food passes from the throat to the stomach. [3]

Laxatives: A substance that promotes bowel movements. [3]

Source: "Genetics Home Reference Glossary," a service of the U.S. National Library of Medicine, available at www.ghr.nlm.nih.gov, 2005. [2] "Digestive Diseases Dictionary," National Institute of Diabetes and Digestive and Kidney Diseases, available at www.digestive.niddk.nih.gov, 2000. [3] "Dictionary of Cancer Terms," National Cancer Institute, available at www.nci.nih.gov; cited December 2004.

What are some effects of bulimia?

Bulimia has serious medical and psychological implications. Some of the major damage that results from bulimia includes:

♣ It's A Fact!!

Bulimia Nervosa In Males

Bulimia nervosa is a severe, life-threatening disorder characterized by re-current episodes of binge eating followed by self-induced vomiting or other purging methods (e.g. laxatives, diuretics, excessive exercise, fasting) in an at-tempt to avoid weight gain. An individual struggling with bulimia is intensely afraid of gaining weight and exhibits persistent dissatisfaction with his body and appearance, as well as a significant distortion in the perception of the size or shape of his body.

Behavioral Characteristics

- Recurrent episodes of binge eating: eating an amount of food that is definitely larger than most people would eat during a similar period of time and under similar circumstances

- A sense of lack of control over eating during binge episodes

- Recurrent purging or compensatory behaviors to prevent weight gain: secretive self-induced vomiting, misuse of laxatives, diuretics, or fasting, compulsive exercise (possibly including excessive running, body build-ing, or weight lifting)

- Hoarding of food, hiding food, and eating in secret

- Frequently weighing self

- Preoccupation with food

- Focus on certain body parts; e.g., buttocks, thighs, and stomach

- Disgust with body size or shape

- Distortion of body size; i.e., feels fat even though he may be thin

Physical Effects

- Electrolyte imbalance caused by dehydration (can lead to irregular heartbeats, heart problems, and even to death)

Emotional And Mental Characteristics

- Intense fear of becoming fat or gaining weight
- Performance and appearance oriented
- Works hard to please others
- Depression
- Social isolation
- Possible conflict over gender identity or sexual orientation
- Strong need to be in control
- Difficulty expressing feelings
- Feelings of worthlessness—uses weight, appearance, and achievement as measures of worth
- Rigid, inflexible "all or nothing" thinking

Physical Characteristics

- Weight fluctuations
- Loss of dental enamel due to self-induced vomiting
- Edema (fluid retention or bloating)
- Constipation
- Swollen salivary glands
- Cardiac arrhythmia due to electrolyte imbalances
- Esophageal tears, gastric (stomach) rupture
- Lack of energy, fatigue

- Inflammation of the esophagus from frequent vomiting

- Tooth and gum problems

- Chronic irregular bowel movements and constipation from laxative abuse

Emotional Effects (Some Of Which May Also Be Causes)

- Shame and guilt

- Depression

- Low self-esteem

- Impaired family and social relationships

- Perfectionism

- "All or nothing" thinking

What causes bulimia?

Bulimia often begins as what seems to be a good idea: a way to manage weight without dieting. It continues as a means of self-control, which paradoxically becomes habitual and out of control. Some of the precursors to bulimia include:

- Feeling out of control because of difficulties at home

- Suppressed anger

- Unmet needs

- Feeling undeserving

- Major life changes, such as divorce, family problems, loss of a relationship, a move

Because bulimia sometimes occurs in more than one family member, there is also research being conducted to determine whether this is genetic or learned behavior.

What should you do if a family member or friend suffers from bulimia?

Confronting a bulimic may encourage her to seek help and begin the process to recovery. Before confronting, have a plan. Decide:

- Why the concern
- Who will be involved
- Where to confront
- How to talk
- When is a convenient time

What is the treatment for bulimia?

Like all bad habits, the longer someone takes part in them, the harder they are to break. Recognizing and addressing the problem as soon as possible is most important. Because bulimia involves both the mind and body, medical doctors, mental health professionals, and dietitians often are involved in the patient's treatment.

Goals of treatments for bulimia are likely to include:

- Psychoeducation about the medical implications of bulimia
- Identification of triggers for binging and purging behavior
- Interrupting the rituals of bulimic episodes
- Challenging weight and body image beliefs
- Improving self-esteem and ability to communicate needs and feelings

Treatment provides a support system and ends the isolation and shame commonly felt by bulimics. Some bulimia treatment programs include an OA (Overeaters Anonymous) 12-Step Program, self-help groups conducted by the Eating Disorders Association, or self-help groups run by hospital outpatient units. Some programs also use antidepressant medications to treat bulimia.

Chapter 12

Frequently Asked Questions About Bulimia

What is bulimia?

Bulimia (buh-LEE -me-ah) nervosa, typically called bulimia, is a type of eating disorder. Someone with bulimia eats a lot of food in a short amount of time (called bingeing) and then tries to prevent weight gain by purging. Purging might be done in these ways:

- Making oneself throw up

- Taking laxatives, pills, or liquids that increase how fast food moves through your body and leads to a bowel movement [BM])

A person with bulimia may also use these ways to prevent weight gain:

- Exercising a lot

- Eating very little or not at all

- Taking pills to pass urine

About This Chapter: Text in this chapter is from "Frequently asked Questions about Bulimia Nervosa," a fact sheet produced by the National Women's Health Information Center (NWHIC), a component of the U.S. Department of Health and Human Services (DHHS), Office on Women's Health, August 2004; available online at http://www.4woman.gov/faq/Easyread/bulnervosa-etr.htm.

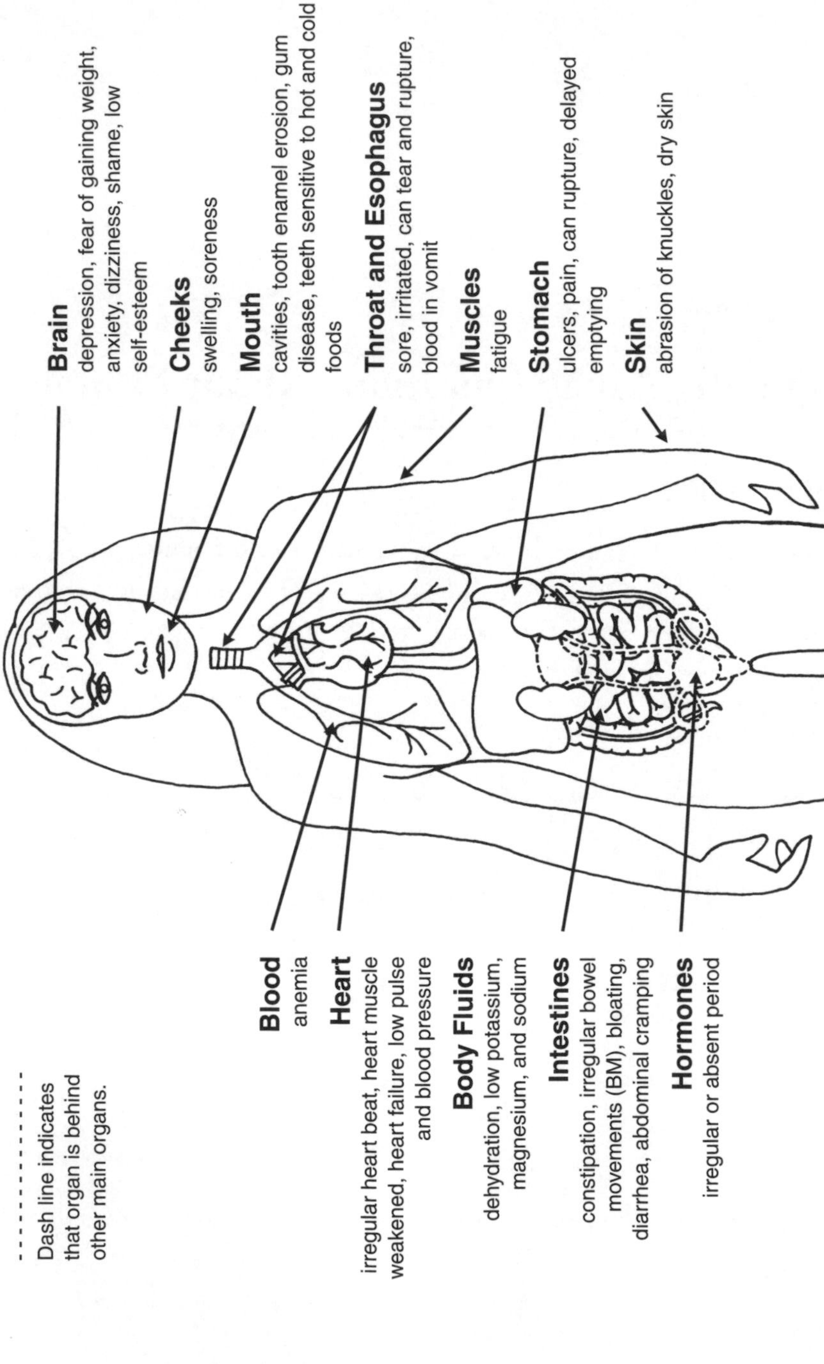

Brain
depression, fear of gaining weight, anxiety, dizziness, shame, low self-esteem

Cheeks
swelling, soreness

Mouth
cavities, tooth enamel erosion, gum disease, teeth sensitive to hot and cold foods

Throat and Esophagus
sore, irritated, can tear and rupture, blood in vomit

Muscles
fatigue

Stomach
ulcers, pain, can rupture, delayed emptying

Skin
abrasion of knuckles, dry skin

- - - - - - - - - -
Dash line indicates that organ is behind other main organs.

Blood
anemia

Heart
irregular heart beat, heart muscle weakened, heart failure, low pulse and blood pressure

Body Fluids
dehydration, low potassium, magnesium, and sodium

Intestines
constipation, irregular bowel movements (BM), bloating, diarrhea, abdominal cramping

Hormones
irregular or absent period

Figure 12.1. How Bulimia Affects Your Body

What causes it?

Bulimia is more than just a problem with food. Purging and other behaviors to prevent weight gain are ways for people with bulimia to feel more in control of their lives and to ease stress and anxiety. While there is no single known cause of bulimia, many things may have a role in its development:

- **Biology:** There are studies being done to look at many genes, hormones, and chemicals in the brain that may have an effect on the development of, and recovery from, bulimia.

- **Culture:** Some cultures in the U.S. have an ideal of extreme thinness. Women may define themselves on how beautiful they are.

- **Personal feelings:** Someone with bulimia may feel badly about herself, feel helpless, and hate the way she looks.

- **Stressful events or life changes:** Things like starting a new school or job, being teased, or traumatic events like rape, can lead to the onset of bulimia.

- **Families:** The attitude of parents about appearance and diet affects their kids. Also, a person is more likely to develop bulimia if a mother or sister has it.

What are signs of bulimia?

People with bulimia may be underweight, overweight, or have a normal weight. This makes it harder to know if someone has this disorder. However, someone with bulimia may have these signs.

Uses extreme measures to lose weight:

- Uses diet pills, or takes pills to urinate or have a bowel movement (BM)
- Goes to the bathroom all the time after she eats (to throw up)
- Exercises a lot, even during bad weather, tiredness, sickness, or injury

Shows signs of throwing up:

- Swelling of the cheeks or jaw area
- Cuts and calluses on the back of the hands and knuckles
- Teeth that look clear

Acts differently:

• Is depressed

• Doesn't see friends or participate in activities as much

What happens to someone who has bulimia?

Bulimia can be very harmful to the body. Look at the picture to find out how bulimia affects your health.

Can someone who had bulimia get pregnant?

Bulimia can cause problems with a woman's period. She may not get it every 4 weeks or it may stop. But researchers don't think this affects a woman's chances of getting pregnant after she recovers.

Does bulimia hurt a baby when the mother is pregnant?

If a woman with active bulimia gets pregnant, these problems may result:

• Miscarriage

• High blood pressure in the mother

• Baby isn't born alive

• Low birth weight

• Low Apgar score, which are tests done after birth to make sure the baby is healthy

• During the delivery, the baby tries to come out with feet or buttocks first

• Birth by C-section

• Baby is born early

• Depression after the baby is born

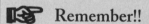 **Remember!!**

Someone with bulimia can get better.

A person with bulimia can get better. Different types of therapy have worked to help people with bulimia. This may include individual, group, and family therapy. A class of medicines, also used for depression, like Zoloft, has been effective when used with therapy. These medicines change the way certain chemicals work in the brain.

Chapter 13

How Serious Is Bulimia?

Most studies report that patients with bulimia that is not accompanied by severe weight loss have a much better outlook than patients with anorexia. Some studies have suggested that between 60% and 80% of bulimic patients are in remission within three months of treatment. However, relapse is common, and over half of women with bulimia continue to battle disordered eating habits for years. In one study, bulimia itself persisted in 10% to 25% of patients after treatment.

Direct Adverse Effects Of Bulimic Behavior On The Body

The following are medical problems directly associated with bulimic behavior, including self-induced vomiting and laxative abuse:

- Teeth erosion, cavities, and gum problems

- Water retention, swelling, and abdominal bloating

- Occasionally, fluid loss with low potassium levels. This occurs from excessive vomiting or laxative use. In severe cases it can cause extreme weakness, near paralysis, or lethal heart rhythms.

- Acute stomach distress

About This Chapter: Information in this chapter is excerpted from "Eating Disorders: Anorexia and Bulimia." © 2003 A.D.A.M., Inc. Reprinted with permission.

- Problems in swallowing. This is an area of possible concern because of repetitive assaults on the esophagus (the food pipe) from forced vomiting. It is not clear, however, if this problem is common.

- Rupture of the esophagus, or food pipe. (Cases have been reported with forced vomiting but are not common.)

- Weakened rectal walls. In rare cases, walls may weaken to the extent that they protrude through the anus. This is a serious condition that requires surgery.

- Irregular periods. (It should be noted that menstrual irregularities in patients with bulimia do not have the serious effects, particularly bone loss, as they do in patients with anorexia.)

Long-Term Health Problems

Studies have been mixed on the long-term health consequences for bulimic people who maintain normal weight and who do not go on to become anorexic. Some report no major problems. A 2002 study, however, reported that eating disorders during adolescence put these young people at risk for a variety of psychologic and medical problems later on, even in those without severe eating disorders. Health problems included circulatory disorders (such as high blood pressure), neurologic symptoms (such as seizures), chronic fatigue, headache, frequent flus and colds, and insomnia, regardless of weight loss. Even worse, only 22% of the subjects had received any psychiatric treatment. The study did not break down specific eating disorders, but related the health problems with specific behaviors. Furthermore, another 2002 study

---

✎ What's It Mean?

Potassium: A metallic element that is important in body functions such as regulation of blood pressure and of water content in cells, transmission of nerve impulses, digestion, muscle contraction, and heartbeat.

Source: "Genetics Home Reference Glossary," a service of the U.S. National Library of Medicine, available at www.ghr.nlm.nih.gov, 2004.

reported that bulimic patients were at higher risk for bone fractures. (The risk was lower than with anorexia and, unlike in anorexia, it returned to normal within a year of diagnosis and treatment.)

Long-Term Psychiatric Problems

In the 2002 study mentioned above, eating disorders, even with normal weight, were associated with a higher risk for anxiety and depressive disorders and with suicide attempts.

♣ **It's A Fact!!**
In all cases, patients who have both bulimia and anorexia are in greatest danger of health risks.

Effect On Pregnancy

Most pregnant women with a history of eating disorders have healthy pregnancies, although they face higher risks for a number of complications, including cesarean sections, postpartum depression, miscarriages, and complicated deliveries. Their babies may also have a higher risk for low birth weight, prematurity, and malformation.

Self-Destructive Behavior

A number of self-destructive behaviors occur with bulimia:

- **Smoking:** Many teenage girls with eating disorders smoke because it is thought to help prevent weight gain.

- **Impulsive Behaviors:** Women with bulimia are at higher-than-average risk for dangerous impulsive behaviors, such as sexual promiscuity, self-cutting, and kleptomania. Some studies have reported such behaviors in half of those with bulimia.

- **Alcohol and Substance Abuse:** An estimated 30% to 70% of patients with bulimia abuse alcohol, drugs, or both. This rate is higher than that of the general population and for people with anorexia. It should be noted, however, that this higher rate of substance abuse might be a distortion because studies are conducted only on diagnosed patients. Bulimia tends not to get diagnosed. And reports of bulimia in the community (where the incidence of the eating disorder is higher than statistics suggest) indicate that substance abuse is actually lower than in people with anorexia.

Abuse Of Over-The-Counter Medications

Women with bulimia frequently abuse over-the-counter medications, such as laxatives, appetite suppressants, diuretics, and drugs that induce vomiting (e.g., ipecac). None of these drugs is without risk. For example, ipecac poisonings have been reported, and some people become dependent on laxatives for normal bowel functioning. Diet pills, even herbal and over-the-counter medications, can be hazardous, particularly if they are abused.

Chapter 14

Binge Eating Disorder

Jana's room is her oasis. It's where she listens to music, does her homework, and talks on the phone to her friends. It's pretty messy in there—she has clothes piled on the chair, her desk is overflowing with books and papers, and the towering stack of CDs looks like it's about to topple. For the most part, it looks like a typical teen's room—except for what's under the bed. That's where Jana keeps her secret stash of snacks and tosses the leftover candy wrappers, chip bags, and cookie crumbs.

Jana has just polished off a whole package of cookies and a large bag of chips—and she hasn't even finished her homework yet. She's searching for more chips to eat while she does her math. She hates that she's overweight, but she can't seem to stop bingeing on junk food. Somehow, the food seems to ease her tension. In the back of her mind, she knows that in an hour or so she's going to feel guilty and disgusted with herself, but right now it feels like she just can't stop eating.

Understanding Binge Eating

If you gorged yourself on chocolate during Halloween or ate so much of your grandma's pumpkin pie during Thanksgiving that you had to wear elastic-waist

About This Chapter: This information was provided by TeensHealth, one of the largest resources online for medically reviewed health information written for parents, kids, and teens. For more articles like this one, visit www.TeensHealth.org, or www.KidsHealth.org. © 2003 The Nemours Center for Children's Health Media, a division of The Nemours Foundation.

pants for the rest of the day, you know what it feels like to overeat. Most people overeat from time to time. Teens are notorious for being hungry frequently—in fact, they need to eat more to support the major growth of muscle and bone that's happening. A teen's normally increased appetite is just his or her body's way of signaling that it needs more nutrients to fuel growth.

But binge eating, also called compulsive overeating, is different from normal appetite increases or overeating now and then. Teens with a binge eating problem eat unusually large amounts of food and don't stop eating when they become full. They binge not just from time to time, but regularly. And binge eating involves more than just eating a lot—with binge eating, a person feels out of control and powerless to stop eating while he or she is doing it. That's why binge eating is also called compulsive overeating. With binge eating, a person may feel a compulsion (a powerful urge) to overeat.

Teens with a binge eating problem may overeat when they feel stressed, upset, hurt, or angry. Many find it comforting and soothing to eat food, but after a binge they are likely to feel incredibly guilty and sad about the out-of-control eating. Teens who binge eat may do so to deal with (or avoid dealing with) difficult emotions. For this reason, some say binge eating is about having an unhealthy relationship with food.

The Problem With Binge Eating

Binge eating can lead to other problems, too—such as weight gain, unhealthy dieting, and emotional distress.

Weight Gain

Gaining weight is a natural consequence of regular binge eating. Most people who binge eat are overweight, and over time many become obese. Being overweight may make someone more prone to health problems such as diabetes, high blood pressure, joint problems, and breathlessness. And being overweight as a kid or teen makes it more likely that someone will be overweight or obese as an adult. Not all people who are overweight have a binge eating problem—but many do.

Unhealthy Dieting

Concerns about weight gain may lead teens who binge eat to diet. Extreme diets and yo-yo dieting (a pattern of repeatedly losing and then regaining weight) have their own health risks, especially for teens. Plus, dieting may make binge eaters so hungry that they end up bingeing again.

Emotional Distress

Regular binge eating may lead to low energy, low self-esteem, or depression. Feelings of helplessness, hopelessness, or worthlessness may surface when a person feels little control to put the brakes on overeating. These painful feelings may make the binge eating worse and can spill over into other areas of a person's life. Some teens who binge eat don't have the coping skills to express or tolerate difficult emotions. When eating is used as a way to deal with (or not deal with) emotions, a person may be less likely to learn and practice healthier coping skills.

How Is Binge Eating Different From Other Eating Disorders?

Anorexia nervosa, bulimia nervosa, and binge eating are eating disorders that can affect teens. There are some similarities among these eating disorders and some key differences, too. All three involve unhealthy patterns of eating. Each has its own pattern that makes it different from the others.

People with bulimia nervosa (sometimes called binge-purge syndrome) binge on food and then vomit or use laxatives to try to keep themselves from gaining weight. They may also try to burn off the extra calories by exercising compulsively as a way of making up for eating binges. Teens who binge eat also consume huge amounts of food but they don't throw it up afterward. Although they may eat compulsively, they don't usually exercise compulsively like someone who has bulimia. Both binge eating and bulimia involve eating excessive amounts of food, feeling out of control while eating, and feeling guilty or ashamed afterward.

Anorexia nervosa is an eating disorder that involves extreme preoccupation with thinness, weight loss, fear of getting fat, and a distorted body image.

Unlike bulimia and binge eating, which involve out-of-control overeating, teens with anorexia starve themselves to feel more in control of their relationship with food. With anorexia, a person believes he or she is fat—even though that person may actually be dangerously thin. With both bulimia and anorexia, a person's self-esteem depends too much on body shape and weight. Like teens with bulimia, some teens with anorexia may also exercise compulsively to lose weight.

All three of these eating disorders involve unhealthy eating patterns that begin gradually and build to the point where a person feels unable to control

♣ It's A Fact!!

Binge Eating Disorder In Males

Binge eating disorder is a severe, life-threatening disorder characterized by recurrent episodes of compulsive overeating or binge eating. In binge eating disorder, the purging to prevent weight gain that is characteristic of bulimia nervosa is absent.

Behavioral Characteristics

- Recurrent episodes of binge eating
- Eating much more rapidly than normal
- A sense of lack of control over eating during binge episodes
- Eating large amounts of food when not feeling physically hungry
- Hoarding food
- Hiding food and eating in secret; e.g., eating alone or in the car, hiding wrappers
- Eating until feeling uncomfortably full
- Eating throughout the day with no planned mealtimes

Emotional And Mental Characteristics

- Feelings of disgust, guilt, or depression during and after overeating
- Binge eating often triggered by uncomfortable feelings such as anger, anxiety, or shame
- Binge eating used as a means of relieving tension, or to "numb" feelings

them. All can lead to serious health consequences, and all involve emotional distress for the person.

How Common Is Binge Eating?

Both guys and girls can have eating disorders. Anorexia and bulimia appear to be more common among girls than guys. Binge eating seems to be just as likely to occur in guys as girls. It's hard to know just how many teens may have a binge eating problem. Because people often feel guilty

- Rigid, inflexible "all or nothing" thinking
- Strong need to be in control
- Difficulty expressing feelings and needs
- Perfectionistic
- Works hard to please others
- Avoids conflict, tries to "keep the peace"
- Disgust about body size, often teased about their body while growing up
- Feelings of worthlessness
- Social isolation
- Depression
- Moodiness and irritability

Physical Characteristics
- Heart and blood pressure problems
- Joint problems
- Abnormal blood-sugar levels
- Fatigue
- Difficulty walking or engaging in physical activities

Source: © 2002 National Eating Disorders Association. All rights reserved. For additional information, visit http://www.NationalEatingDisorders.org.

or embarrassed about the out-of-control eating, many don't talk about it or seek help.

At least 4 million Americans are thought to have a binge eating disorder. It's estimated that between 30% and 90% of all people who are obese have binge eating problems.

What Causes Binge Eating?

There is no known single cause for binge eating. Most experts believe that a combination of factors is responsible, including genetics and biology, emotional issues, and learned behaviors.

Experts believe that some people may be more prone to over-eating because the hypothalamus (pronounced: hi-poh-tha-luh-mus), the part of the brain that controls appetite, may fail to send proper messages about hunger and fullness. Serotonin, a normal brain chemical that affects mood and some compulsive behaviors, may also play a role in binge eating. These are some of the biological factors that may make someone more likely to have a binge eating problem.

✎ What's It Mean?

Diabetes: A disease in which the body does not properly control the amount of sugar in the blood. As a result, the level of sugar in the blood is too high. This disease occurs when the body does not produce enough insulin or does not use it properly. [1]

High Blood Pressure (Hypertension): A condition present when blood flows through the blood vessels with a force greater than normal. High blood pressure can strain the heart, damage blood vessels, and increase the risk of heart attack, stroke, kidney problems, and death. [2]

Laxative: A substance that promotes bowel movements. [1]

Metabolism: The total of all chemical changes that take place in a cell or an organism. These changes produce energy and basic materials needed for important life processes. [1]

Nutrient: A chemical compound (such as protein, fat, carbohydrate, vitamins, or minerals) that make up foods. These compounds are used by the body to function and grow. [1]

Source: [1] "Dictionary of Cancer Terms," National Cancer Institute, available at www.nci.nih.gov; cited December 2004. [2] "Diabetes Dictionary," National Institute of Diabetes and Digestive and Kidney Diseases, available at www.diabetes.niddk.nih.gov, 2003.

Patterns of overeating often begin in childhood, sometimes as a result of unhealthy eating habits learned in the family. It's normal to associate food with nurturing and love. But in some families, food may be overused as a way to soothe or comfort. When this is the case, kids may grow up with a habit of overeating to soothe themselves when they're feeling pressured because they may not have learned healthier ways to deal with stress. Some kids may grow up believing that unhappy or upsetting feelings should be suppressed and may use food to quiet unsettling feelings rather than express them. These are some of the ways emotions and learning may play a role in binge eating.

What Are The Signs And Symptoms?

Binge eating is defined as eating more food than most people would eat in a short period of time (such as 2 hours), while feeling a lack of control over eating. Someone is said to have a binge eating disorder if the binge eating happens frequently (at least twice a week), continues over a period of time (at least 6 months), and causes distress or problems in the person's life. Teens who have a binge eating problem may do the following:

- Eat much more rapidly than normal

- Eat until uncomfortably full

- Eat large amounts of food even when not hungry

- Eat alone because of embarrassment

- Feel disgusted with themselves or depressed or guilty after a binge eating episode

- Gain weight excessively

Getting Help For A Binge Eating Problem

It's common for binge eating to begin during the teen years, even though many people don't get treatment for the problem until they are adults. Often people get treatment because they are seeking help to lose weight. In most cases, unhealthy overeating habits that are part of a binge eating pattern start during childhood. The sooner someone with a binge eating problem receives treatment, the better, because some of the long-term health problems associated with binge eating and with being overweight can be reduced or eliminated.

Teens can start to get help with binge eating by letting a trusted adult know about the problem. Many teens who binge eat consider going on extreme diets, but this is not a healthy practice and can lead to additional health problems. A checkup with a doctor is an important first step in having an overeating problem evaluated and getting guidance on how to lose weight safely. In addition to asking questions about eating habits, a doctor may ask about feelings about school, parents, and other aspects of life. The doctor may also check a person's overall health and nutritional status.

> ☞ **Remember!!**
>
> If you think a friend might have a problem with binge eating, it may be difficult to talk about it, but your concern and support may be just what your friend needs to get help from a professional. Offering your heartfelt caring, being willing to listen, and just being there are important parts of being a good friend in any difficult situation.
>
> The good news is that help is available for teens who have problems with binge eating. With the right guidance, commitment, and practice, it is possible to overcome old habits and replace them with healthier behaviors. Teens can overcome overeating and enjoy food without having it control their lives.

A variety of health professionals often work together to help people with binge eating disorder meet their individual goals for managing eating, weight, and feelings. Nutrition specialists or dietitians can help people learn about healthy eating behaviors, nutritional needs, portion sizes, metabolism, and exercise. They can also help teens design an eating plan that's structured and specific and monitor their progress. Psychologists and other therapists can help teens understand the connections between emotions, thoughts, and eating behaviors and can help teens begin to control binge eating. Therapists can also help teens learn healthy ways to respond to stress and deal with compulsions.

If a teen is depressed, taking care of the depression will be an important part of the therapy. For some teens, antidepressant medications might be prescribed along with therapy. Sometimes certain family members can be a big help by talking with the person and his or her therapist about shared eating patterns, feelings (and beliefs about how feelings should be expressed), and family relationships. Doing this can help a person to examine some of the eating patterns that may have been influenced by family—and to shed the patterns that he or she no longer wants to follow. As with any eating disorder, there is no quick fix for binge eating. Treatment can take several months or longer while a person learns a healthier approach to food.

Dealing With Binge Eating

If you're a teen with a binge eating problem, you may feel that the temptations to overeat are always present. Unlike a problem with drugs, alcohol, or smoking, in which part of the treatment is avoiding the substance altogether, teens still have to eat. So part of dealing with a binge eating disorder is learning how to have a healthy relationship with food.

People with binge eating disorder may find it helpful to surround themselves with supportive family members and friends. Critical comments and judgments from others about eating are rarely helpful and usually add to a person's feelings of self-criticism, making matters worse. Trying a new extracurricular activity or hobby is a great way to meet people, have some fun, and boost self-esteem. Finding a way to express feelings, whether through conversation, music, art, dance, or writing, can also be helpful.

Chapter 15

Frequently Asked Questions About Binge Eating Disorder

What is binge eating disorder?

People with binge eating disorder often eat an unusually large amount of food and feel out of control during the binges. People with binge eating disorder also may:

- eat more quickly than usual during binge episodes.
- eat until they are uncomfortably full.
- eat when they are not hungry.
- eat alone because of embarrassment.
- feel disgusted, depressed, or guilty after overeating.

What causes binge eating disorder?

No one knows for sure what causes binge eating disorder. Researchers are looking at the following factors that may affect binge eating:

About This Chapter: Text in this chapter is from "Frequently asked Questions about Binge Eating Disorder," a fact sheet produced by the National Women's Health Information Center (NWHIC), a component of the U.S. Department of Health and Human Services (DHHS), Office on Women's Health, January 2005; available online at http://www.4woman.gov/faq/bingeeating.htm.

- **Depression.** As many as half of all people with binge eating disorder are depressed or have been depressed in the past.

- **Dieting.** Some people binge after skipping meals, not eating enough food each day, or avoiding certain kinds of food.

- **Coping skills.** Studies suggest that people with binge eating may have trouble handling some of their emotions. Many people who are binge eaters say that being angry, sad, bored, worried, or stressed can cause them to binge eat.

- **Biology.** Researchers are looking into how brain chemicals and metabolism (the way the body uses calories) affect binge eating disorder. Research also suggests that genes may be involved in binge eating, since the disorder often occurs in several members of the same family.

Certain behaviors and emotional problems are more common in people with binge eating disorder. These include abusing alcohol, acting quickly without thinking (impulsive behavior), and not feeling in charge of themselves.

What are the health consequences of binge eating disorder?

People with binge eating disorder are usually very upset by their binge eating and may become depressed. Research has shown that people with binge eating disorder report more health problems, stress, trouble sleeping, and suicidal thoughts than people without an eating disorder. People with binge eating disorder often feel badly about themselves and may miss work, school, or social activities to binge eat.

People with binge eating disorder may gain weight. Weight gain can lead to obesity, and obesity raises the risk for these health problems:

- Type 2 diabetes

- High blood pressure

- High cholesterol

- Gallbladder disease

> **♣ It's A Fact!!**
> Among adolescent and young adult women of America, as much as 4 percent suffer from binge eating disorder.
>
> Source: National Women's Health Information Center, October 23, 2000.

- Heart disease

- Certain types of cancer

What is the treatment for binge eating disorder?

People with binge eating disorder should get help from a health care provider, such as a psychiatrist, psychologist, or clinical social worker. There are several different ways to treat binge eating disorder:

- Cognitive-behavioral therapy teaches people how to keep track of their eating and change their unhealthy eating habits. It teaches them how to cope with stressful situations. It also helps them feel better about their body shape and weight.

♣ **It's A Fact!!**

Several studies have found that people with binge eating disorder may find it harder than other people to stay in weight loss treatment. Binge eaters also may be more likely to regain weight quickly. For these reasons, people with the disorder may require treatment that focuses on their binge eating before they try to lose weight. Even those who are not overweight are frequently distressed by their binge eating, and may benefit from treatment.

Source: National Women's Health Information Center, October 23, 2000.

- Interpersonal psychotherapy helps people look at their relationships with friends and family and make changes in problem areas.

- Drug therapy, such as antidepressants, may be helpful for some people.

Other treatments include dialectical behavior therapy, which helps people regulate their emotions; drug therapy with the anti-seizure medication topiramate; exercise in combination with cognitive-behavioral therapy; and support groups.

Many people with binge eating disorder also have a problem with obesity. There are treatments for obesity, like weight loss surgery (gastrointestinal surgery), but these treatments will not treat the underlying problem of binge eating disorder.

Chapter 16

Lesser-Known Eating Disorders

Orthorexia Nervosa

Whereas anorexia nervosa is an obsession with the quantity of food one eats, it is also possible to be obsessed with eating foods of a certain quality. Orthorexia nervosa, a new term coined by Steven Bratman, M.D., refers to this obsession with eating "proper" foods. ("Ortho" means straight and "orexia" refers to appetite.)

While it is normal for people to change what they eat to improve their health, treat an illness or lose weight, individuals with orthorexia nervosa may take the concern too far. It is common for individuals who are on diets to be concerned with what types of food they are eating, but this concern should quickly decrease as they near or achieve their desired weight. In the case of orthorexia nervosa, people remain consumed with what types of food they allow themselves to eat, and feel badly about themselves if they fail to stick to their diet.

About This Chapter: "Orthorexia Nervosa" is reprinted with permission from the Palo Alto Medical Foundation teen health website, http://www.pamf.org/teen/. © 2003. All rights reserved. "Night-Eating Syndrome" is reprinted with permission from http://www.anred.com. © 2004 Anorexia Nervosa and Related Eating Disorders, Inc. All rights reserved. "Laxative Abuse" from a document titled "Laxatives and Enemas: Not the Way to Go," is reprinted with permission from http://www.anred.com. © 2002 Anorexia Nervosa and Related Eating Disorders, Inc. All rights reserved.

People suffering from this obsession may find themselves:

- Spending more than three hours a day thinking about healthy food.

- Planning tomorrow's menu today.

- Feeling virtuous about what they eat, but not enjoying it much.

- Continually limiting the number of foods they eat.

- Experiencing a reduced quality of life or social isolation (because their diet makes it difficult for them to eat anywhere but at home).

- Feeling critical of others who do not eat as well they do.

- Skipping foods they once enjoyed in order to eat the "right" foods.

- Feeling guilt or self-loathing when they stray from their diet.

- Feeling in "total" control when they eat the correct diet.

While orthorexia nervosa isn't yet a formal medical condition, many doctors do feel that it explains an important and growing health phenomenon. If you think you or a friend suffers from something that sounds or feels like this description of orthorexia nervosa, you should visit either a nutritionist or doctor to discuss it further with them. They can help.

Night-Eating Syndrome

Signs And Symptoms

- The person has little or no appetite for breakfast. Delays first meal for several hours after waking up. Is not hungry or is upset about how much was eaten the night before.

- Eats more food after dinner than during that meal.

♣ **It's A Fact!!**
Night-eating syndrome is thought to be stress related and is often accompanied by depression. Especially at night the person may be moody, tense, anxious, nervous, agitated, etc.
Source: ANRED, 2004.

- Eats more than half of daily food intake during and after dinner but before breakfast. May leave the bed to snack at night.

- This pattern has persisted for at least two months.

- Person feels tense, anxious, upset, or guilty while eating.

- Has trouble falling asleep or staying asleep. Wakes frequently and then often eats.

- Foods ingested are often carbo- hydrates: sugary and starch.

- Behavior is not like binge eating, which is done in relatively short epi- sodes. Night-eating syndrome involves continual eating throughout evening hours.

- This eating produces guilt and shame, not en- joyment.

✔ **Quick Tip**

If you are seeking help for night- eating syndrome, you would be wise to schedule a complete physical exam with your physician and also an evaluation with a counse- lor trained in the field of eating disorders. In ad- dition, a dietitian can help develop meal plans that distribute intake more evenly throughout the day so that you are not so vulnerable to caloric loading in the evening.

Source: ANRED, 2004.

How many people have night-eating syndrome?

Perhaps only 1–2% of adults in the general population have this problem, but research at the University of Pennsylvania School of Medicine suggests that about 6% of people who seek treatment for obesity have NES. Another study suggests that 27% of people who are overweight by at least 100 pounds have the problem.

Comments

Night-eating syndrome has not yet been formally defined as an eating disorder. Underlying causes are being identified, and treatment plans are still being developed. It seems likely that a combination of biological, genetic, and emotional factors contribute to the problem. Stress appears to be a cause or trigger of NES, and stress-reduction programs, including mental health therapy, seem to help.

Researchers are especially interested in the foods chosen by night eaters. The heavy preference for carbohydrates, which trigger the brain to produce so-called "feel-good" neurochemicals, suggests that night eating may be an unconscious attempt to self-medicate mood problems.

NES may run in families. At this time, it appears to respond to treatment with the SSRI sertraline (a prescription medication). NES is remarkable for characteristic disturbances in the circadian (24 hour period) rhythm of food intake while the circadian sleep rhythm remains normal.

Laxative Abuse

By abusing laxatives and enemas, some people with eating disorders try to rush food through their bodies before the calories can be absorbed. These practices are harmful, even potentially fatal, and they don't work to remove calories.

I have been using laxatives and enemas to control my weight. My mother says I am putting myself in danger. Is she just trying to control me?

Listen to your mother. This time she is right.

- Laxatives and enemas have no place in modern health care except in medical conditions monitored by physicians.

- People with eating disorders abuse laxatives because they believe they can remove food from their bodies before the calories are absorbed (They can't. See below.) Also, many are constipated. The little bit of food they allow themselves does not provide enough bulk to stimulate regular bowel movements.

- The misuse of laxatives and enemas can cause serious, sometimes irreversible, sometimes fatal problems.

- Many people can kick the laxative/enema habit, even after long-term use. To manage problems, work with a physician.

Why can't laxatives help me control my weight? After I use the bathroom, I always weigh less than I did before.

A healthy bowel receives food residue from the stomach and small intestine. As the bowel fills, fecal matter stimulates nerve endings, causing muscle contractions that expel the residue from the body in a bowel movement.

Laxatives and enemas artificially stimulate nerve endings in the large bowel, which is also called the colon. The colon is one of the last structures in the digestive tract. By the time food arrives there, nothing is left but indigestible fiber and other non-nutritive material.

Laxatives remove lots of water from the colon as well as food residue. The scales indicate weight loss after a laxative-induced bowel movement, but it is false weight loss. The ounces or pounds return as the body rehydrates after liquid intake consumption. If the person refuses to drink liquids, s/he risks dehydration, which can lead to fainting spells and in some cases death.

Laxatives and enemas cannot stimulate the small intestine, the part of the gastrointestinal (GI) tract where food is digested and where nutrients and calories are absorbed. The small intestine does not even have the kinds of nerves that occur in the colon and respond to artificial stimulation.

In one experiment, a group of laxative abusers ate a high calorie meal. A group of normal people ate the same food, which totaled several thousand calories. The laxative abusers took their purgatives of choice. The normal people let nature take its course. Researchers collected all the material passed in bowel movements and tested it for calorie content. Even after consuming thousands of calories and massive amounts of laxatives, the laxative abusers managed to remove only about 100 extra calories from their bodies, the amount found in one small cookie.

How can I hurt myself my continuing to use laxatives and enemas?

- You can upset your electrolyte balance. Electrolytes are minerals like sodium, potassium that are dissolved in the blood and other body fluids. They must be present in very specific amounts for proper functioning of nerves and muscles, including the heart muscle.

- Laxatives and enemas (and also vomiting) can upset this balance, resulting in muscle cramps, tremors, spasms, irregular heartbeat, and in some cases cardiac arrest. The heart stops, and unless the person receives immediate emergency medical treatment, s/he dies.

- Laxatives and enemas (and also vomiting) remove needed fluid from the body. The resulting dehydration can lead to tremors, weakness, blurry vision, fainting spells, kidney damage, and in some cases death. Severe dehydration requires medical treatment. Drinking fluid may not hydrate cells and tissues quickly enough to prevent organ damage or death.

- Laxatives irritate intestinal nerve endings, which in turn stimulate muscle contractions that move the irritant through the gut and out of the body. After a while the nerve endings no longer respond to stimulation. The person must now take greater and greater amounts of laxatives to produce bowel movements. S/he has become laxative dependent and without them may not have any bowel movements at all.

✎ What's It Mean?

Benign Tumor: A noncancerous growth that does not invade nearby tissue or spread to other parts of the body. [1]

Cancer: A term for diseases in which abnormal cells divide without control. Cancer cells can invade nearby tissues and can spread through the bloodstream and lymphatic system to other parts of the body. [1]

Constipation: A condition in which the stool becomes hard and dry. A person who is constipated usually has fewer than three bowel movements in a week. Bowel movements may be painful. [2]

Source: [1] "Dictionary of Cancer Terms," National Cancer Institute, available at www.nci.nih .gov; cited December 2004. [2] "Digestive Diseases Dictionary," National Institute of Diabetes and Digestive and Kidney Diseases, available at www.digestive. niddk.nih.gov, 2000.

- Laxatives and enemas strip away protective mucus that lines the colon, leaving it vulnerable to infection.

- Enemas can stretch the colon, which over time becomes a limp sack with no muscle tone. No longer can it generate the muscle contractions necessary to move fecal matter out of the body.

- Laxatives abusers seem to have more trouble with the following problems than do nonusers: irritable bowel syndrome (rectal pain, gas, and episodes of constipation and diarrhea) and bowel tumors (both benign and cancerous).

How can I stop the laxative and enema habit?

- Ask your doctor for help. Don't let shyness or embarrassment stop you.

- As your doctor advises either taper off or go cold turkey. Expect to be anxious when time passes with no bowel movement and increasing feelings of fullness, bloat, and discomfort. Your body needs time to regulate itself and relearn how to respond to natural cues. Be reassured that most people who stick with their doctor's recommendations manage to stop laxatives and enemas and resume normal functioning after an initial period of discomfort.

- Make sure you eat enough food, especially high-fiber items like whole grains, fresh fruits, and fresh vegetables. Eat the skin and peels too; they are usually high in fiber. An inexpensive, effective way to increase fiber in your diet is to add a few spoonfuls of unprocessed bran to soups, stews, and cereals. Don't go overboard with bran, however. It can generate intestinal gas, which will increase your discomfort.

- Drink a hot beverage (lemon juice in hot water is good), and then walk briskly for thirty minutes. The hot liquid and muscle movements in your legs and abdomen will help stimulate muscle contractions in the intestines.

- Drink lots of water during the day. Doctors recommend eight to ten glasses. Don't count caffeine beverages in your total; caffeine pulls water out of your body instead of adding it to cells and tissues.

- Before breakfast, take a walk. Walking gets your intestinal muscles working so they can move the contents of your GI tract along and out of your body. A cup of hot water and lemon juice helps get things going too.

- Eat breakfast! After breakfast, sit on the toilet for 5–10 minutes. Breakfast initiates a reflex that triggers the intestines to evacuate their contents.

- Let your therapist help you deal with the anxiety that this recovery process may create. Remember that the human body has tremendous powers of restoration, but they sometimes take a while to kick in.

Part Three

Athletics And Eating Disorders

Chapter 17

Athletes With Eating Disorders: An Overview

In a sense, eating disorders are diets and fitness or sports programs gone horribly wrong. A person wants to lose weight, get fit, excel in his or her sport, but then loses control and ends up with body and spirit ravaged by starvation, binge eating, purging, and frantic compulsive exercise. What may have begun as a solution to problems of low self-esteem has now become an even bigger problem in its own right.

Statistics

Several studies suggest that participants in sports that emphasize appearance and a lean body are at higher risk for developing an eating disorder than are non-athletes or folks involved in sports that require muscle mass and bulk.

Eating disorders are significant problems in the worlds of ballet and other dance, figure skating, gymnastics, running, swimming, rowing, horse racing, ski jumping, and riding. Wrestlers, usually thought of as strong and massive, may binge eat before a match to carbohydrate load and then purge to make weight in a lower class.

One study of 695 male and female athletes found many examples of bulimic attitudes and behavior. A third of the group was preoccupied with

✎ What's It Mean?

Carbohydrate: A sugar molecule. Carbohydrates can be simple, such as glucose, or complex, such as starch. [1]

Cardiac Arrest: The sudden cessation of the heart's pumping action, possibly due to a heart attack, respiratory arrest, electrical shock, extreme cold, blood loss, drug overdose, or a severe allergic reaction. [2]

Laxative: A substance that promotes bowel movements. [1]

Metabolism: The total of all chemical changes that take place in a cell or an organism. These changes produce energy and basic materials needed for important life processes. [1]

Source: [1] "Dictionary of Cancer Terms," National Cancer Institute, available at www.nci.nih.gov; cited December 2004. [2] "Glossary," Agency for Healthcare Research and Quality, U.S. Department of Health and Human Services, available at www.ahrq.gov, 2000.

food. About a quarter binged at least once a week. Fifteen percent thought they were overweight when they were not. About twelve percent feared losing control, or actually did lose control, when they ate. More than five percent ate until they were gorged and nauseated.

In this study, five and a half percent vomited to feel better after a binge and to control weight. Almost four percent abused laxatives. Twelve percent fasted for twenty-four hours or more after a binge, and about one and a half percent used enemas to purge.

Another research project done by the National Collegiate Athletic Association (NCAA) looked at the number of student athletes who had experienced an eating disorder in the previous two years. Ninety-three percent of the reported problems were in women's sports. The sports that had the highest number of participants with eating disorders, in descending order, were women's cross country, women's gymnastics, women's swimming, and women's track and field events.

The male sports with the highest number of participants with eating disorders were wrestling and cross country.

Male And Female Athletes: Different Risk Factors

The female athlete is doubly at risk for the development of an eating disorder. She is subject to the constant social pressure to be thin that affects all females in western countries, and she also finds herself in a sports milieu that may overvalue performance, low body fat, and an idealized, unrealistic body shape, size, and weight. Constant exposure to the demands of the athletic subculture added to those bombarding her daily on TV, in movies, in magazines, and transmitted by peers, may make her especially vulnerable to the lures of weight loss and unhealthy ways of achieving that loss.

Males also develop eating disorders but at a much reduced incidence (approximately 90% female; 10% male). Males may be protected somewhat by their basic biology and different cultural expectations.

Many sports demand low percentages of body fat. In general, men have more lean muscle tissue and less fatty tissue than women do. Males also tend to have higher metabolic rates than females because muscle burns more calories faster than fat does. So women, who in general carry more body fat than men, with slower metabolisms and smaller frames, require fewer calories than men do.

All of these factors mean that women gain weight more easily than men, and women have a harder time losing weight, and keeping it off, than men do. In addition, women have been taught to value being thin. Men, on the other hand, usually want to be big, powerful, and strong; therefore, men are under less pressure to diet than women are—and dieting is one of the primary risk factors for the development of an eating disorder.

Special Concerns: Wrestlers And Quick Weight Loss

Everyone who uses drastic and unhealthy methods of weight loss is at risk of dying or developing serious health problems, but the deaths of three college wrestlers in the latter part of 1997 triggered re-examination of the extreme weight-loss efforts common in that sport. Athletes in other sports have died too; runners and gymnasts seem to be at high risk. The death of three young men in different parts of the U.S. in the late 1990s has put the problem once again before the public.

News reports say that the three were going to school in North Carolina, Wisconsin, and Michigan. Authorities believe they were trying to lose too much weight too rapidly so they could compete in lower weight classes. The wrestling coach at Iowa State University has been quoted as saying, "When you have deaths like this, it calls into question what's wrong with the sport. Wrestlers believe that, foremost, it's their responsibility to make weight, and that mind set may come from the fact that they find themselves invincible." They share that mind set with others who use dangerous methods of weight loss, both athletes and non-athletes.

☞ **Remember!!**

Everyone who uses drastic and unhealthy methods of weight loss is at risk of dying or developing serious health problems.

Two of the young men were wearing rubber sweat suits while they worked out in hot rooms. One died from kidney failure and heart malfunction. The other succumbed to cardiac arrest after he worked out on an exercise bike and refused to drink liquids to replenish those he lost by sweating. One was trying to lose four pounds, the other six.

Wrestlers share a mentality with people who have eating disorders. They push themselves constantly to improve, to be fitter, to weigh less, and to excel. They drive themselves beyond fatigue. One coach reports that "wrestlers consider themselves the best-conditioned athletes that exist, and they like the fact they can go where no one's gone before. The instilled attitude among these kids is that if they push and push, it'll pay off with a victory." No one expects to die as a consequence of weight loss, but it happens.

When a clamor arose for the NCAA to do something, to make rules prohibiting drastic methods of weight loss, a representative said, "We could make every rule in the book, but we can't legislate ethics. That's where the wrestlers and coaches have to put the onus on themselves."

What price victory? It takes wisdom indeed to realize that in some circumstances the price is too high.

Chapter 18

Identifying Athletes At Risk For Eating Disorders

Sports Associated With Eating Disorders

- Eating disorders and disordered eating are significant problems for many athletes.

- Female athletes are especially at risk in sports that emphasize a thin body or appearance, such as gymnastics, ballet, figure skating, swimming, and distance running.

- Male athletes are especially at risk in body building and wrestling.

- A greater risk is associated with sports in which anaerobic activities predominate over aerobic activities.

Gender And Eating Disorders Among Athletes

- 90% of eating disorders occur among women.

- There is some evidence, however, that male athletes are at least equally at risk as female athletes for certain types of eating disorders.

About This Chapter: "Athletes and Eating Disorders," by Pauline S. Powers, M.D. and Craig Johnson, Ph.D. © 2005 Screening for Mental Health, Inc. All rights reserved. Reprinted with permission.

- A study of National Collegiate Athletic Association (NCAA) athletes found that:

  - Binge eating occurred more often in male athletes than in female athletes.

  - More than three times as many male athletes as female athletes used saunas or steam baths to lose weight.

  - The same percentage of males and females used steroids to improve athletic performance.

  - Female athletes were four times more likely than males to use vomiting to lose weight.

  - White female athletes have significantly lower self esteem than black male or female athletes or white male athletes.

- Female athletes who abuse anabolic-androgenic steroids may develop significant psychiatric symptoms including hypomania or depression.

Causes Of Eating Disorders Among Athletes

1. The idealization of thinness in our society

    - Judges in gymnastics and figure skating have progressively rewarded thinner athletes.

2. The unsubstantiated belief that lower body fat enhances performance

3. Pre-selection

    - Individuals who are preoccupied with weight and appearance may be more likely to participate in athletics.

4. Exercise

    - Animal studies have shown that a dramatic increase in activity can precipitate a decrease in appetite and severe weight loss.

5. Body dissatisfaction

    - Athletes at risk for eating disorders are often those who are particularly anxious and critical of their own athletic performance and who express these concerns by dissatisfaction with their bodies.

♣ **It's A Fact!!**

Closely Connected!

The athlete who is considered a "good athlete" and the athlete at risk of developing disordered eating share many of the same characteristics. It can be difficult to know which characteristics are helpful to performance and which may be harmful to health.

A "good" athlete:

- Is willing to train and exercise harder and longer than her teammates.

- Performs through pain and injury.

- Is selflessly committed to her team.

- Complies completely with coaching instructions in order to please others.

- Accepts nothing less than perfection.

- Is willing to lose weight to improve performance.

An athlete with disordered eating:

- Is a perfectionist with high goals.

- Has a strong desire to please others.

- Bases her self worth on achievement and performance.

- Is willing to tolerate pain and sacrifice herself to meet her goals.

- Is critical of herself and has high expectations in sport and life.

- Places emphasis on maintaining an "ideal body weight" or optimal body fat.

Source: Adapted from materials created by Dr. Ron Thompson and Dr. Roberta Trattner Sherman for the International Academy of Eating Disorders Conference, 2000. Reprinted with permission.

6. Perfectionism

    • Among female athletes, a history of perfectionism confers additional risk for an eating disorder.

7. Mood

    • Depressed mood in both male and female athletes may mask disordered eating attitudes.

Effects Of Eating Disorders In Athletes

• Eating disorders may result in symptoms that interfere with athletic performance.

✎ What's It Mean?

Amenorrhea: The lack of a menstrual period. This term is used to describe the absence of a period in young women who haven't started menstruating by age 16, or the absence of a period in women who used to have a regular period. Causes of amenorrhea include pregnancy, breastfeeding, and extreme weight loss caused by serious illness, eating disorders, excessive exercising, or stress. Hormonal problems (involving the pituitary, thyroid, ovary, or adrenal glands) or problems with the reproductive organs may be involved. [1]

Anabolic-Androgenic Steroids (Anabolic Steroids): The familiar name for synthetic substances related to the male sex hormones. They promote the growth of skeletal muscle and the development of male sexual characteristics. [2]

Electrolyte: A substance that breaks up into ions (electrically charged particles) when it is dissolved in body fluids or water. Some examples of electrolytes are sodium, potassium, chloride, and calcium. Electrolytes are primarily responsible for the movement of nutrients into cells and the movement of wastes out of cells. [3]

Estrogen: A hormone that promotes the development and maintenance of female sex characteristics. [3]

- Fatigue, weakness, lightheadedness, broken bones, leg cramps, and irregular heart rate are among the symptoms which may impair athletic capacity.

- These symptoms are the result of various physiological complications of eating disorders, including low thyroid hormones, poor heart and circulatory function, osteoporosis, and electrolyte imbalance.

The Female Athlete Triad

- The triad of amenorrhea, disordered eating, and osteoporosis is particularly likely to occur in female athletes.

Hypomania: Part of a mild form of bipolar disorder in which the person's mood is elevated and does not cause the person to be disconnected from reality. [4]

Osteoporosis: A condition that is characterized by a decrease in bone mass and density, causing bones to become fragile. [3]

Steroids: A class of drugs that are available legally only by prescription, to treat conditions that occur when the body produces abnormally low amounts of testosterone, such as delayed puberty and some types of impotence. They are also prescribed to treat body wasting in patients with AIDS and other diseases that result in loss of lean muscle mass. [5]

Thyroid: A gland located beneath the voice box (larynx) that produces thyroid hormone. The thyroid helps regulate growth and metabolism. [3]

Source: [1] "Menstruation and the Menstrual Cycle," U.S. Department of Health and Human Services, Office on Women's Health, available at www.4woman.gov, 2002. [2] "Anabolic Steroid Abuse," Research Report Series, National Institute on Drug Abuse, U.S. Department of Health and Human Services, available at www.nida.nih.gov, 2004. [3] "Dictionary of Cancer Terms," National Cancer Institute, available at www.nci.nih.gov; cited December 2004. [4] Editor. [5] "Info Facts," National Institute on Drug Abuse, U.S. Department of Health and Human Services, available at www.nida.nih.gov, 2004.

Treatment Of Athletes With Eating Disorders And The Coach's Place On The Treatment Team

Research suggests that the most effective treatment for an eating disorder is multidisciplinary. A treatment team, instead of a solitary practitioner, designs and executes a treatment plan that addresses the multidimensional nature of anorexia nervosa and bulimia.

The Treatment Team At Work

As the client and treatment team members combat the eating disorder, a physician monitors and treats physical problems associated with starving, stuffing, and purging. If necessary, a psychiatrist prescribes medications that help correct underlying mood disturbances such as depression and anxiety. A mental health therapist helps the client unravel and solve emotional and psychological problems. A dietitian provides nutritional counseling and debunks myths surrounding food and dieting. A family therapist helps identify and change patterns of communications that have been troublesome and unsatisfying. A group therapy facilitator helps the client see that s/he is not alone in her/his disorder and that s/he can learn from peers.

An athlete's coach is enormously important in her/his life. The coach at different times is teacher, parent figure, confidant, disciplinarian, and demigod. The coach decides when an athlete will compete, how much s/he will compete, and what s/he must do to compete. Because the coach is so significant to the athlete, s/he must not be omitted from the treatment team.

Advantages Of Including The Athlete's Coach On The Treatment Team

If the coach does not know what is going on, s/he can unintentionally sabotage progress. For example, s/he must be kept informed of food and weight requirements while the athlete is in treatment and of any restrictions on physical activity.

Because a coach is so powerful in the life of an athlete, her/his cooperation is needed. Without it, therapeutic concern about an impaired body and mind will be subordinated to sports issues such as keeping one's place on the team, scholarships, opportunities to compete at more advanced levels, the possibility of a professional career in sports, and sometimes the chance for money-making endorsements.

Managing Health And Participation In Sports: A Difficult Challenge

Athletes want to compete and win, and their coaches want them to do so. Indeed, the career of a coach may depend, for better or for worse, on the success or failure of her/his athletes. Sometimes, when an eating disorder is severe and health is compromised, the medical members of a treatment team will want to remove the athlete from participation in trainings, workouts, and competitions. It is absolutely essential that they and the coach come to a mutual understanding and agreement. The bottom line is always the best interests of the athlete, and that may be harder to determine than is first apparent.

Two Different Worlds

The primary goal of physicians and mental health workers is to restore their clients to physical and psychological health. They may see the impaired athlete as having a destructive commitment to a trivial activity. The athlete and coach, as well as the athlete's family, on the other hand, often see sports achievement as worthy of single-minded determination and significant sacrifice. If the treatment team, including the coach, and the athlete are to work smoothly together and ultimately defeat the eating disorder, they must come to some mutual understanding and agreement about the place of athletics, including discipline and dedication, in the life of the athlete.

- Multiple factors cause the amenorrhea seen in female athletes, including exercise, low weight, low body fat content, stress, hormonal changes, inadequate nutrition, and imbalance in nutritional composition.

- Amenorrhea, or irregular periods, in female athletes should be taken seriously because even brief episodes are associated with osteoporosis and infertility problems.

- Estrogen supplementation, without weight gain, does not seem to reverse the vulnerability to osteoporosis.

Detection And Treatment

- Athletes are often aware of the symptoms of eating disorders, but do not want to acknowledge the symptoms for fear that they will be required to stop their sport.

- Except in extreme cases, the athlete can continue the sport while in treatment.

- The American College of Sports Medicine has encouraged all individuals working with physically active girls and women to be educated about the triad of amenorrhea, disordered eating, and osteoporosis, and to develop plans to prevent, recognize, treat, and reduce its risks.

- Coaches and team physicians are often in a position to identify an eating disorder early and assist the athlete in seeking appropriate treatment.

Chapter 19

Compulsive Exercise

We all know the benefits of exercise. It makes our hearts healthier, our bones stronger, prevents or delays the development of certain diseases, and improves our mental well being and self-image. Teens in the United States today are less fit than they were a generation ago. Many are showing early signs of cardiovascular risk factors such as no physical activity, excess weight, high cholesterol, and cigarette smoking. Inactive teens are apt to become inactive adults. However, inactive teens aren't the only ones exhibiting unhealthy behavior. There is a growing number of the teen population who are taking things to the opposite extreme and turning exercise from a healthy activity into an unhealthy obsession.

What Is Compulsive Exercise?

Compulsive exercise is when someone no longer chooses to exercise but feels compelled to do so and struggles with guilt and anxiety if she doesn't work out. Social events, bad weather, or an illness doesn't deter a compulsive exerciser. In a sense, exercising takes over her life because she plans her life around it.

When done correctly, exercise can be part of a safe and healthy way to control weight. Unfortunately many teens, especially girls, have unrealistic expectations of what their ideal body image should be based on what they see on television and in magazines. Compulsive exercise, also known as anorexia athletica, is often compared with eating disorders because the people who partake in it do so to feel more in control of their lives and their bodies. Most teens who exercise compulsively are females who try to deal with their emotional issues by pushing their bodies to their physical limits. While compulsive exercise doesn't necessarily accompany an eating disorder, the two are often seen together. In most cases, the excessive workouts start as a way to control weight and become more and more extreme, eventually leading to decreased eating.

Physical Signs Of Overdoing It

Too much exercise, especially the same kind of exercise, can cause repetitive injuries to the tendons, ligaments, bones, cartilage, and joints. Don't allow yourself to mask your injury by loading up on pain relievers just so you can play in the big game. Minor injuries that aren't given time to heal can result in long-term damage. Overdoing it can also cause your body to break down muscle instead of fat, especially when you are not fueling it with enough food.

Girls who exercise compulsively may throw off their bodies' hormone balance and stop having periods, which can lead to premature bone loss and osteoporosis later in life. When coupled with an eating disorder, excessive exercise can lead to serious stress on the heart, which can be fatal if left untreated.

So how do you know if your fitness routine is over the top? Do you:

• Force yourself to work out, even if you don't feel well?

• Prefer to exercise rather than be with your friends?

• Become upset if you miss a workout?

• Base the amount you exercise on how much you eat?

• Have trouble sitting still because you don't think you're burning enough calories?

- Worry that you'll gain weight if you skip exercising for a day?

- Never seem satisfied with your physical achievements?

- Withdraw from social and academic activities with friends or family in order to exercise?

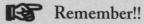 **Remember!!**

Don't allow yourself to mask an injury by loading up on pain relievers just so you can play in the big game. Minor injuries that aren't given time to heal can result in long-term damage.

- Use diet aids, herbs, steroids, or chemicals to help enhance yourself physically? These products are extremely dangerous and can cause liver problems, increased heart rate, increased blood pressure, heart attack, and stroke.

- Seem constantly preoccupied with your weight and exercise routine?

If you answered yes to any of these, you may have a problem and need to be evaluated.

Getting Help

Start with your doctor. The doctor may recommend medical treatment if your body is severely undernourished or she detects heart problems. Since compulsive exercise is so closely linked with eating disorders, help can be found at hospitals and community agencies that specialize in these issues. Compulsive exercising is part of a distorted body image and low self-esteem, which often calls for extensive help from a trained mental health professional who can help you learn how to deal with your emotions and recognize the many positive attributes you possess.

Treating a compulsion to exercise takes time—often months or even years. Therapy can help improve your body image and self-esteem. Appointments with a dietitian or nutritionist can help you learn healthy eating habits. And to encourage your new, healthy approach to diet and fitness, involve yourself in meal planning and preparation and find fun physical activities that you can do like swimming, biking, rollerblading and hiking. A visit with a sports medicine specialist to discuss safe guidelines is also helpful.

Muscle Dysmorphic Disorder (Bigorexia)

What Is Muscle Dysmorphic Disorder?

A subtype of body dysmorphic disorder, which in itself is a variant of obsessive-compulsive disorder. Sometimes called bigorexia, muscle dysmorphia is the opposite of anorexia nervosa. People with this disorder obsess about being small and undeveloped. They worry that they are too little and too frail. Even if they have good muscle mass, they believe their muscles are inadequate.

New research indicates that people with MDD really do see themselves as small. Apparently something has gone awry with the brain's ability to map body boundaries.

✎ What's It Mean?

Body Dysmorphic Disorder: A serious illness when a person is preoccupied with minor or imaginary physical flaws, usually of the skin, hair, and nose. A person with BDD tends to have cosmetic surgery, and even if the surgeries are successful, does not think they are and is unhappy with the outcomes. [1]

Cartilage: A tough, flexible tissue that lines joints and gives structure to the nose, ears, larynx, and other parts of the body. [2]

Cholesterol: A fat-like substance in the body. The body makes and needs some cholesterol, which also comes from foods such as butter and egg yolks. Too much cholesterol may cause gallstones. It also may cause fat to build up in the arteries. This may cause a disease that slows or stops blood flow. [3]

Hormone: A chemical made by glands in the body. Hormones circulate in the bloodstream and control the actions of certain cells or organs. Some hormones can also be made in a laboratory. [4]

Ligaments: Shiny, flexible bands of fibrous tissue connecting together articular extremities of bones. [5]

Osteoporosis: A condition that is characterized by a decrease in bone mass and density, causing bones to become fragile. [4]

In efforts to fix their perceived smallness, people with muscle dysmorphia lift weights, do resistance training, and exercise compulsively. They may take steroids or other muscle-building drugs, a practice with potentially lethal consequences.

Who Gets Muscle Dysmorphic Disorder?

Both genders, but more males than females. Perhaps part of the reason for this discrepancy is related to the fact that the culturally defined ideal male is big and strong while the ideal female is small and thin. Almost everyone with MDD also suffers from depression.

Steroids: A class of drugs that are available legally only by prescription, to treat conditions that occur when the body produces abnormally low amounts of testosterone, such as delayed puberty and some types of impotence. They are also prescribed to treat body wasting in patients with AIDS and other diseases that result in loss of lean muscle mass. [6]

Tendons: Fibrous bands or cords of connective tissue at the ends of muscle fibers that serve to attach the muscles to bones and other structures. [5]

Source: [1] "Body Dysmorphic Disorder (BDD)—When poor body image is an illness," U.S. Department of Health and Human Services, Office on Women's Health, available at www.4woman.gov, 2004. [2] "Dictionary of Cancer Terms," National Cancer Institute, available at www.nci.nih.gov; cited February 2005. [3] "Digestive Diseases Dictionary," National Institute of Diabetes and Digestive and Kidney Diseases, available at www.digestive.niddk.nih.gov, 2000. [4] "Dictionary of Cancer Terms," National Cancer Institute, available at www.nci.nih.gov; cited December 2004. [5] "Genetics Home Reference Glossary," a service of the U.S. National Library of Medicine, available at www.ghr.nlm.nih.gov, 2004. [6] "Info Facts," National Institute on Drug Abuse, U.S. Department of Health and Human Services, available at www.nida.nih.gov, 2004.

Consequences Of Muscle Dysmorphic Disorder

The constant preoccupation with perceived smallness interferes with school and career accomplishments. It robs friendships and romantic relationships of spontaneity and enjoyment. Since the person is exceedingly self-conscious at all times, she cannot relax and enjoy life without worrying about how other people may be seeing, and criticizing, the perceived smallness.

In almost all cases, people with muscle dysmorphia are not small at all. Many have well-developed musculature, and some even compete in body building competitions.

People with MDD cannot or will not stop their excessive exercise even when they are injured. If they abuse steroids in the service of building bulk, they will not give up this unhealthy practice even when they fully understand the risks involved.

Treatment Of Muscle Dysmorphic Disorder

Many people with this problem resist getting treatment stating that they are content with the way they are. Some admit they are afraid that if they give up the drugs and exercise, they will wither away to frailty.

Family members and concerned friends may be able to persuade the person to at least get an evaluation by focusing on the problems caused by the behaviors, such as job loss, relationship failure, and physical harm.

Nonetheless, about half of people with this problem are so convinced of their perceived smallness, so ruled by a true delusion, that they refuse help and continue their excessive exercise and steroid use.

For those who enter treatment, cognitive-behavioral therapy combined with medication holds promise. The same combination can also target co-existing depression. The best place to start is with an evaluation by a physician. Ask for a referral to a mental health counselor who is familiar with these disorders. After both professionals have completed their evaluations, consider their recommendations and choose a course of action that is in your own best interests.

Chapter 20

Sports And Women Athletes: The Female Athlete Triad

With dreams of Olympic trials and college scholarships in her mind, Hannah joined the track team her freshman year and trained hard to become a lean, strong sprinter. When her coach told her losing a few pounds would improve her performance, she didn't hesitate to start counting calories and increasing the duration of her workouts. She was too busy with practices and meets to notice that her period had stopped—she was more worried about the stress fracture in her ankle slowing her down.

Although Hannah thinks her intense training and disciplined diet are helping her performance, they may actually be hurting her—and her health.

What Is Female Athlete Triad?

There's no doubt about it—playing sports and exercise are part of a balanced, healthy lifestyle. Girls who play sports are healthier; get better grades; are less likely to experience depression; and use alcohol, cigarettes, and drugs

About This Chapter: This information was provided by TeensHealth, one of the largest resources online for medically reviewed health information written for parents, kids, and teens. For more articles like this one, visit www.TeensHealth.org, or www.KidsHealth.org. © 2003 The Nemours Center for Children's Health Media, a division of The Nemours foundation.

less frequently. But for some girls, not balancing the needs of their bodies and their sports can have major consequences.

Some girls who play sports or exercise are at risk for a problem called female athlete triad. Female athlete triad—also known as female athletic

Cathy Rigby   ♣ It's A Fact!!

In the 1968 Summer Olympics at Mexico City, a blond, pigtailed 15-year-old girl earned the highest U.S. scores in gymnastics. She captured the hearts of millions of people around the world and changed the course of women's gymnastics in the United States. That teenage athlete was Cathy Rigby, the first American woman to win a medal in World Gymnastics competition. She holds 12 international medals, eight of which are gold. While Cathy excelled in the Olympics, she also suffered from an eating disorder.

"We didn't know very much about nutrition. Neither did the coaches," Cathy said, recalling how her eating disorder started. The coaches would tell the athletes what their weight should be, somewhat arbitrarily. Cathy weighed about 94 pounds at the time and was eating one meal a day to maintain her weight at the prescribed 90 pounds. One night, near the end of training camp, the team went out for pizza to celebrate. "I had three pieces and panicked, knowing I would be weighed-in the next day." Cathy knew one girl on the team was taking laxatives but had no idea it was her way of maintaining her weight. Another girl said she threw up everything she ate. That night Cathy tried the latter method, but it didn't work. "When I hit puberty and went up to about 104 pounds two or three months later, I worked a little harder at either starving myself or becoming bulimic."

Cathy's recovery began in the early '80s after she went through a divorce. "I tried to get professional help before that. Even the psychologists and psychiatrists back then, I think, had to look it up." Her early experiences with treatment met with little success. It wasn't until she remarried that a break came. Her desire not to repeat her past failed marriage, along with the persistent encouragement of the man who is now her husband, Tom McCoy, eventually led to a treatment situation that worked. "The two of us got help for it—him to understand it and deal with me and not try to feed me scrambled eggs."

triad—is a combination of three conditions: disordered eating, amenorrhea (pronounced: ay-meh-nuh-ree-uh, which means loss of a girl's period), and osteoporosis (a weakening of the bones). A female athlete can have one, two, or all three parts of the triad.

Today, a successful actress and mother of four, Cathy is free of her eating disorder. In her appearances at colleges and universities, she talks about her experiences in a positive way. "What I try to do is to lure people into the story," she said. Gymnastics is "a sport that demands absolute control, both emotionally and physically." It can be difficult to tell when the quest for excellence crosses over into obsession—when the passion for the sport becomes overshadowed by greed or abusive control. Cathy echoes the thoughts of other experts when she points out "the very thing that makes anybody a great athlete many times predisposes them to become affective-compulsive people." The powerful emotions, interaction with the coach and parents, and the strain of reaching for an almost unattainable goal can be more difficult to balance than any part of a gymnastic routine. "Even in the best of situations, it's a little dysfunctional. It's a lot of pressure," she said.

Cathy Rigby has come a long way since she was one of those super-competitive teenagers. Now she says, "I don't want to compete against somebody else. I want to do the best I can for myself. This is a competitive world and that's unrealistic, but there's always going to be somebody better—there will always be somebody worse." Her advice for young athletes is to "maintain that joy and passion that you have the minute you walk into a gym." It can be extremely difficult to keep everything in perspective. Cathy was able to overcome her problems when she "started to focus on other things that I wanted in my life, not just something that I thought would please somebody else." Perhaps the most difficult thing to learn is "to reach your own goals, your own gold medals of achievement."

Source: Excerpted with permission from "Little Girls in Pretty Boxes" by David M. Edwards and Mary Allen, originally published in the Winter 1996 issue of *Treatment Today* magazine. Copyright 1996 Quest Publishing Company, Inc.

Triad Factor #1: Disordered Eating

Girls who have the disordered eating that accompanies female athlete triad often have many of the signs and symptoms of anorexia nervosa or bulimia nervosa, such as low body weight for their height and age and episodes of binge eating and purging. But girls with female athlete triad try to lose weight primarily to improve their athletic performance. Sometimes the disordered eating that accompanies this condition isn't technically an eating disorder. Many girls with female athlete triad are simply trying to become better at their chosen sports. But like teens with eating disorders, girls with female athlete triad may use behaviors such as calorie restriction, purging, and exercise to lose weight.

Triad Factor #2: Amenorrhea

Because a girl with female athlete triad is simultaneously exercising intensely and reducing her weight, she may experience decreases in estrogen, the hormone that helps to regulate the menstrual cycle. As a result, a girl's periods may become irregular or stop altogether. (In many cases, of course, a missed period indicates another medical condition—pregnancy. If you have missed a period and you are sexually active, you should talk to your doctor.) Some girls who participate intensively in sports may never even get their first period because they've been training so hard—this is called primary amenorrhea. Other girls may have had periods, but once they increase their training and change their eating habits, their periods may stop—this is called secondary amenorrhea.

Triad Factor #3: Osteoporosis

Low estrogen levels and poor nutrition can also lead to osteoporosis, the third aspect of the triad. Osteoporosis is a weakening of the bones due to the loss of bone density and improper bone formation. This condition can ruin a female athlete's career because it may lead to stress fractures and other injuries due to weakened bones. Because of poor nutrition, a girl's body may not be able to repair the injuries efficiently.

Usually, the teen years are a time when girls should be building up their bone mass to their highest levels—called peak bone mass. Female athlete triad can lead to a lower level of peak bone mass and a lot of time on the sidelines. After she becomes an adult, a girl may also develop health problems related to osteoporosis at an earlier age than she would have otherwise.

Who Gets Female Athlete Triad?

Most girls have concerns about the size and shape of their bodies, but girls who develop female athlete triad have certain risk factors that set them apart. Being a highly competitive athlete and participating in a sport that requires you to train extra hard is a risk factor. Girls with female athlete triad often care so much about their sports that they would do almost anything to improve their performances. Martial arts and rowing are examples of sports that classify athletes by weight class, so focusing on weight becomes an important part of the training program and can put a girl at risk for disordered eating.

Participation in sports where a thin appearance is valued can also put a girl at risk for female athlete triad. Sports such as gymnastics, figure skating, diving, and ballet are examples of sports that value a thin, lean body shape. Some girls may even be told by coaches or judges that losing weight would improve their scores.

Even in sports where body size and shape aren't as important for judging purposes, such as distance running and cross-country skiing, girls may be pressured by teammates, parents, partners, and coaches who mistakenly believe that "losing just a few pounds" would improve their performance. Losing those few pounds generally doesn't improve performance at all—people who are fit and active enough to compete in sports generally have more muscle than fat, so it's the muscle that gets starved when a girl cuts back on food. Plus, if a girl loses weight when she doesn't need to, it interferes with healthy body processes such as menstruation and bone development.

♣ **It's A Fact!!**

The condition female athlete triad was first recognized by the American College of Sports Medicine in 1992. Before then, doctors considered disordered eating separately from a girl's athletic participation, but health pros now know that athletic participation and the disordered eating in girls with female athlete triad are interrelated.

In addition, for some competitive female athletes, problems such as low self-esteem, a tendency toward perfectionism, and family stress place them at risk for disordered eating.

What Are The Signs And Symptoms?

If a girl has risk factors for female athlete triad, she may already be experiencing some symptoms and signs of the disorder, such as:

- Weight loss.

- No periods or irregular periods.

- Fatigue and decreased ability to concentrate.

- Stress fractures (fractures that occur even if a person hasn't had a significant injury).

- Muscle injuries.

Girls with female athlete triad often have signs and symptoms of eating disorders, such as:

- Eating alone.

- Preoccupation with food and weight.

♣ It's A Fact!!
National Ballet School Program: A Case Study

A program conducted at the National Ballet school in Toronto demonstrates how early intervention, nutrition education, and counseling can greatly reduce the chances of dancers developing eating disorders.[1] In small group meetings several times a year, students were encouraged to discuss their experiences regarding unrealistic demands on their behavior or appearance, and their feelings of powerlessness, shame, and fear. Students who became preoccupied with shape, weight, or food were encouraged to request help promptly.

Before the program was started, the incidence of new cases of anorexia or bulimia was about 1.6 per year for 100 girls ages 12 to 18. For the past 8 years, there has been only one case of anorexia and one of bulimia.[2]

Notes

1. Piran, N. et al. (eds.). *Preventing Eating Disorders: A Handbook of Interventions and Special Challenges.* Philadelphia: Brunner/Mazel, 1999.

2. Piran, N. *On Prevention and Transformation.* Toronto Department of Applied Psychology, Ontario Institute for Studies in Education.

Source: Excerpted from "Physical Education Teachers, Coaches, and Dance Instructors," Eating Disorders Information Sheet, The National Women's Health Information Center (NWHIC), 2004.

- Continuous drinking of water and diet soda.

- Frequent trips to the bathroom during and after meals.

- Using laxatives.

- Presence of lanugo hair (fine, soft hair that grows on the body).

- Tooth enamel that's worn away from frequent vomiting.

- Anemia (fewer red blood cells in the blood than normal).

- Sensitivity to cold.

- Heart irregularities and chest pain.

What Do Doctors Do?

It may be easy for girls with female athlete triad to keep their symptoms a secret because information about their periods and any damage done to bones usually isn't visible to friends and family. And lots of girls become very skilled at hiding their disordered eating habits.

✎ What's It Mean?

Estrogen: A hormone that promotes the development and maintenance of female sex characteristics.

Hormone: A chemical made by glands in the body. Hormones circulate in the bloodstream and control the actions of certain cells or organs. Some hormones can also be made in a laboratory.

Laxative: A substance that promotes bowel movements.

Nutrient: A chemical compound (such as protein, fat, carbohydrate, vitamins, or minerals) that make up foods. These compounds are used by the body to function and grow.

Source: "Dictionary of Cancer Terms," National Cancer Institute, available at www.nci.nih.gov; cited December 2004.

A doctor may recognize that a girl has female athlete triad during a regular exam. An extensive physical examination is a crucial part of diagnosing the triad. A doctor who suspects a girl has female athlete triad will probably ask questions about her periods, her nutrition and exercise habits, any medications she takes, and her feelings about her body. Because poor nutrition can affect the body in many ways, a doctor might also test for blood problems and nutritional imbalances. Because osteoporosis can put a girl at higher risk for bone fractures, a doctor who suspects female athlete triad may also request tests to measure bone density.

Tips For Female Athletes   ✔ Quick Tip

Here are a few tips to help teen athletes stay on top of their physical condition:

- **Keep track of your periods.** It's easy to forget when you had your last visit from Aunt Flo, so keep a little calendar in your gym bag and mark down when your period starts and stops and if the bleeding is particularly heavy or light. That way, if you start missing periods, you'll know right away and you'll have accurate information to give to your doctor.

- **Don't skip meals or snacks.** You're constantly on the go between school, practice, and competitions, so it may be tempting to skip meals and snacks to save time. But eating now will improve your performance later, so stock your locker or bag with quick and easy favorites such as bagels, string cheese, unsalted nuts and seeds, raw vegetables, energy bars, and fruit.

- **Visit a dietitian or nutritionist who works with teen athletes.** He or she can help you get your dietary game plan into gear and can help you determine if you're getting enough key nutrients such as iron, calcium, and protein. And, if you need supplements, a nutritionist can recommend the best choices.

- **Do it for you.** Pressure from teammates, parents, or coaches can turn an activity you took up for fun into a nightmare. If you're not enjoying your sport, make a change. Remember: It's your body and your life. Any damage you do to your body now, you—not your coach or teammates—will have to live with later.

Doctors don't work alone to help a girl with female athlete triad—coaches, parents, physical therapists, pediatricians and adolescent medicine specialists, nutritionists and dietitians, and mental health specialists all work together to treat the physical and emotional problems that a girl with female athlete triad faces.

It might be tempting for a girl with female athlete triad to shrug off several months of missed periods, but getting help right away is important. In the short term, a girl with female athlete triad may have muscle weakness, stress fractures, and reduced physical performance. Over the long term, a girl with female athlete triad may suffer from bone weakness, damage to her reproductive system, and heart problems.

A girl who is recovering from female athlete triad may work with a dietitian to help get to and maintain a healthy weight and ensure she's eating enough nutrients for health and good athletic performance. Depending on how much the girl is exercising, she may have to reduce the length of her workouts. Talking to a psychologist or therapist can help a girl deal with depression, pressure from coaches or family members, or low self-esteem and can help her find ways to deal with her problems other than restricting her food intake or exercising excessively.

Some girls with female athlete triad may need to take hormones to supply their bodies with estrogen so they can get their periods started again. In such cases, birth control pills are often used to regulate a girl's menstrual cycle. Calcium and vitamin D supplementation is also common for a girl who has suffered bone loss as the result of female athlete triad.

What If I Think Someone I Know Has Female Athlete Triad?

A girl with female athlete triad can't just ignore the disorder and hope it goes away—she needs to get help from a doctor and other health professionals. If your friend, sister, or teammate has signs and symptoms of female athlete triad, discuss your concerns with her and encourage her to seek treatment. If she refuses to seek treatment, you may need to mention your concern to her parent, coach, teacher, or school nurse.

Looking for ways to be supportive to your friend with female athlete triad? You may worry about being nosy, but don't: Your concern is a sign that you're a caring friend. Lending an ear may be just what your friend needs.

Part Four

Prevention And Treatment
Of Eating Disorders

Chapter 21

Reducing Your Risk Of Eating Disorders

To begin, accept what is not in your control:

1. Accept your body's genetic predisposition. All bodies are wired to be fatter, thinner, or in between. This includes fatter in some places and thinner in others. Regardless of efforts to change it, over time your body will fight to maintain or resume the shape it was born to be. You may force your body into sizes and shapes that you prefer, but you can't beat Mother Nature without a tremendous cost.

2. Understand that all bodies change developmentally in ways that are simply not in your control through healthy means. You may positively influence changes of puberty, pregnancy and lactation, menopause, and aging by making healthy lifestyle choices, but you will not "control" these changes, no matter how much you try.

3. Never diet. Hunger is an internally regulated drive and demands to be satisfied. If you limit the food needed to satiate hunger completely, it will backfire, triggering preoccupation with food and ultimately an overeating or compulsive eating response. You may lose weight in the short run, but 95% of weight that is lost through dieting is regained, plus added pounds. Dieters who go off their diets only to binge are not weak willed.

About This Chapter: "Tips for Developing a Healthy Body Image," by Kathy Kater, LICSW. © 2004 BodyImageHealth.org. All rights reserved. Reprinted with permission.

They are mammals whose built-in starvation response has kicked in—both physically and psychologically, going after what has been restricted. Scientific evidence has been available on this since the early 1950s, but most people are not aware of the biologically predictable results of dieting.

Then focus your attention and energy on what is within your power to achieve:

4. Satisfy hunger completely with plenty of wholesome, nutrient-rich foods chosen from all the food groups. In today's world, surrounded by taste stimulating, cheap, cleverly advertised, readily available, low-nutrient entertainment foods, learning to feed your body versus merely "eat" is an essential difference.

5. Limit sedentary entertainment. Move aerobically, if possible, on a regular basis. Everyone who is not medically limited, regardless of size, can, and should, develop a reasonable level of fitness and maintain it throughout the life cycle.

6. Understand that if you eat well and maintain an active lifestyle over time, your best, natural weight will be revealed. Set a goal to eat well and be active. Don't be swayed by whether or not this makes you thin. Healthy, well fed, active bodies are diverse in size and shape, from fat to thin and everything in between. Don't let anyone tell you otherwise.

7. Choose role models that reflect a realistic standard against which you can feel good about yourself. If the "Ugly Duckling" had continued to compare herself to the ducks, she'd still be miserable, no matter how beautifully she developed.

8. Maintain your integrity as a human being. In spite of advertisements seducing you to believe that image is everything, never forget that how you look is only one part of who you are. Develop a sense of identity based on all the many things you can do, the values you believe in, and the person that you are deep inside.

9. Become media savvy. Educate yourself about the hidden power of advertisements. Advertisers spend tons of money on strategies specifically

✔ Quick Tip

What Can You Do To Help Prevent Eating Disorders?

- Learn all you can about anorexia nervosa, bulimia nervosa, and binge eating disorder. Genuine awareness will help you avoid judgmental or mistaken attitudes about food, weight, body shape, and eating disorders.

- Discourage the idea that a particular diet, weight, or body size will automatically lead to happiness and fulfillment.

- Choose to challenge the false belief that thinness and weight loss are great, while body fat and weight gain are horrible or indicate laziness, worthlessness, or immorality.

- Avoid categorizing foods as "good/safe" vs. "bad/dangerous." Remember that we all need to eat a balanced variety of foods.

- Decide to avoid judging others and yourself on the basis of body weight or shape. Turn off the voices in your head that tell you that a person's body weight says anything about their character, personality, or value as a person.

- Avoid conveying an attitude that says, "I will like you better if you lose weight, or don't eat so much, etc."

- Become a critical viewer of the media and its messages about self-esteem and body image. Talk back to the television when you hear a comment or see an image that promotes thinness at all costs. Rip out (or better yet, write to the editor) about advertisements or articles in your magazines that make you feel bad about your body shape or size.

- If you think someone has an eating disorder, express your concerns in a forthright, caring manner. Gently but firmly encourage the person to seek trained professional help.

- Be a model of healthy self-esteem and body image. Recognize that others pay attention and learn from the way you talk about yourself and your body. Choose to talk about yourself with respect and appreciation. Choose to value yourself based on your goals, accomplishments, talents, and character. Avoid letting the way you feel about your body weight and shape determine the course of your day. Embrace the natural diversity of human bodies and celebrate your body's unique shape and size.

Source: Excerpted from "What Can You Do To Help Prevent Eating Disorders?" © 2002 National Eating Disorders Association. All rights reserved. For additional information visit http://www.NationalEatingDisorders.org.

Anorexia Nervosa   ✔ Quick Tip

- Don't diet. Instead, design a meal plan that gives your body all the nutrition it needs for health and growth. Also, get 30 to 60 minutes of exercise or physical activity three to five days a week. More than that is too much.

- Ask someone you trust for an honest, objective opinion of your weight. If they say you are normal weight or thin, believe them.

- When you start to get overwhelmed by feeling fat, push beyond the anxiety and ask yourself what you are really afraid of. Then take steps to deal with the threat, if it is real, or dismiss it if it is not real.

Bulimia Nervosa And Binge Eating Disorder

- Don't let yourself get too hungry, too angry, too lonely, too tired, or too bored. All these states are powerful binge triggers. Watch for them, and when they first appear, deal with them in a healthy manner instead of letting the tension build until bingeing and purging become the release of choice.

- Stay busy and avoid unstructured time. Empty time is too easily filled with binge food.

- Make sure that every day you touch base with friends and loved ones. Enjoy being with them. It sounds corny, but hugs really are healing.

- Take control of your life. Make choices thoughtfully and deliberately. Make your living situation safe and comfortable.

- Every day do something fun, something relaxing, and something energizing.

- Keep tabs on your feelings. Several times a day ask yourself how you feel. If you get off track, do whatever the situation requires to get back to your comfort zone.

Source: Excerpted from "Self-help tips." Reprinted with permission from http://www.anred.com. © 2003 Anorexia Nervosa and Related Eating Disorders, Inc. All rights reserved.

designed to make you feel there is something wrong with you. Why? If they first advertise an unrealistic standard of beauty that leaves you feeling deficient by comparison, a product that promises to improve your condition is an easy sale. Don't be sold these bill of goods.

10. Encourage your friends and to join you in developing a healthy, realistic body image. Use the collective energy your group would have spent on hating your bodies to make the world a better place. Help others to develop healthy body image attitudes and learn positive lifestyle habits, too.

Chapter 22

Body Image And Self-Esteem

I'm fat. I'm too skinny. I'd be happy if I were taller, shorter, had curly hair, straight hair, a smaller nose, bigger muscles, longer legs.

Is there something wrong with me?

Do any of these statements sound familiar? Are you used to putting yourself down? If so, you're not alone. As a teen, you're going through a ton of changes in your body, and as your body changes, so does your image of yourself. Read on to learn more about how your body image affects your self-esteem and how you can develop a healthy body image.

Why Are Self-Esteem And Body Image Important?

You may have heard the term self-esteem on talk shows or seen it in your favorite magazine. But what does it mean? Self-esteem involves how much a person values herself, and appreciates her own worth. Self-esteem is important because when you feel good about yourself, you enjoy life more.

Although self-esteem applies to every aspect of how you see yourself, it is often mentioned in terms of appearance or body image. Body image is how

About This Chapter: This information was provided by TeensHealth, one of the largest resources online for medically reviewed health information written for parents, kids, and teens. For more articles like this one, visit www.TeensHealth.org, or www.KidsHealth.org. © 2001 The Nemours Center for Children's Health Media, a division of The Nemours Foundation.

you see and feel about your physical appearance. We tend to relate self-esteem to body image for several reasons. First of all, most people care about how other people see them. Unfortunately, many people judge others by things like the clothes they wear, the shape of their body, or the way they wear their hair. If a person feels like he or she looks different than others, then body image and self-esteem may be affected negatively.

Teens with a poor body image may think negative thoughts like, "I'm fat, I'm not pretty enough, I'm not strong enough."

What Shapes Self-Esteem?

The Effects Of Puberty

Some teens struggle with their self-esteem when they begin puberty. That's because the body undergoes many changes when puberty starts. These rapid changes and the desire for acceptance make it difficult for teens to judge whether they are "normal" when they look at other teens around them. And many people worry about what's normal during puberty. But puberty doesn't proceed at the same pace for everyone.

Puberty usually begins with a growth spurt. Usually, this happens to girls first but guys tend to catch up with their own spurts around the ages of 13 or 14. In general, puberty for both sexes takes between 2 to 5 years to complete but every teen has her own genetic timetable for the changes of puberty.

The sexual development of girls typically starts around age 9 to 10 with the appearance of budding breasts, pubic hair, and later the start of menstruation. Other changes include wider hips, buttocks and thighs, and a greater proportion of body fat. These changes can make a girl feel self-conscious about her body. She may feel like her maturing body draws attention to her, and feel uncomfortable or embarrassed. Or she may feel as though her body is weird and different than her friends' bodies. Unhealthy "crash" dieting or eating disorders can result.

Meanwhile, guys will begin to notice their shoulders getting wider, muscles developing, voices deepening, testicles getting larger, and penises growing longer and wider. Guys who are dissatisfied with their development may become obsessed with weight training and may take steroids or other drugs to help boost their physiques and athletic performance.

✔ Quick Tip
What Am I Doing?

Question: I am 18 years old, and I have just begun a steady workout program. Because within 2 weeks people started noticing a difference, I began to feel better about myself. I was not overweight, but now I am feeling like I should lose more weight. I eat, just not as much as I am used to. Occasionally I get hungry, but feel guilty about whatever I put in my mouth. Help, what am I doing?

Answer: Exercise can be a wonderful part of life, enhancing both physical and mental health. It sounds as though the natural positive experience that you may have had within yourself as you began to work out has become confused by the reactions of other people.

The myth of our culture is that size is the most important ingredient of beauty and the key to a positive reaction from others. I wonder if the change in you that people responded to was a change in size, or a change in vitality, or attitude. It may be that they were reacting to something about your energy rather than something about your appearance.

In any case, it is a shame that the positive reactions you have received from other people do not give you a feeling of happiness, satisfaction, and connectedness. Instead, you seem to be beginning to struggle with eating disorder thinking (for example feeling that you need to lose weight when you are not overweight, feeling guilty about whatever you eat). Why not see a therapist or counselor to get a better understanding of why you are worrying about food, weight and dieting? It would be wise to address these concerns now and learn other ways to improve your relationship with yourself and others before you become reliant on the myth that focusing on your body is the way to feel better about yourself.

Source: © 2002 The Renfrew Center. All rights reserved. Reprinted with permission. For additional information, call 1-800-RENFREW or visit http://www.renfrewcenter.com.

The Effects Of Culture

Media images from TV, movies, and advertising may affect self-esteem. Girls may struggle with media images of teen girls and women who are unrealistically thin. Many women and teen girls in magazines, the news, or on TV are unusually thin, which may lead girls who are not thin to believe that something is wrong with them. It's important to realize that self-worth should not be determined by body size. It's more important to lead a healthy lifestyle by exercising regularly and eating nutritiously than to try to change your body to fit an unrealistic ideal.

Guys can also have body image problems. Although girls may feel pressured to be smaller, guys may feel pressured to become larger and look stronger. Sports and other guys may put pressure on guys to gain muscle mass quickly, which can lead them to feel unhappy or dissatisfied with their bodies.

Sometimes low self-esteem is too much to bear. Instead of getting help, some teens may drink or do drugs to help themselves feel better, especially in social situations.

> ### ✎ What's It Mean?
>
> Puberty: The process of developing from a child to sexual maturity, when a person becomes capable of having children.
>
> Source: "4Girls Web Site Glossary," 4Girls Health, U.S. Department of Health and Human Services, Office on Women's Health, available at www.4girls.gov, 2004.

The Effects Of Home And School

Your home or school life may also affect your self-esteem. Some parents spend more time criticizing than praising their children. Sometimes this criticism reduces a teen's ability to have a positive body image—the teen may model her own "inner voice" after that of a parent, and learn to think negative thoughts about herself.

It's hard to succeed at school when the situation at home is tense, so sometimes teens who suffer from abuse at home may have problems in school, both of which contribute to poor self-esteem.

Teens may also experience negative comments and hurtful teasing or bullying from classmates and peers. This can definitely affect a person's self-esteem, but it's important to remember that the people who are being hurtful probably have low self-esteem as well, and putting others down may make them feel better about themselves.

Sometimes racial and ethnic prejudice is the source of hurtful comments. These comments come from ignorance on the part of the person who makes them, but sometimes they can negatively affect a person's body image and self-esteem.

Checking Your Own Self-Esteem And Body Image

If you have a positive body image, you probably like the way you look and accept yourself the way you are. This is a healthy attitude that allows you to explore other aspects of growing up, such as increasing independence from your parents, enhanced intellectual and physical abilities, and an interest in dating.

When you believe in yourself, you're much less likely to let your own mistakes get you down. You are better able to recognize your errors, learn your lessons, and move on. The same goes for the way you treat others. Teens who feel good about themselves and have good self-esteem are less likely to use putdowns to hurt themselves or anyone else.

A positive, optimistic attitude can help you develop better self-esteem. For example, saying, "Hey, I'm human," instead of "Wow, I'm such a loser," when you've made a mistake. Or avoiding blaming others when things don't go as expected.

Knowing what makes you happy and how to meet your goals can make you feel capable, strong, and in control of your life. A positive attitude and a healthy lifestyle are a great combination for developing good self-esteem.

Tips For Boosting Your Self-Esteem

Some teens think they need to change how they look or act to feel good about themselves. But if you can train yourself to reprogram the way you

👉 **Remember!!**
Where Can I Go If I Need Help?

Sometimes low self-esteem and body image problems are too much to handle alone. Some teens may become depressed, and lose interest in activities or friends. Talk to a parent, coach, religious leader, guidance counselor, therapist, or an adult friend. An adult can help you put your body image in perspective and give you positive feedback about your body, your skills, and your abilities.

If you can't turn to anyone you know, call a teen crisis hotline (check the yellow pages under social services). The most important thing is to get help if you feel like your body image and low self-esteem are affecting your life.

look at your body, you can defend yourself from negative comments—both those that come from others and those that come from you. Remember: when others criticize your body, it's usually because they are insecure about the changes happening to themselves.

The first thing to do is recognize that your body is your own, no matter what shape, size, or color it comes in. If you are very worried about your weight or size, you can check with your doctor to verify that things are OK. But remember that it is no one's business but your own what your body is like—ultimately, you have to be happy with yourself.

Remember, too, that there are things about yourself you can't change—such as your height and shoe size—and you should accept and love these things about yourself. But if there are things about yourself that you do want to change, make goals for yourself. For example, if you want to lose weight, commit yourself to exercising three to four times a week and eating nutritiously. Accomplishing the goals you set for yourself can help to improve your self-esteem.

When you hear negative comments coming from within, tell yourself to stop. Your inner critic can be retrained. Try exercises like giving yourself three compliments every day. While you're at it, every evening list three things in your day that really gave you pleasure. It can be anything from the way the sun felt on your face, the sound of your favorite band, or the way someone laughed at your jokes. By focusing on the good things you do and the positive aspects of your life, you can change how you feel about yourself.

Chapter 23

How Can I Improve My Self-Esteem?

Self-esteem involves how much a person values herself and appreciates her own worth and importance. For example, a teen with healthy self-esteem is able to feel good about her character and her qualities and take pride in her abilities, skills, and accomplishments. Self-esteem is the result of comparing how we'd like to be and what we'd like to accomplish with how we actually see ourselves.

Everyone experiences problems with self-esteem at certain times in their lives—especially teens who are still figuring out who they are and where they fit into the world. How a teen feels about herself can be related to many different factors, such as her environment, her body image, her expectations of herself, and her experiences. For example, if a person has had problems in her family, has had to deal with difficult relationships, or sets unrealistic standards for herself, this can lead to low self-esteem.

Recognizing that you can improve your self-esteem is a great first step in doing so. Learning what can hurt self-esteem and what can build it is also important. Then, with a little effort, a person can really improve the way she feels about herself.

About This Chapter: This information was provided by TeensHealth, one of the largest resources online for medically reviewed health information written for parents, kids, and teens. For more articles like this one, visit www.TeensHealth.org, or www.KidsHealth.org. © 2001 The Nemours Center for Children's Health Media, a division of The Nemours Foundation.

Constant criticism can harm self-esteem—and it doesn't always come from others! Some teens have an "inner critic," a voice inside that seems to find fault with everything they do—and self-esteem obviously has a hard time growing in such an environment. Some people have modeled their inner critic's voice after a critical parent or teacher whose acceptance was important to them. The good news is that this inner critic can be retrained, and

---

✔ **Quick Tip**

Tips For Becoming A Critical Viewer Of The Media

Media messages about body shape and size will affect the way we feel about our bodies and ourselves only if we let them. One of the ways we can protect our self-esteem and body image from the media's often narrow definitions of beauty and acceptability is to become a critical viewer of the media messages we are bombarded with each day. When we effectively recognize and analyze the media messages that influence us, we remember that the media's definitions of beauty and success do not have to define our self-image or potential.

What To Remember To Be A Critical Viewer

- All media images and messages are constructions. They are NOT reflections of reality. Advertisements and other media messages have been carefully crafted with intent to send a very specific message.

- Advertisements are created to do one thing—convince you to buy or support a specific product or service.

- To convince you to buy a specific product or service, advertisers will often construct an emotional experience that looks like reality. Remember that you are only seeing what the advertisers want you to see.

- Advertisers create their message based on what they think you will want to see and what they think will affect you and compel you to buy their product. Just because they think their approach will work with people like you doesn't mean it has to work with you as an individual.

- As individuals, we decide how to experience the media messages we encounter. We can choose to use a filter that helps us understand what the advertiser wants us to think or believe and then choose whether we want

because it now belongs to you, you can be the one to decide that the inner critic will only give constructive feedback from now on.

It may help to pinpoint any unrealistic expectations that may be affecting your self-esteem. Do you wish you were thinner? Smarter? More popular? A better athlete? Although it's easy for teens to feel a little inadequate physically, socially, or intellectually, it's also important to recognize what you can

to think or believe that message. We can choose a filter that protects our self-esteem and body image.

Help Promote Healthier Body Image Messages In The Media

- Talk back to the TV when you see an ad or hear a message that makes you feel bad about yourself or your body by promoting only thin body ideals.

- Write a letter to an advertiser you think is sending positive, inspiring messages that recognize and celebrate the natural diversity of human body shapes and sizes. Compliment their courage to send positive, affirming messages.

- Make a list of companies who consistently send negative body image messages and make a conscious effort to avoid buying their products. Write them a letter explaining why you are using your "buying power" to protest their messages. Tear out the pages of your magazines that contain advertisements or articles that glorify thinness or degrade people of larger sizes. Enjoy your magazine without negative media messages about your body.

- Talk to your friends about media messages and the way they make you feel. Ask yourself, are you inadvertently reinforcing negative media messages through the ways you talk to yourself (and the mirror), the comments you make to children or friends, or the types of pictures you have on the refrigerator?

change and what you can't, and to aim for accomplishments rather than perfection. You may wish to be a star athlete, but it may be more realistic to set your sights on improving your game in specific ways this season. If you are thinking about your shortcomings, try to start thinking about other positive aspects of yourself that outweigh them. Maybe you're not the tallest person in your class and maybe you're not class valedictorian, but you're awesome at volleyball or painting or playing the guitar. Remember—each person excels at different things and your talents are constantly developing.

If you want to improve your self-esteem, there are some steps you can take to start empowering yourself:

- Remember that self-esteem involves much more than liking your appearance. Because of rapid changes in growth and appearance, teens often fall into the trap of believing their entire self-esteem hinges on how they look. Don't miss the inner beauty that's more than skin deep in yourself and in others.

- Think about what you're good at and what you enjoy, and build on those abilities. Take pride in new skills you develop and talents you have. Share what you can do with others.

- Exercise! You'll relieve stress, and be healthier and happier.

- Try to stop thinking negative thoughts about yourself. When you catch yourself being too critical, counter it by saying something positive about yourself.

- Take pride in your opinions and ideas—and don't be afraid to voice them.

- Each day, write down three things about yourself that make you happy.

- Set goals. Think about what you'd like to accomplish, then make a plan for how to do it. Stick with your plan and keep track of your progress. If you realize that you're unhappy with something about yourself that you can change, then start today. If it's something you can't change (like your height), then start to work toward loving yourself the way you are.

- Beware the perfectionist! Are you expecting the impossible? It's good to aim high, but your goals for yourself should be within reach.

> **Remember!!**
>
> Healthy self-esteem means feeling good about your character and your qualities and taking pride in your abilities, skills, and accomplishments.

- Make a contribution. Tutor a classmate who's having trouble, help clean up your neighborhood, participate in a walk-a-thon for a good cause, the list goes on. Feeling like you're making a difference can do wonders to improve self-esteem.

- Have fun—enjoy spending time with the people you care about and doing the things you love.

It's never too late to build or improve self-esteem. In some cases, a teen may need the help of a mental health professional, like a therapist or psychologist, to help heal emotional hurt and build healthy, positive self-esteem. A therapist can help a teen to learn to love herself and realize that her differences make her unique.

So, what's the payoff? Self-esteem plays a role in almost everything you do—teens with high self-esteem do better in school and enjoy it more and find it easier to make friends. They tend to have better relationships with peers and adults, feel happier, find it easier to deal with mistakes, disappointments, and failures, and are more likely to stick with something until they succeed. Improving self-esteem takes work, but the payoff is feeling good about yourself and your accomplishments.

Chapter 24

Helping A Friend With An Eating Disorder

Talking to a friend about suspected eating problems is difficult to do, but is something that a true friend would do. Here are some guidelines to assist friends in this process.

Before

- Decide upon one or two caring individuals who will approach the person you are concerned about. Close, trusted friends or family members are usually best. This individual(s) should be prepared to encourage the person to seek further help with a trained mental health professional.

- The individual(s) chosen should also convey a sensible attitude concerning weight-related issues and a healthy, realistic approach to eating and exercise.

- Establish a private, safe environment.

- Consider rehearsing what will be said.

About This Chapter: Text in this chapter is from "Eating Disorders: Helping a Friend," © 2002 University of Wisconsin-Eau Claire Counseling Services. Reprinted with permission.

During

- Start by letting the person know you are reading and learning about eating disorders.

- Next, express your concerns in a straightforward, yet caring manner. Share two or three specific examples/times when you felt afraid or uneasy. Use an "I" message format:

  Example: "I noticed you've been avoiding meals with us lately. I wonder if we could talk about that?"

  Example: "I feel concerned about the weight you've lost recently. I was hoping we could talk about this."

✔ Quick Tip

Why Is It Anyone's Business?

Question: I have always been heavy, never obese, but I have never been skinny. For the last few years I have tried many different diets and nothing's really worked. Recently I have been experiencing some moderate weight loss. I am eating normally, and I have just begun to exercise more. I weigh myself everyday, and wish that I was thin.

Friends of mine took me to a counselor because they thought that I had an eating disorder. I cannot convince them that I don't. I don't want to lose my friends, but they watch me all the time like I am a criminal. I am happy that I have finally lost some weight, but people seem to think it's a crime. I don't know how to tell them that I don't have a problem and to let me live my own life.

Answer: You sound very frustrated with your friends' persistent worry that you have an eating disorder. You also raise the very delicate issue of whose business it is how your eating, exercise, and weight may have changed. Who decides when it is a problem? After all, it is your body and you really are an authority on what is right or comfortable for your own body. At the same time, unfortunately, one of the symptoms of an eating disorder is distortion or denial about eating disorder symptoms, such as weight loss, excessive exercise, and drive for thinness.

Example: "I feel concerned because it seems like you've been dieting for a long time now. Is it possible for us to discuss this?"

- Then, give the person time to talk and encourage him/her to verbalize feelings. Continue to engage discussion by asking clarifying questions and accepting responses in a non-judgmental manner.

- Be prepared for strong feelings/reactions from the person (i.e., denial, anger, and confusion).

- Throughout the discussion, strive to avoid:
    a. Offering advice or personal opinions.
    b. Lengthy discussions that often end up in power struggles.

You have already seen a counselor, and perhaps it would be helpful to continue to work with her/him, or to consult an eating disorder specialist, or a physician, to get some additional objective feedback about your eating, exercise, weight, and health.

Your friendships seem to be strained by this disagreement about whether you have an eating problem. It is a shame when a person's relationships with the caring people in her/his life become overly focused on eating and weight issues. It can lead to power struggles, cat and mouse games, mutual feelings of mistrust, and increasing isolation for the person suspected of having an eating disorder.

I suggest that you and your friends remember to talk about non-food/weight/exercise topics and feelings. Are you sharing what is going on with your family life? Your social life? Your thoughts and hopes about your future? When you and your friends are able to restore a sense of connection, understanding, and support around these and other dimensions of life, you will probably have an easier time dealing with the issue of their concerns about you.

Source: © 2002 The Renfrew Center. All rights reserved. Reprinted with permission. For additional information, call 1-800-RENFREW or visit http://www.renfrewcenter.com.

✔ Quick Tip

Friend With Bulimia

Question: My roommate (and close friend) has bulimia and is trying really hard to deal with it and change. Even though she wants to get better, it is really stressful to live with someone in the middle of an eating disorder, and I'm afraid it is wrecking our relationship. I want to help her in any way I can but I'm not sure what to do.

Answer: It sounds like you are in a painful and difficult situation. There are things you can do to support your friend in addressing her eating problems, but ultimately the responsibility for change and recovery is hers.

Here are some of the things you can do to help your friend:

Learn more about eating disorders so that you will be more aware of issues and warning signs.

Listen to your friend, and ask about her feelings.

Talk about your concerns for her, and your feelings, as you see her struggling with bulimia.

And most importantly, suggest that she get professional help.

Sadly, it may take time for your friend to be able to use your help and support. You can set a good example by looking for a support group in your area for the loved ones of people struggling with eating disorders.

Source: © 2002 The Renfrew Center. All rights reserved. Reprinted with permission. For additional information, call 1-800-RENFREW or visit http://www.renfrewcenter.com.

c. Offering simplistic solutions (i.e., "Why don't you just eat?").

d. Making "you" statements (i.e., "You have to eat something.").

e. Saying things like "You're getting too skinny." Instead, put it in health terms, (i.e., "I am worried because you seem preoccupied and don't have much energy lately.")

f. Debate concerning food eaten or not eaten, calories consumed, and/or looking for reasons that contributed to the development of an eating disorder. Remember that your primary purpose is to be supportive and to encourage the person to seek further help.

- Toward the end of the discussion, provide information and resources for counseling/treatment. At this point you might offer to go along and wait while he/she has a first appointment.

- Close the discussion by letting him/her know you are willing to talk again.

Example: "I know you feel things are okay, but that will not change my concerns. So, I will bring this up at another time in the near future. We can talk again then."

After

- If the person declines your request to seek further help, remind yourself you have done all that is reasonable for you to do. Realize you will have made important progress in honestly sharing your concerns, providing support, and offering available information and resources.

- Eating disorders are usually not emergency situations. However, if the person is in acute medical danger and/or at risk for suicide, contact help immediately.

Chapter 25

Talking To Your Health Care Provider About Eating Disorders

Below is a list of potential questions that may be used when seeking treatment, changing facilities, etc. This non-exhaustive list can be helpful in generating a list of questions that will be tailored to your needs. Good rapport with your potential therapist is a key element in the treatment process. During the interview, remember to take notes. This will allow you to compare them to other facilities.

Suggested Questions To Ask A Therapist/Psychiatrist When Seeking Treatment

- What are your credentials?

- How long have you been working in this area? (Experience is a must!)

- How did you become involved with treating eating disorders?

- Are you specialized in treating other addictions?

- Are you affiliated with any hospital, organization, private practice, etc.?

About This Chapter: "Things To Think About Regarding Treatment," University of Minnesota Extension Service. Copyright © 1997 Regents of the University of Minnesota. All rights reserved. Despite the older date of this document, the issues identified still represent concerns that you may want to discuss with your health care provider.

- How many patients do you treat in a week, month, year, etc.?

- Do you have patients who are willing to meet and/or talk to me?

- Do you believe patients can get better? (This type of question will establish the therapist's view of eating disorders in patients. Stay away from therapists who view eating disorders as a lack of willpower or bad habits that will never be cured!)

- Do you believe in self-help groups and "anonymous" programs? (Examples are: Overeaters Anonymous, Alcoholics Anonymous, etc.)

- Why do you want to work with someone like me?

- How will my goals be set and by whom?

Suggested Questions To Ask A Therapist Regarding Treatment

- What is the cost of treatment?

- What type(s) of insurance do you accept?

- How much will my insurance cover? (This will establish if there are any hidden costs such as reading materials.)

- Is medication used? If so, why? What type(s), how often, etc.?

- What is the main focus of therapy? (Food, weight, diet, behavior change, etc.)

- What type(s) of treatment do you use? (Examples are cognitive, behavioral, and family therapies.)

- Are there any restrictions? (Will therapy be canceled if I take drugs, relapse, exercise, binge, purge, etc.?)

- How long will treatment take? (Remember that no definite answer may be given.)

- What is your success rate for the given disorder?

- What is the average age of your patients?

- What will happen if a crisis occurs? (Is there a 24-hour help line?)

Suggested Questions To Ask Regarding Group And/Or Family Therapy

There are generally two types of groups:

1. Therapy—A therapy group should be led and facilitated by a qualified counselor.

2. Support—A support group may be led by the members of that group.

    • What are the purposes of the sessions?

    • What type of therapy is this?

    • Any additional costs to participate in group sessions?

    • What can I expect during a session?

    • Who is the group(s) facilitator?

    • Will my family, friends, or significant others be involved?

    • What are the characteristics of the group(s)?

    • What are the ages and gender of the group(s)?

    • Do you encourage sponsorship and outside communication?

✔ Quick Tip

Questions To Ask Your Treatment Provider

After you have chosen a treatment provider, here are some helpful questions that you might want to consider asking in your first meeting. Remember that at any time during treatment, you can raise questions and consult your treatment provider regarding areas of concern.

1. What is the diagnosis?

2. What treatment plan do you recommend?

3. Will you or someone else conduct the treatment? If someone else, does that person work for you or would this be a referral? Will you supervise the treatment?

4. What other professionals will you be collaborating with in the treatment of my eating disorder?

5. What are the alternative treatments?

6. What are the benefits and the risks associated with the recommended treatment? With the alternative treatments?

7. What role will family members or friends play in treatment?

Source: Excerpted from "Seeking Treatment: What Does Treatment Involve? © 2002 National Eating Disorders Association. All rights reserved. For additional information, visit http://www .NationalEatingDisorders.org.

Do I Have An Eating Disorder?

Question: I wonder if I have an eating disorder. My best friend told me she thinks I am becoming anorexic. I was chubby my whole life, and over the last year, I have finally lost weight and kept it off by being really careful about what I eat and making sure to exercise every day. After so many years of hearing how pretty I'd be if I lost a few pounds, now I'm hearing that I've gone too far. Now I'm too thin. I'm only trying to look good. What is wrong with that? I feel like I just can't win.

Answer: It is sometimes hard to know what is winning when it comes to trying to look good. What our culture calls pretty, using models and actresses as examples of what women should look like, is not realistic for most people. Trying to live up to these images can cause frustration and contribute to eating and other health problems.

Many people who do have anorexia or bulimia say that their eating disorder developed after a successful diet. It is dangerous to think that "if losing a little bit of weight is good, then losing more and more weight is better" or "you can never be too thin" because neither statement is true. If you do have an eating disorder, you are at risk for serious medical and psychological problems. I suggest that you pursue this question, so that you can get professional help if you need it.

A good way to begin is to schedule an appointment with your physician. You should discuss your concerns about food, weight, exercise, dieting, and anorexia. Your doctor will assess whether you meet medical criteria for the diagnosis of anorexia, such as being 15% or more below ideal body weight. Some doctors are able to give advice about a healthy balanced diet and appropriate exercise. Your doctor may also give you a referral to a psychotherapist and perhaps a nutritionist to help you with these issues. You have made the first step by asking the question.

Source: © 2002 The Renfrew Center. All rights reserved. Reprinted with permission. For additional information, call 1-800-RENFREW or visit http://www.renfrewcenter.com.

- Do you mix individuals with multiple disorders?

- Are there penalties for missing sessions?

Questions To Ask Regarding Hospitalization

Most hospitals offer an inpatient and outpatient treatment program. Brochures or pamphlets are usually available. Call the targeted location, ask for the eating disorders unit, and request these items by mail. A formal, as well as telephone interview, may be helpful in the information gathering stage. Below are a few questions that may be helpful when seeking both inpatient and outpatient care.

- Name and location of the hospital?

- What are the hospital staff qualifications?

- What types of insurance do they accept?

- Is hospitalization based on an inpatient and outpatient basis?

- What schedule or agenda of activities are there for the patient's day?

- Is there a separate eating disorders unit?

- What is the average length of treatment?

There are many different approaches to the treatment of eating disorders. Some individuals must try several types of treatment before finding the one that is suitable. When looking for a therapist, the first step is to decide which type of treatment regiment will suit your needs. To do this, one must be willing to do a little homework. The long-term benefits may greatly outweigh the time spent calling several therapists. Remember, trust your instinct and follow your heart!

Chapter 26

Treatment for Eating Disorders

What Are The General Guidelines For Treating Eating Disorders?

The first major difficulty in treating eating disorders is often the resistance by everyone involved:

- The anorexic patient often believes that the emaciation is normal and even attractive.

- The bulimic patient may feel that purging is the only way to prevent obesity.

- Even worse, the anorexic condition may be encouraged by friends who envy thinness or by dance or athletic coaches who encourage low body fat.

- The family itself may deny the problem and be obstructive or manipulative, adding to the difficulties of treatment.

It is very important that the patient and any close friends and relatives be informed about the serious potential of these conditions and the importance of receiving immediate help.

About This Chapter: Information in this chapter is excerpted from "Eating Disorders: Anorexia and Bulimia," © 2003 A.D.A.M., Inc. Reprinted with permission.

♣ It's A Fact!!

There is general agreement that good treatment often requires a spectrum of treatment options. These options can range from basic educational interventions designed to teach nutritional and symptom management techniques to long-term residential treatment (living away from home in treatment centers).

Most individuals with eating disorders are treated on an outpatient basis after a comprehensive evaluation. Individuals with medical complications due to severe weight loss or due to the effects of binge eating and purging may require hospitalization. Other individuals, for whom outpatient therapy has not been effective, may benefit from day-hospital treatment, hospitalization, or residential placement.

Treatment is usually conducted in the least restrictive setting that can provide adequate safety for the individual. Many patients with eating disorders also have depression, anxiety disorders, drug and/or alcohol use disorders and other psychiatric problems requiring treatment along with the eating disorder.

Initial Assessment

The initial assessment of individuals with eating disorders involves a thorough review of the patient's history, current symptoms, physical status, weight control measures, and other psychiatric issues or disorders such as depression, anxiety, substance abuse, or personality issues. Consultation with a physician and a registered dietitian is often recommended. The initial assessment is the first step in establishing a diagnosis and treatment plan.

Outpatient Treatment

Outpatient treatment for an eating disorder often involves a coordinated team effort between the patient, a psychotherapist, a physician, and a dietitian (yet, many patients are treated by their pediatrician or physician with or without a mental health professional's involvement).

Similarly, many patients are seen and helped by generalist mental health clinicians without specialist involvement. Not all individuals, then, will receive a multidisciplinary approach, but the qualified clinician should have access to all of these resources.

Day Hospital Care

Patients for whom outpatient treatment is ineffective may benefit from the increased structure provided by a day hospital treatment program. Generally, these programs are scheduled from three to eight hours a day and provide several structured eating sessions per day, along with various other therapies, including cognitive behavioral therapy, body image therapies, family therapy, and numerous other interventions. Day hospital allows the patient to live at home when they are not in treatment, and often continue to work or attend school.

Inpatient Treatment

Inpatient treatment provides a structured and contained environment in which the patient with an eating disorder has access to clinical support 24 hours a day. Many programs are now affiliated with a day hospital program so that patients can "step-up" and "step-down" to the appropriate level of care depending on their clinical needs.

Although eating disorder patients can sometimes be treated on general psychiatric units with individuals experiencing other psychiatric disorders, such an approach often poses problems with monitoring and containing eating disorder symptoms. Therefore, most inpatient programs for eating disordered individuals only treat patients with anorexia nervosa, bulimia nervosa, binge eating disorder, or variants of these disorders.

Residential Care

Residential programs provide a longer-term treatment option for patients who require longer-term treatment. This treatment option generally is reserved for individuals who have been hospitalized on several occasions, but have not been able to reach a significant degree of medical or psychological stability.

Source: Excerpted with permission from "Treatment." © 2005 Academy for Eating Disorders. All rights reserved.

Getting Rid Of Unrealistic Expectations

Patients may drop out of programs if they have unrealistic expectations of being "cured" simply through the therapists' insights. Before a program begins, the following possibilities should be made clear:

- The process is painful and requires hard work on the part of the patient and family.

- A number of therapeutic methods are likely to be tried until the patient succeeds in overcoming these difficult disorders.

- Relapse is common but should not be greeted with despair. (In one study, about 90% of bulimic patients responded to treatments after six years.)

Although the outcome for bulimics is generally more favorable than for anorexics, long-term studies are showing recovery in most people treated for anorexia.

General Treatment Approaches

Psychotherapies: All eating disorders are nearly always treated with some form of psychiatric or psychologic treatment. Depending on the problem, different psychologic approaches may work better than others. A 2001 study reported that patients at greater risk for not completing therapy are those with a history of childhood trauma (e.g., divorce, abuse). Dropout rates were not related to the severity or duration of the disorder.

Medications: A number of medications may be valuable for these patients depending on the type of eating disorder, psychiatric state, and severity of the condition.

What Are Specific Treatments For Patients Who Have Bulimia Without Weight Loss?

Some experts recommend a stepped approach for patients with bulimia, which may follow these stages, depending on the severity and response to initial treatments:

- Support groups. This is the least expensive approach and may be helpful for patients who have mild conditions with no health consequences.

- Cognitive-behavioral therapy (CBT) along with nutritional therapy is the preferred first treatment for bulimia that does not respond to support groups.

- Drugs. The drugs used for bulimia are typically antidepressants known as selective serotonin-reuptake inhibitors (SSRIs). A combination of CBT and SSRIs is very effective if CBT is not helpful.

Patients with bulimia rarely need hospitalization except under the following circumstances:

- Binge-purge cycles have led to anorexia

- Drugs are needed for withdrawal from purging

- Major depression is present

Psychotherapeutic Approaches And Medications For Bulimia

Psychologic Therapy: Cognitive-behavioral therapy (CBT) is the first-line of therapy for most patients with bulimia and is successful in about 60% of cases. In one study of bulimic patients, those who did not respond to CBT tended to be less committed to the treatment, were more preoccupied with their symptoms, and had ritualized eating behaviors. Interpersonal therapy may be tried if CBT fails, although in one study it was no more successful than antidepressants.

Antidepressants: Because of the high incidence of depression in patients with bulimia, antidepressant medication is often recommended for patients who have normal weight or for those who are overweight. They should be used in combination with CBT. (These agents can cause weight loss and should not be used in patients who are underweight, unless it is part of a clinical trial.) The most common antidepressants prescribed for bulimia are selective serotonin reuptake inhibitors (SSRIs). They include fluoxetine (Prozac), sertraline (Zoloft), paroxetine (Paxil), and fluvoxamine (Luvox). Studies are mixed, however, on whether SSRIs offer an additional advantage in reducing binge eating compared to CBT. Prozac has been approved for bulimia and is considered the drug of choice, although some studies suggest that other SSRIs, such as Luvox, may be even more effective.

If the drugs are not effective, the physician should be sure it is not because the patient is vomiting after taking the medication. Some experts believe that these agents should be continued even after symptoms have improved in order to restore healthy brain chemical balances.

Drug Therapy For Bulimia Nervosa

Agents to Prevent Vomiting: In one study, ondansetron, a drug that prevents vomiting, reduced the binge-purge episodes by half. The drug may cause depression in people already on SSRI antidepressants. More studies are needed.

Sibutramine: Sibutramine (Meridia) is a drug used for weight loss. It does so by keeping two important brain chemicals, serotonin and norepinephrine, in balance, which helps to increase metabolism. Some evidence suggests that the actions of this drug may be useful for people who binge. Note, however, that for bulimic patients this agent should be used only for those with normal or above normal weight and never for those who are anorexic.

Inositol: Inositol is a B vitamin that is being investigated for bipolar disorder, anxiety, and depression. A 2001 study suggests that it may also have benefits for bulimic patients.

Alternative Approaches To Bulimia

Hypnosis: A study on women with bulimia showed that they had a high susceptibility to hypnosis, suggesting that it might be beneficial as part of their treatment. People with anorexia, on the other hand, seem to be very resistant to the state of vulnerability required in this process.

Light Therapy: Some researchers have noted an association between bulimia and seasonal affective disorder (depression that intensifies in the darker winter months). This suggests that therapy using intense directed light may be useful. Studies report, however, that while light therapy relieves depression, it has little effect on binge-purging behavior. Some experts suggest it may be more useful in combination with medication and psychotherapy.

Guided Imagery: A technique called guided imagery reduced frequency of binges and vomiting by almost 75% in one study. This method uses audiotapes to evoke images that will reduce stress and help achieve specific goals.

What Are Specific Treatments For Patients With Anorexia?

The treatment goals for patients with anorexia require a team approach and include the following:

- Treatment of any existing medical conditions. Physicians should immediately check and treat any medical problems related to the condition, such as bone loss, imbalances in important electrolytes, and any hormonal deficiencies, including thyroid and reproductive hormones.

- Nutritional rehabilitation

- Psychotherapy

Many moderately to severely ill anorexic patients require hospitalization, particularly under the following circumstances:

- When weight loss continues even with outpatient treatment

- When weight is 30% below ideal body weight

- When depression is severe or the patient is suicidal

- When symptoms of medical complications (e.g., disturbed heart rate, low potassium levels, altered mental status, low blood pressure, severe sensations of cold)

In some severe cases, patients with anorexia may need to be hospitalized involuntarily. A 2000 study reported that such patients respond as well as patients who were admitted voluntarily. And, most later agreed that such treatment had been necessary.

Duration of Inpatient Treatment: For people with severe anorexia, many experts believe that 10 to 12 weeks of hospitalization with full nutritional support are required to reach ideal body weight. Unfortunately, the pressures of managed care force most patients out much earlier before they have reached even a suboptimal weight. Insurance companies rarely cover more than 15 days in the hospital, which places patients with severe anorexia at great risk for relapse and serious health consequences. It is particularly critical for women with both diabetes and anorexia to achieve 100% of ideal weight before being released.

✎ What's It Mean?

Bipolar Disorder: Also known as manic-depressive illness, is a brain disorder that causes unusual shifts in a person's mood, energy, and ability to function. [1]

Calcium: A mineral found in teeth, bones, and other body tissues. [2]

Cholesterol: A fat-like substance in the body. The body makes and needs some cholesterol, which also comes from foods such as butter and egg yolks. Too much cholesterol may cause gallstones. It also may cause fat to build up in the arteries. This may cause a disease that slows or stops blood flow. [3]

Diabetes: A disease in which the body does not properly control the amount of sugar in the blood. As a result, the level of sugar in the blood is too high. This disease occurs when the body does not produce enough insulin or does not use it properly. [2]

Electrolyte: A substance that breaks up into ions (electrically charged particles) when it is dissolved in body fluids or water. Some examples of electrolytes are sodium, potassium, chloride, and calcium. Electrolytes are primarily responsible for the movement of nutrients into cells and the movement of wastes out of cells. [2]

Estrogen: A hormone that promotes the development and maintenance of female sex characteristics. [2]

Glucose: A primary source of energy for living organisms. It is naturally occurring and is found in fruits and other parts of plants. [4]

Low Blood Pressure: When a person's blood pressure is too low, there is not enough blood flow to the heart, brain, and other vital organs. Symptoms include dizziness and lightheadedness. [5]

Malnutrition: A disorder caused by a lack of proper nutrition or an inability to absorb nutrients from food. [2]

Metabolism: The total of all chemical changes that take place in a cell or an organism. These changes produce energy and basic materials needed for important life processes. [2]

Nutrients: A chemical compound (such as protein, fat, carbohydrate, vitamins, or minerals) that make up foods. These compounds are used by the body to function and grow. [2]

Postmenopausal: Refers to the time after menopause. Menopause is the time in a woman's life when menstrual periods stop permanently, also called "change of life." [2]

Potassium: A metallic element that is important in body functions such as regulation of blood pressure and of water content in cells, transmission of nerve impulses, digestion, muscle contraction, and heartbeat. [2]

Progestin: Any natural or laboratory-made substance that has some or all of the biologic effects of progesterone, a female hormone. [2]

Prostate: A gland in the male reproductive system just below the bladder. The prostate surrounds part of the urethra (the canal that empties the bladder) and produces a fluid that forms part of semen. [2]

Schizophrenia: A severe emotional disorder of psychotic depth characteristically marked by a retreat from reality with delusion formation, hallucinations, emotional disharmony, and regressive behavior. [4]

Thyroid: A gland located beneath the voice box (larynx) that produces thyroid hormone. The thyroid helps regulate growth and metabolism. [2]

Source: [1] "Bipolar Disorder," The National Institute of Mental Health, U.S. Department of Health and Human Services, available at www.nimh.nih.gov, 2004. [2] "Dictionary of Cancer Terms," National Cancer Institute, available at www.nci.nih.gov; cited December 2004. [3] "Digestive Diseases Dictionary," National Institute of Diabetes and Digestive and Kidney Diseases, available at www.digestive.niddk.nih.gov, 2000. [4] "Genetics Home Reference Glossary," a service of the U.S. National Library of Medicine, available at www.ghr.nlm.nih.gov, 2004. [5] Editor.

Team Approaches: A multidisciplinary team approach with consistent support and counseling is essential for long-term recovery from all severe eating disorders. Depending on the severity and type of disorder, team members may include the following:

- Physicians specializing in relevant medical complications

- Dietitians

- Cognitive-behavioral therapists (Bulimia is best treated with a combination of antidepressants and cognitive therapy.)

- Psychotherapists

- Nurses

All should be skilled in treating eating disorders. Studies have found that people treated by such specialists have a lower mortality rate than those treated only as psychiatric patients.

Restoring Normal Weight And Nutritional Intervention

Nutritional intervention is essential. Weight gain is associated with fewer symptoms of anorexia and with improvements in both physical and mental function. Restoring good nutrition can help reduce bone loss. Restoring weight is also essential before the patient can fully benefit from additional psychotherapeutic treatments.

Goals for Weight Gain and Good Nutrition: One approach to weight gain involves the following steps:

- The weight-gain goal, usually one to two pounds a week, is strictly set by the physician or health professional. This goal is absolute, no matter how convincingly the patient (or even family members) may argue for a lower-weight goal.

- Patients who are severely malnourished may need to begin with a calorie count as low as 1,500 calories a day, however, in order to reduce the chances for stomach pain and bloating, fluid retention, and heart failure.

- Eventually, the patient is given foods containing as many as 3,500 calories or more a day.

- More calories than normal may be required to put on weight. In some cases, severe dieting has caused the metabolism to adapt to malnutrition and resist the effects of overfeeding. Some anorexic patients also may naturally have a higher metabolism than other individuals.

- Dietary supplements may be needed. Zinc supplementation has been shown to help increase body mass. Patients should receive calcium plus a multivitamin. Oral phosphates are also useful. Although eating is the problem, discussions of the disorder are never held during meals, which are times for relaxed social interaction.

Some physicians recommend cyproheptadine (Periactin), an antihistamine, which may stimulate appetite. (It is not useful for patients with bulimia and may even slow recovery.) One interesting study suggested that eating yogurt with active cultures of so-called good bacteria may boost immune factors that may help prevent infections.

Tubal Feedings: Feeding tubes that pass through the nose to the stomach are not commonly used, since many experts believe they discourage a return to normal eating habits and because many patients interpret their use as punishing forced feeding. A 2002 study reported, however, that when patients were given such tube feedings at night with oral feedings during the day, they gained twice as much weight as patients who were being fed orally only. More research is needed to see if benefits persist when patients return home.

Intravenous Feedings: Intravenous feedings may be needed in life-threatening situations. This involves inserting a needle into the vein and infusing fluids containing nutrients directly into the bloodstream. Overzealous administration of glucose solutions can trigger the so-called refeeding syndrome, in which phosphate levels drop severely and cause a condition called hypophosphatemia. Emergency symptoms include irritability, muscle weakness, bleeding from the mouth, disturbed heart rhythms, seizures, and coma.

The Role Of Exercise In Recovery

The role of exercise in recovery is complex, since for those with anorexia, excessive exercise is often a component of the original disorder. However, very controlled exercise regimens may be used as both a reward for developing good eating habits and as a way to reduce the stomach and intestinal distress that accompanies recovery. Exercise should not be performed if severe medical problems still exist and if the patient has not gained significant weight.

Psychologic Approaches And Medications For Patients With Anorexia

Psychologic Therapies Used in Anorexia: Some studies suggest that for adolescents with anorexia, family therapy that employs cognitive-behavioral techniques works best. For those with late-onset anorexia, individual supportive therapy may be more effective, particularly since many people with anorexia lack a sense of self-survival. Family therapy is important for younger and older individuals. It should be noted that people with severe anorexia often have mental deficits and may not respond well to psychologic therapies until they have regained weight.

Antidepressants: Studies have not reported many benefits from selective serotonin reuptake inhibitors (SSRIs), the antidepressants that are often useful for patients with bulimia. Some SSRIs cause weight loss. Furthermore, experts fear that the effects of starvation may intensify their side effects and reduce their effectiveness. Nevertheless, few studies have actually been conducted using SSRIs in anorexia, particularly using some of the newer agents. Some, in fact, suggest that SSRIs may help prevent relapse in patients who have been treated and have restored weight. And a small study using sertraline (Zoloft) reported improvement in patients who were initially treated with the SSRI. These agents may also be specifically useful for people with anorexia who also have obsessive-compulsive disorder (OCD) or similar features. More work is needed to determine if there is a possible role for these agents.

Anti-Anxiety Agents: Patients with anxiety disorders and anorexia may also benefit from other agents that treat anxiety.

Atypical Antipsychotics: Certain agents, called atypical antipsychotics, are currently used for schizophrenia and bipolar disorders. Not only are they useful for stabilizing mood but they also produce significant weight gain. Specific agents that may be helpful for patients with severe treatment-resistant anorexia include olanzapine (Zyprexa).

Agents To Restore Hormonal Function And Bone Density

Oral Contraceptives: Although abnormal reproductive hormone balances appear to be more important in bone loss than low weight, the use of oral contraceptives (OCs), which contain estrogen and progestin, have had mixed results, with many showing no improvement. Still, it is important to try to restore normal menstruation in women with anorexia nervosa.

Calcium and Vitamin D: Patients should take supplements of 1,000 to 1,500 mg of calcium and a multivitamin containing 400 IU of vitamin D.

Other Agents for Restoring Bone Density: Other drugs are useful for bone restoration, including parathyroid hormone and bisphosphonates, although research on these agents have been conducted primarily on post-menopausal women.

Investigative Agents: One 2002 study reported that recombinant human IGF-I (rhIGF-I), which is a growth hormone, was effective in restoring bone, particularly in combination with oral contraceptives.

Dehydroepiandrosterone (DHEA) is a weak male hormone that is reduced in anorexia and, like estrogen, has positive effects on bone density. In a 2002 study, patients with anorexia who took DHEA experienced both improved bone density and improved psychological well being. Long-term effects of taking DHEA are unknown. Possible adverse effects include male characteristics (acne, facial hair), unfavorable effects on cholesterol, and a possible growth-stimulating effect on breast or prostate cancer.

Chapter 27

Psychological Therapies For Eating Disorders

Eating disorders are nearly always treated with some form of psychiatric or psychologic treatment. Depending on the problem, different psychologic approaches may work better than others.

Cognitive-Behavioral Therapy

Cognitive-behavioral therapy (CBT) works on the principle that a pattern of false thinking and belief about one's body can be recognized objectively and altered, thereby changing the response and eliminating the unhealthy reaction to food. One approach for bulimia is the following:

- Over a period of four to six months the patient builds up to three meals a day, including foods that the patient has previously avoided.

- During this period, the patient monitors and records the daily dietary intake along with any habitual unhealthy reactions and negative thoughts toward eating while they are occurring.

- The patient also records any relapses (binges or purging). Such lapses are reported objectively and without self-criticism and judgment.

About This Chapter: Information in this chapter is excerpted from "Eating Disorders: Anorexia and Bulimia," © 2003 A.D.A.M., Inc. Reprinted with permission.

- The patient discusses the responses with a cognitive therapist at regular sessions. Eventually the patient is able to discover the false attitudes about body image and the unattainable perfectionism that underlies the opposition to food and health.

- Once these habits are recognized, food choices are broadened and the patient begins to challenge any entrenched and automatic ideas and responses. The patient then replaces them with a set of realistic beliefs along with actions based on reasonable self-expectations.

An interesting Swedish study reported significant success in a small group of patients with anorexia and bulimia using specific behavioral techniques

✔ **Quick Tip**

I Can't Disappoint My Parents

Question: I force myself to throw up at least once every 2 days, sometimes 3 times a day. I want to stop, but I feel so guilty after I've eaten that I do it again.

I'm a teenager, and I'm getting straight As. I'm in all honors classes, in sports, and everyone likes me. My parents are so proud of me. Is there any way that I can get help without my parents finding out? I know I need help, but I can't disappoint my parents, they went through my problems with anorexia with me, and I don't want them to go through their child messing up again. I don't want them to think less of me. What do you suggest I do?

Answer: It is sad to hear what you are going through with bulimia. It sounds so lonely to have to deal with your feelings and your symptoms in secret.

Many people feel ashamed of their eating disorder, and this keeps them from reaching out for the support and help they need. The confidentiality of psychotherapy can allow someone to share the whole truth of who they are, including all kinds of feelings, symptoms and experiences. This is an important part of the healing process. One goal of therapy is often to be able to open up to other people who care about you so that you can develop healthy, supportive relationships. Often family therapy is used to help address family issues such as

that were based on the premises that dieting and exercise stimulate regions in the brain to produce feelings of pleasure and reward. In the study, patients were initially severely restricted from physical activity (anorexic patients were in wheelchairs and bulimic patients could only walk slowly). Meals were monitored using a scale connected to a computer to measure the amount of food taken off the plate and to match intake against a scale. The patients were then trained to eat more by watching their progress on the screen. After each meal, they rested for an hour in a warm room to restore body temperature (which is low in anorexia). A higher percentage of patients remained in remission than those who did not have this treatment. This approach warrants more research.

fear of disappointment causing a breakdown in communication. I have been amazed at how much growth and closeness that can develop when families engage in family psychotherapy and learn how to help one another in constructive ways.

While an adult can work through issues in the privacy of individual therapy and include family members, if and when, they feel ready to do so, it is very difficult for a teenager who lives at home to get professional help without the family knowing about it. It may be possible for you to work with a nurse or counselor at your school, and request that they keep your meetings confidential. Perhaps they will know of resources in your community, or maybe they can help you find a way to let your parents know that you need help.

I hope that you can get past your own feelings of disappointment that you continue to suffer with an eating disorder. Recovery from eating disorders is possible, but it often takes a lot of time and effort. My advice to you is to continue to risk reaching out for help. I hope that your parents and other people in your life will prove to be good allies in your struggle to be a whole and healthy person.

Interpersonal Therapy

Interpersonal therapy deals with depression or anxiety that might underlie the eating disorders along with social factors that influence eating behavior. This therapy does not deal with weight, food, or body image at all. The goals are the following:

- To express feelings
- To discover how to tolerate uncertainty and change

♣ It's A Fact!!

Therapists And Health Professionals

Many different professionals can assist individuals in different ways. Below is summary of the different roles of health professionals.

When seeking therapy, many people ask what the differences are between therapists, such as counselors, social workers, psychologists, and psychiatrists. The professional difference is largely in qualifications, but the model or style(s) of therapy they employ depends on many factors, such as their interests, personal characteristics, specialist training, etc. Two practitioners may have the same qualifications, but employ different therapeutic techniques.

Because different therapists work in different ways, it is important that people choose someone they feel comfortable working with. Sometimes this can take time, and a person may see several counselors, psychologists, or psychiatrists before they find someone they feel comfortable with.

Psychologists: Psychologists must have completed a doctoral degree in psychology and appropriate post graduate studies (usually specializing in a particular area(s). Psychologists are subject to licensing in most states.

Psychiatrists: A psychiatrist is a physician who has completed a three or four year post-graduate training program in psychiatry, and passed a national certification exam in psychiatry. Because they are medically qualified, psychiatrists can prescribe drug treatments such as anti-depressants.

Counselors: Counselors may have any of a variety of qualifications or educational backgrounds. General courses in counseling techniques, or welfare

- To develop a strong sense of individuality and independence

- To address any relevant sexual issues or traumatic or abusive event in the past that might be a contributor of the eating disorder

Studies generally report that it is not as effective as cognitive therapy for bulimia and binge eating, but may be useful for some patients with anorexia. The skill of the therapist plays a strong role in its success.

studies, etc. can range from three months to four years. Some states require counselors to be licensed; others do not have formal definitions for counselors.

Medical Practitioners: A qualified medical practitioner is a physician with either a M.D. or D.O. degree, and has a state license to practice medicine. Medical practitioners are concerned with people's physical health. They may offer a medical examination, medical advice, education, and referrals to specialist medical practitioners or therapists. Many medical practitioners also treat psychiatric diseases, and they are also able to prescribe drug treatments such as anti-depressants. The majority of psychiatric medical care in the United States is provided by non-psychiatrist physicians.

Dietitians: A dietitian can offer information about foods, the way the body uses them, nutritional management, and dietetic counseling. A dietitian can be useful for people with eating disorders to re-educate them about the value and necessity of food, and also to develop meal plans. Generally, a dietitian has completed a four-year course in nutrition and dietetics.

Social Workers: A social worker's main function is to assist people practically. This may involve helping them with their finances, getting in touch with people, or helping them with difficult relationships. Some social workers may also provide counseling or psychological therapy.

Family Therapy

Because of the major role family attitudes play in eating disorders, one of the first steps in treating the patient with early-onset anorexia is to also treat the family. Family therapy is certainly useful for both younger and older patients.

If the patient is hospitalized, experts recommend that family therapy start after the patient has gained weight, but before discharge. It should usually continue after the patient has left the hospital.

The feelings of intense guilt and anxiety that caregivers experience are probably similar to those produced by living with a person who is suicidal.

✔ Quick Tip

Should I Tell My Mother?

Question: I haven't been eating that much for the last few months. I keep looking at myself at the mirror to see how fat I am. I feel I'm fat because I see guys checking out girls who are way thinner than me. Every morning I feel a little hungry (7:00 a.m.) and just starve myself until like 5:00 p.m. I don't know what to do because now when I am hungry, I feel sick and dizzy. I haven't told my mother about this, but I am willing to tell her if I have some support from you. Please answer my questions and offer some suggestions on what I should do.

Answer: I certainly want to support you in trying to talk with your mother about what is going on with you. I can't be sure how it will work out for you, but in general, I do believe it is worth it to take a chance and reach out to someone close to you when you are in this kind of situation. Your feelings of sickness and dizziness are telling you that you have a problem, and you and your mother may be able to work together to deal with this. You may also want, or need, to talk to someone outside of your family, like a doctor or a therapist.

The first step is to talk to your mother. It is very important to tell her what you have been doing (starving yourself) and how it has been affecting you (feeling sick and dizzy). You are not eating enough, and you need to eat more. This is

An over-involved parent may even support the patient's eating disorder for various reasons:

- Some parents may be afraid of releasing some underlying anger or grief directed at the patient.

- Other parents may identify with the goal of thinness and not even perceive that their child is unhealthily underweight.

In such cases, it is extremely important that the family fully understand the danger of this disorder and that they are collaborating in their child's illness, or even death, by encouraging this state.

---

not something your mother can do for you, but perhaps you can think of ways that she can be encouraging to you about this. Would it be helpful to talk to a doctor or a nutritionist? Would you like to have company or support at meal-times? You may not know what will be helpful ahead of time, so you will probably have to experiment and continue to talk with each other about what works and what doesn't.

You may also want to risk telling your mother what you have been thinking (that you are fat) and what you have been feeling (about yourself, about boys). Perhaps there are other things going on that are making you feel unhappy or unsure of yourself that would be good to talk with your mother about. Again, it may not be easy for you and your mother to know how to talk about the things that are bothering you. Often parents and children have to learn and relearn how to talk to each other as they each grow older.

I encourage you to reach out to your mother and hope you are able to be patient with yourself, with your mother, and with the communication process.

Source: © 2002 The Renfrew Center. All rights reserved. Reprinted with permission. For additional information, call 1-800-RENFREW or visit http://www.renfrewcenter.com.

Chapter 28

Medications For Eating Disorders

Medications have been proven to be very effective in some psychiatric disorders such as depression. In eating disorders, the evidence for using medication is not as strong. Still, medications can be an important part of eating disorder treatment. There are basically three functions for medication in treating people with eating disorders; each of these is covered below.

For bulimia nervosa, psychotherapy is typically the foundation of treatment. Medication may be used along with psychotherapy, or may be useful in situations where psychotherapy has not been effective. Most antidepressants are helpful in reducing bulimic symptoms. For example, fluoxetine (better known by its commercial name, Prozac) has shown promise in treating bulimia nervosa (BN), whether as an adjunct to psychotherapy or as the sole treatment intervention. Interestingly, the doses of fluoxetine that help bulimia appear to be higher than the doses typically used to treat depression.

> ♣ **It's A Fact!!**
> For bulimia nervosa, psychotherapy is typically the foundation of treatment. Medication may be used along with psychotherapy, or may be useful in situations where psychotherapy has not been effective.

About This Chapter: Reprinted with permission from the Department of Pediatrics at the University of Arkansas for Medical Sciences College of Medicine. © 2003 University of Arkansas for Medical Sciences. All rights reserved.

There is little evidence that medications are helpful in directly treating the symptoms of anorexia nervosa (AN).

Many medications have been tried, including antidepressants, neuroleptics (such as risperidone/Risperdal and olanzapine/Zyprexa), and antihistamines (including cyproheptadine). Hopefully, in coming years, new medications and new research will make medication a more useful and effective option for people with AN.

♣ **It's A Fact!!**
There is little evidence that medications are helpful in directly treating the symptoms of anorexia nervosa.

Medication definitely has a role in treating conditions that occur at the same time as AN or BN. Treatment of these conditions, such as depression or anxiety, may facilitate more effective treatment of the eating disorder. For instance, malnutrition may sometimes cause symptoms of low energy and poor concentration in AN that my mimic depression, but sometimes depression occurs simultaneously with AN. If someone is struggling with a depressive disorder marked by hopelessness and poor concentration, the return of hope and the ability to focus can be a springboard for recovery from the eating disorder.

If you have an eating disorder and are interested in exploring medication options in treatment, consult the physician treating you.

Part Five

Other Health Issues Related To Eating Disorders

Chapter 29

Dental Problems Associated With Eating Disorders

An estimated 5 to 10 million teenaged girls and women and 1 million teenaged boys and men in the U.S. are struggling with eating disorders, according to the National Eating Disorders Association (NEDA). The two most common eating disorders, especially among young American women, are bulimia and anorexia nervosa. Both disorders stem from psychological issues, which result in the sufferer's depriving the body of essential nutrients.

People suffering from an eating disorder are often able to hide their problem from family and friends. However, many bulimics and anorexics are finding it difficult to hide the disorder from their dentists. In fact, dental professionals first diagnose 28% of all bulimic cases.

Bulimia is characterized by compulsive overeating (binging) followed by self-induced vomiting, whereas anorexia nervosa is marked by extreme weight loss usually achieved through a severely restricted caloric intake. Yet, both diseases produce signs and symptoms that can be detected in the mouth during a routine oral examination, such as dry mouth and swollen salivary glands. Lips may become reddened, dry, and cracked.

About This Chapter: Excerpted with permission from the Dear Doctor column provided by the University of Alabama at Birmingham Office of Medical Publications. © 2004 UAB Health System. All rights reserved.

In addition, repeated vomiting exposes teeth to stomach acids that erode tooth enamel, the hard protective covering of the tooth. Teeth may become rounded and soft, and fillings may start to protrude above a tooth's surface. The teeth may change in color, shape, and length, and also can become brittle, translucent, and sensitive to temperature.

> **♣ It's A Fact!!**
> Dental professionals first diagnose 28% of all bulimic cases.

Left untreated, extreme cases of eating disorders may expose the innermost layer of the teeth, the pulp, which can result in infection or even pulp death. If pulp death occurs, the patient may need a root canal or tooth extraction.

Some of the common signs and symptoms of dental problems associated with eating disorders include:

- erosion of dental enamel.

- hypersensitivity to cold/hot.

- salivary gland enlargement.

- dryness of the mouth and decreased salivary flow.

- redness of the throat and palate.

- reddened, dry, and cracked lips, and fissures at angles to the lips.

Eating disorders can become chronic, debilitating, and even life-threatening conditions. The most effective and long-lasting treatment for an eating disorder is some form of psychotherapy or counseling, coupled with careful attention to medical and nutritional needs.

Early diagnosis and intervention may enhance recovery. By referring patients with suspected eating disorders to appropriate healthcare professionals, dentists may play a crucial role in helping to save their patients' lives.

Dental experts recommend that people with eating disorders do the following, while seeking treatment, to prevent further damage:

1. Immediately after vomiting, rinse their mouth with sodium bicarbonate or magnesium hydroxide (place 1 teaspoon in half a glass of water and rinse, or use a proprietary preparation).

2. Brush daily with fluoride toothpaste.

3. After brushing, apply stannous fluoride gel (i.e., Floran), or rinse with neutral sodium fluoride rinse, such as Orofluor or Dentamint.

4. Floss daily.

5. If necessary, consider restoration of teeth with resins or crowns.

6. Have regular dental checkups.

Chapter 30

Osteoporosis Associated With Eating Disorders

What Is Osteoporosis?

Osteoporosis is a condition in which the bones become less dense and more likely to fracture. Fractures from osteoporosis can result in significant pain and disability. It is a major health threat for an estimated 44 million Americans, 68% of whom are women.

Risk factors for developing osteoporosis include: thinness or small frame; family history of the disease; being postmenopausal or having had early menopause; abnormal absence of menstrual periods; prolonged use of certain medications, such as glucocorticoids, low calcium intake, physical inactivity, smoking, and excessive alcohol intake.

Osteoporosis is a silent disease that can often be prevented. However, if undetected, it can progress for many years without symptoms until a fracture occurs. It has been called "a pediatric disease with geriatric consequences," because building healthy bones in one's youth is important to help prevent osteoporosis and fractures later in life.

About This Chapter: Text in this chapter is from "What People with Anorexia Nervosa Need to Know About Osteoporosis," a fact sheet produced by the National Institutes of Health Osteoporosis and Related Bone Diseases—National Resource Center, 2002. Available online at http://www.osteo.org.

The Anorexia Nervosa-Osteoporosis Link

Anorexia nervosa has significant physical consequences. Affected individuals can experience nutritional and hormonal problems that negatively impact bone density. Low body weight causes the body to stop producing estrogen, resulting in a condition known as amenorrhea, or absent menstrual periods. Low estrogen levels contribute to significant losses in bone density. Severe anorexia has resulted in osteoporosis in patients as early as their 20s.

In addition, glucocorticoid levels tend to be higher in anorexic individuals. Sufferers tend to produce excessive amounts of the adrenal hormone cortisol, which is known to trigger bone loss. Other factors such as a decrease in the production of growth hormone and other growth factors, low body weight (apart from estrogen loss), calcium deficiency and malnutrition contribute to bone loss in girls and women with the disorder. Weight loss, restricted dietary input, and testosterone deficiency may be responsible for the low bone density found in males with the disorder.

Studies suggest that osteopenia (low bone mass) is common in anorexic individuals and that it occurs early in the course of the disease. Up to two-thirds of teens with the disorder have bone density values significantly below the norm. Anorexic girls are less likely to reach their peak bone density and, therefore, are at increased risk for osteoporosis and fracture throughout life.

Osteoporosis Management Strategies

Up to half of peak bone density is achieved in adolescence. Anorexia typically originates in mid to late adolescence, a critical period for bone development. The longer the duration of the disorder the greater the bone loss and the less likely it is that bone mineral density will ever return to normal.

The primary goal of medical therapy for anorexic individuals is weight gain and (in females) the return of normal menstrual periods. However, attention to other aspects of bone health is also important.

Nutrition and Exercise: A well-balanced diet rich in calcium and vitamin D is important for healthy bones. Good sources of calcium include low-fat dairy products, dark green, leafy vegetables, and calcium fortified foods and beverages. Also, supplements can help ensure that the calcium requirement is met each day.

✎ What's It Mean?

Calcium: A mineral found in teeth, bones, and other body tissues. [1]

Estrogen: A hormone that promotes the development and maintenance of female sex characteristics. [1]

Geriatric: Relating to the elderly. [2]

Glucocorticoid: A compound that belongs to the family of compounds called corticosteroids (steroids). Glucocorticoids affect metabolism and have anti-inflammatory and immunosuppressive effects. They may be naturally produced (hormones) or synthetic (drugs). [1]

Hormone: A chemical made by glands in the body. Hormones circulate in the bloodstream and control the actions of certain cells or organs. Some hormones can also be made in a laboratory. [1]

Malnutrition: A disorder caused by a lack of proper nutrition or an inability to absorb nutrients from food. [1]

Menopause: The transition in a woman's life when production of the hormone estrogen in her body falls permanently to very low levels, the ovaries stop producing eggs, and menstrual periods stop for good. [3]

Pediatric: Relating to children. [2]

Postmenopausal: Refers to the time after menopause. [1]

Testosterone: A hormone that promotes the development and maintenance of male sex characteristics. [1]

Source: [1] "Dictionary of Cancer Terms," National Cancer Institute, available at www.nci.nih.gov; cited December 2004. [2] Editor. [3] "NWHIC Web Site Glossary," U.S. Department of Health and Human Services, Office on Women's Health, available at www.4woman.gov, 2004.

Vitamin D plays an important role in calcium absorption and bone health. It is synthesized in the skin through exposure to sunlight. Individuals may require vitamin D supplements in order to ensure an adequate daily intake.

Like muscle, bone is living tissue that responds to exercise by becoming stronger. The best exercise for bones is weight-bearing exercise that forces you to work against gravity. Some examples include walking, stair climbing and dancing.

Regular exercises such as walking can help prevent bone loss and provide many other health benefits. However, the potential benefits of exercise need to be weighed against the risk of fractures, delayed weight gain and exercise-induced amenorrhea in anorexics and those recovering from the disorder.

Healthy Lifestyle: Smoking is bad for bones, as well as the heart and lungs. In addition, smokers may absorb less calcium from their diets. Alcohol can also negatively affect bone health. Those who drink heavily are more prone to bone loss and fracture, both because of poor nutrition as well as increased risk of falling.

Bone Density Test: Specialized tests known as bone mineral density (BMD) tests measure bone density in various sites of the body. These tests can detect osteoporosis before a fracture occurs and predict one's chances of fracturing in the future.

Medication: There is no cure for osteoporosis. However, there are medications available for the prevention and treatment of the disease in postmenopausal women, men, and women and men taking glucocorticoid medication. Some studies suggest that there may be a role for estrogen preparations among girls and young women with anorexia. However, experts agree that estrogen should not be a substitute for nutritional support.

Chapter 31

Diabetes And Eating Disorders

Because both diabetes and eating disorders involve attention to body issues, weight management, and control of food, some people develop a pattern in which they use the disease to justify or camouflage the disorder. Because the complications of diabetes and eating disorders can be serious, even fatal, responsible, healthy behavior is essential.

How many people have both an eating disorder and diabetes?

We are not sure, but the combination is common. Some clinicians think that eating disorders are more common among folks with diabetes than they are in the general population. Research is currently underway to find out if this is so.

Does diabetes cause anorexia nervosa or bulimia?

No, diabetes does not cause eating disorders, but it can set the stage, physically and emotionally, for their development. Once people develop eating disorders, they can hide them in the overall diabetic constellation. This makes treatment and even diagnosis difficult. In some of these cases the eating disorder has gone undetected for years, sometimes coming to light only when life-altering complications appear.

What are some of those life-altering complications?

Blindness, kidney disease, impaired circulation, nerve death, and amputation of limbs. Death, of course, is the ultimate life-altering complication.

People who have both diabetes and an eating disorder eat in ways that would make their doctors wince. Many believe that being fat, a perceived immediate threat, is far worse than the consequences noted above which may never happen, or if they do, will happen years down the road. Like Scarlett O'Hara, they will worry tomorrow.

Many of these people superstitiously believe they will escape complications. They are wrong.

♣ It's A Fact!!
What is diabetes?

Diabetes is a disorder of metabolism—the way our bodies use digested food for growth and energy. Most of the food we eat is broken down into glucose, the form of sugar in the blood. Glucose is the main source of fuel for the body.

After digestion, glucose passes into the bloodstream, where it is used by cells for growth and energy. For glucose to get into cells, insulin must be present. Insulin is a hormone produced by the pancreas, a large gland behind the stomach.

When we eat, the pancreas automatically produces the right amount of insulin to move glucose from blood into our cells. In people with diabetes, however, the pancreas either produces little or no insulin, or the cells do not respond appropriately to the insulin that is produced. Glucose builds up in the blood, overflows into the urine, and passes out of the body. Thus, the body loses its main source of fuel even though the blood contains large amounts of glucose.

There are three main types of diabetes—type 1, type 2, and gestational.

Source: Excerpted from "Diabetes Overview," National Institute of Diabetes and Digestive and Kidney Diseases, available at www.diabetes.niddk.nih.gov, 2005.

What is the main mechanism that connects diabetes and eating disorders?

People who take insulin to control their diabetes can misuse it to lose weight. If they cut back the required dosage, blood sugar will rise and spill over into the urine. These folks will lose weight, but the biochemical process is particularly dangerous. Reducing insulin causes body tissues to dissolve and be flushed out in urination.

Once diabetics discover that they can manipulate their weight this way, they are reluctant to stop even if they know about potential consequences because weight loss is rewarding in our fat-phobic culture. They decide to maintain the weight loss, and that decision can serve as the trigger for a full-blown eating disorder.

What are the similarities between diabetes and eating disorders?

Both demand that people pay close attention to body states, weight management, types and amounts of food consumed, and the timing and content of meals. Both encourage people to embrace some foods as "safe" and "good" and fear others as "dangerous" and "bad."

Control is a central issue in both diabetes and eating disorders. Diabetics may feel guilty, anxious, or out of control if their blood sugar swings more than a few points. Anorexics and bulimics may feel the same way if their weight fluctuates. People with both problems may become consumed with strategies to rigidly control both weight and blood sugar.

Children with diabetes may have parents they perceive as overprotective and overcontrolling. The parents of young people with eating disorders are often described in similar terms. In both kinds of families over involvement and enmeshment can lead children to rebellion and dramatic, potentially catastrophic, acts of independence.

People with eating disorders are preoccupied with weight, food, and diet. So are folks with diabetes. In fact, the latter can use their diabetes to hide anorexia or bulimia because, after all, they are supposed to be watching what they eat, and they can blame poorly controlled diabetes for alarming weight loss.

♣ It's A Fact!!

Type 1 Diabetes

Type 1 diabetes is an autoimmune disease. An autoimmune disease results when the body's system for fighting infection (the immune system) turns against a part of the body. In diabetes, the immune system attacks the insulin-producing beta cells in the pancreas and destroys them. The pancreas then produces little or no insulin. A person who has type 1 diabetes must take insulin daily to live. Type 1 diabetes accounts for about 5 to 10 percent of diagnosed diabetes in the United States. It develops most often in children and young adults, but can appear at any age.

Type 2 Diabetes

The most common form of diabetes is type 2 diabetes. About 90 to 95 percent of people with diabetes have type 2. This form of diabetes is associated with older age, obesity, family history of diabetes, previous history of gestational diabetes, physical inactivity, and ethnicity. About 80 percent of people with type 2 diabetes are overweight. Type 2 diabetes is increasingly being diagnosed in children and adolescents. When type 2 diabetes is diagnosed, the pancreas is usually producing enough insulin, but for unknown reasons, the body cannot use the insulin effectively, a condition called insulin resistance. After several years, insulin production decreases. The result is the same as for type 1 diabetes—glucose builds up in the blood and the body cannot make efficient use of its main source of fuel.

Gestational Diabetes

Gestational diabetes develops only during pregnancy. Women who have had gestational diabetes have a 20 to 50 percent chance of developing type 2 diabetes within 5 to 10 years.

Source: Excerpted from "Diabetes Overview," National Institute of Diabetes and Digestive and Kidney Diseases, available at www.diabetes.niddk.nih.gov, 2005.

Are there any other problems related to a combination of diabetes and eating disorders?

Yes. When people misuse insulin to lose weight, sometimes that weight loss seems to improve diabetes, at least temporarily, by reducing or eliminating the need for insulin. It's interesting to note that starvation was a primary treatment for diabetes before commercial production of supplemental insulin. This weight loss method is not without problems, however. If continued, the person experiences life-threatening organ failure and death.

What kind of treatment should people have who have both diabetes and an eating disorder?

Getting them into treatment is the first step. Many of these folks are embarrassed to admit that they have been doing something as unhealthy as an eating disorder. Often they defiantly hang onto starving and stuffing behaviors in spite of real threats to life and health. Families sometimes collude by denying that anything is wrong.

Nevertheless, it is important to begin treatment early. Eating disorders can be treated, and people do recover from them, but the longer symptoms are ignored, the harder it is to turn them around and the harsher the effects on the body.

The best treatment is team treatment. That means that many professionals are involved with the patient and perhaps with the family as well: a physician to manage the diabetes and the effects of starving and stuffing, a mental health therapist to help define and deal with underlying emotional issues, a family therapist to help the family, and a dietitian to provide nutritional counseling and education.

The first priority is restoration of physical health. For people with anorexia that means weight gain back to healthy levels. For both anorexics and bulimics the next step is implementation of balanced, varied, and healthy meal plans that provide adequate calories and nutrients. After physical health is stabilized, treatment can focus on the underlying psychological issues.

Most treatment for eating disorders is outpatient, but if the patient is suicidal, severely depressed, or in any kind of medical danger, hospitalization is appropriate until the crisis has passed. Medication may be used to ease depression and anxiety, but a physician must carefully monitor it.

☞ Remember!!
In Summary

Diabetes and eating disorders are a nasty combination with very real potential for catastrophic complications, including death. The good news, however, is that in most cases diabetes can be controlled, and eating disorders can be treated. Many people recover from anorexia nervosa and bulimia, but almost always professional help is required.

If you are concerned about yourself, arrange right now to talk to your physician. Don't let shame or embarrassment stop you from telling the truth. The doctor has heard your story many times before. Ask for a referral to a mental health professional who works with people with eating disorders. Contact that person and ask for an evaluation. Then follow up on any treatment recommendations that come from the evaluation. Other people have made this journey successfully. You can too.

Chapter 32

Substance Abuse And Eating Disorders

More than five million Americans, predominately (but not solely) women, suffer from eating disorders—anorexia nervosa, bulimia nervosa, and binge eating disorder. Millions more periodically display symptoms of eating disorders or constantly worry about their weight.

This is a life-threatening problem. The death rate of a young woman with anorexia has been found up to 12 times greater than that of a woman of the same age without anorexia—and up to twice that of a young woman with any other psychiatric disorder.

More than five million women currently use illicit drugs; some 1.5 million are addicts. At least three million are alcoholics and several million more abuse alcohol. Some 30 million women are addicted to nicotine. More than one million girls ages 12 to 17 are current illicit drug users; more than one and a half million girls are addicted to nicotine; and more than 1.2 million binge drink or are heavy alcohol users.

The tobacco companies understood the relationship between smoking and weight control long before the public health experts. Nicotine pushers began pitching cigarettes as a route to thinness in the 1920s when they first tried to reach women as a market. Lucky Strike ads told women to "Reach for a Lucky instead of a sweet."

When the 1964 Surgeon General's report spotlighted the harmful effects of smoking, and the male market leveled off, tobacco companies targeted women. They created Virginia Slims with its tag line "slimmer, longer, not like those fat cigarettes men smoke." They placed their ads in women's magazines

---

✤ It's A Fact!!

FACT: Between 12 and 18 percent of individuals with anorexia and between 30 and 70 percent of those with bulimia abuse tobacco, alcohol, pills, or over the counter substances.

FACT: The adolescent years are when women are at greatest risk of eating disorders. These are precisely the years when they are at greatest risk of substance abuse.

FACT: During substance abuse treatment and early recovery, it is not unusual for an individual to turn to binge eating.

FACT: A student who has dieted in sixth grade is more than 20 percent likelier to drink alcohol in the ninth grade than one who has never dieted.

FACT: The more often and more severely an incoming college female diets, the more likely she is to use drugs and abuse alcohol. 72 percent of severe freshmen dieters and bulimics have used alcohol in the past month, compared with less than 44 percent of those who did not diet. Freshmen women with bulimia are more than four times likelier to have smoked in the last month than those who did not diet. The more severe the dieter, the more likely the abuse will involve more than one substance.

FACT: A *People* magazine survey revealed that 12 percent of women consider smoking a weight reduction method.

FACT: Girls who smoke to suppress their appetites are among the largest group of new nicotine addicts. Among white teenagers who smoke, girls are three times likelier than boys to smoke to suppress their appetites.

FACT: Women who smoke are more than twice as likely as men to cite weight concerns as a reason not to quit.

that rarely reported on the health dangers of tobacco. Thanks in part to these ads, the rate at which girls started smoking rose sharply from between 1967 and 1973: among 12 year old girls, by 110 percent; among 17 year old girls, by 35 percent.

Polls repeatedly show that the number one wish for females ages 11 to 17 is to lose weight. Sixty percent of 12 and 13 year old girls with low self-esteem are watching their weight and on diets. Tobacco companies manipulate this desire, capitalizing on girls' low self-esteem, a risk factor for both eating disorders and substance abuse.

✎ What's It Mean?

Comorbidity: The coexistence of syndromes or diagnosable disorders.

Source: "Glossary Of Terms," Crisis Intervention in Child Abuse and Neglect, Administration for Children and Families, U.S. Department of Health and Human Services, available at www.nccanch.acf.hhs.gov, 2004.

The slogan for Misty cigarettes is "Slim 'n' Sassy." Capri claims "There's no slimmer way to smoke" and calls its cigarettes, "The Slimmest Slim in Town." Virginia Slims' famous tag line is "You've come a long way, Baby." But as Gloria Steinham once pointed out, "If we've come such a long way, why are we still smoking?"

Cigarettes and eating disorders are linked in more ways than the tobacco companies let on. Cigarette smoking and eating disorders share many of the same health consequences—osteoporosis, heart problems, and infertility.

The most sordid exploitation of the connection between eating disorders and substance abuse is found in the fashion industry. Drug use—especially heroin and cocaine—is not uncommon, and for many models it is the chosen route to wafer thinness. Grotesque as it may be, heroin chic—the thin, hollow-eyed, emaciated figure caricatured as social X-rays by novelist Tom Wolfe—has been promoted as the standard of beauty by fashion photographers and their principals.

These facts and commercial exploitation provide ample evidence of a need for professionals to be sensitive to the increased risks of substance abuse among patients with eating disorders—and vice versa—and for researchers to explore the relationship between the two conditions. Though research has assembled some prevalence estimates, researchers still do not know or fully

---

♣ It's A Fact!!

Shifting Addictions

Those who are chemically dependent agree that craving is a strong drive in their addiction. The craving results in preoccupation. The preoccupation of addiction is actually an obsession—intense recurring thoughts about alcohol or other drugs.

Since addiction involves harmful consequences, it isn't very long until family members, employers, friends, or co-workers are telling them to cut back or stop altogether. But the physical craving and mental obsession take controlling alcohol or other drug use beyond the realm of willpower. So instead, some of them have simply substituted other addictive behaviors.

Examples

- The young woman who gradually substitutes bingeing on bakery goods to cut back on her drinking.

- The middle-aged man who quits using cocaine only to find himself eating compulsively, eventually gaining sixty pounds.

For other individuals the reverse may be the case:

- The adolescent who starves herself and finds that she can eat more normally when she drinks.

- The overweight young adult who is obsessed with his appearance and finds that cocaine not only makes him feel high, but also cuts off his appetite.

A third scenario involves those who attempt to switch addictions, only to suffer the progression of both:

understand all of the driving forces behind the comorbidity of eating disorders and substance abuse.

There is an important CASA finding—an individual who gets through age 21 without using drugs, smoking cigarettes, or abusing alcohol is virtually certain never to do so.

- The young man who substitutes bingeing on sugary snacks to cut back on drinking, only to find himself bingeing on both food and alcohol.

- The adolescent who starves herself and discovers that she can eat more normally when she drinks, only to compound her anorexia with alcoholism.

If alcoholism and other kinds of drug dependency are not bad habits but addictions, can we say the same thing about eating disorders?

Addictions Are Not All The Same

Many of those in recovery from dual addictions have found that the progression of alcoholism and an eating disorder is similar, although the behavior and consequences are different.

Eating disorders involve a choice of addictive behaviors, just like chemical dependency. The person with chemical dependency might depend on wine and beer, but might also take Valium and sleeping pills. The person with an eating disorder might depend on bingeing and starving, but might also overeat and exercise excessively.

For many, addictive eating behaviors change over time and sometimes follow different patterns. The addict could compulsively overeat, binge and purge (bulimia), or starve (anorexia).

Source: From *Facing an Eating Disorder in Recovery* by Tim Sheehan, Ph.D., Copyright 1991 by HAZELDEN FOUNDATION. Reprinted by permission of Hazelden Foundation, Center City, MN.

Chapter 33

Eating Disorders And Pregnancy

I have an eating disorder, but I want to have a family someday. Will I be able to have babies?

Because dieting, excessive exercise, stress, and low weight negatively impact a woman's endocrine (hormone) system, you may have trouble conceiving a baby and carrying it to term. The closer to normal your weight is, and the healthier your diet, the better your chances of a successful pregnancy. If you are underweight or overweight, and if you do not eat a wide variety of healthy foods, you and your baby may have problems.

A recent study in Denmark suggests that even eight years after successful ED treatment, the chances of having a high-risk pregnancy are the same as those for women who receive treatment immediately before they conceive. (Secher, et al. *American Journal of Obstetrics and Gynecology*, January 2004). It appears that a history of disordered eating may predict reproductive trouble even years after treatment and progress in recovery. In the U.S., about 20 percent of women patients who ask for help at fertility clinics have had an eating disorder.

If I do manage to get pregnant before I'm recovered, could I hurt my baby by being eating disordered?

You might. Women with eating disorders have higher rates of miscarriage than do healthy, normal women. Also, your baby might be born prematurely, meaning that it would not weigh as much, or be as well developed, as babies who are born full term. Low birth weight babies are at risk of many medical problems, some of them life threatening.

An article in the January 2002 *New England Journal of Medicine* reports that premature babies have neurological and developmental problems well into early adulthood, and possibly longer. Some of the problems include lower IQs, learning disabilities, and cerebral palsy. Additional problems include increased chances of infant death and failure to thrive in the first year following birth. Even if low birth weight babies seem to be healthy, they may not reach full-expected adult stature, remaining small and short throughout their lives.

✎ What's It Mean?

Basal: The amount of heat given off by a person at rest in a comfortable environment. [1]

Bipolar Disorder: Also known as manic-depressive illness, is a brain disorder that causes unusual shifts in a person's mood, energy, and ability to function. [2]

Cesarean Section (C-section): Procedure where the baby is delivered through an abdominal incision. [3]

Calcium: A mineral found in teeth, bones, and other body tissues. [4]

Cerebral Palsy: A developmental disability that applies to a wide range of physical disabilities caused by damage to the brain during its development. [5]

Coronary: Structures that encircle another structure (such as the coronary arteries, which encircle the heart); commonly used to refer to a heart attack. [6]

Diabetes: A disease in which the body does not properly control the amount of sugar in the blood. As a result, the level of sugar in the blood is too high. This disease occurs when the body does not produce enough insulin or does not use it properly. [4]

Babies born to women with active eating disorders seem to be at higher risk of birth defects than those born to asymptomatic mothers. In particular, major handicaps such as blindness and mental retardation are common in those who survive.

I know this sounds selfish, but could I hurt myself by trying to have a baby before I am recovered?

You are wise to think ahead. If you become pregnant now, you could seriously deplete your own body. The baby will take nourishment from you, and if you don't replenish your own reserves, you could find yourself struggling with the depression and exhaustion associated with malnutrition. You would also have to deal with the physical and emotional demands of pregnancy. You might find yourself overwhelmed and feeling out of control.

Fetus: The developing offspring from 7 to 8 weeks after conception until birth. [4]

High Blood Pressure (Hypertension): A condition present when blood flows through the blood vessels with a force greater than normal. High blood pressure can strain the heart, damage blood vessels, and increase the risk of heart attack, stroke, kidney problems, and death. [7]

Hormone: A chemical made by glands in the body. Hormones circulate in the bloodstream and control the actions of certain cells or organs. Some hormones can also be made in a laboratory. [4]

Insulin: A hormone made by the islet cells of the pancreas. Insulin controls the amount of sugar in the blood by moving it into the cells, where it can be used by the body for energy. [4]

IQ (Intelligence Quotient) Tests: A series of tests used to determine the general intelligence of a person compared to other people the same age. [8]

Malnutrition: A disorder caused by a lack of proper nutrition or an inability to absorb nutrients from food. [4]

continued on next page

According to an article in the September 2001 *American Journal of Psychiatry*, pregnant women with active eating disorders or a history of eating disorders are at increased risk of delivery by caesarean section and postpartum depression. This makes taking care of themselves and their infants difficult to impossible.

Are there any specific medical problems I might have trouble with?

Your teeth and bones might become weak and fragile because the baby's need for calcium takes priority over yours. If you don't replenish calcium with dairy products and other sources, you could find yourself with stress fractures and broken bones in later years. Once calcium is gone from your bones, it is difficult, if not impossible, to replace it.

Pregnancy can exacerbate other problems related to the eating disorder such as potentially fatal liver, kidney, and cardiac damage. A woman who is eating disordered, pregnant, and diabetic is at especially high risk for serious problems.

What's It Mean? continued from previous page

Manic Depression: Also known as bipolar disorder, is a brain disorder that causes unusual shifts in a person's mood, energy, and ability to function. [2]

Metabolism: The total of all chemical changes that take place in a cell or an organism. These changes produce energy and basic materials needed for important life processes. [4]

Miscarriage: An unplanned loss of a pregnancy. Also called a spontaneous abortion. [3]

Neurological: Having to do with nerves or the nervous system. [4]

Nutrient: Chemical compounds (such as protein, fat, carbohydrate, vitamins, or minerals) that make up foods. These compounds are used by the body to function and grow. [4]

Postpartum Depression: A serious condition that requires treatment from a health care provider. With this condition, feelings of the baby blues (feeling sad, anxious, afraid, or confused after having a baby) do not go away or get worse. [3]

Prenatal: Prior to birth. [8]

All pregnant women should receive prenatal care. Those who have one or more of the above complicating factors should consult with a physician as soon as they think they might be pregnant. To increase their own, and the baby's, chances of life and health, they should follow recommendations scrupulously.

That's pretty scary, but I'm more concerned about my baby than I am about myself. Assuming it was born healthy, would it be OK from then on?

Maybe. There is evidence suggesting that babies born to eating disordered mothers may be retarded or slow to develop. Physically they may be smaller, weaker, and slower growing than other children their age. Intellectually they may lag behind peers and classmates. Emotionally they may remain infantile and dependent. They also may not develop effective social skills and successful relationships with other people.

Triglyceride: A neutral fat that serves as a metabolic energy source. [9]

Unipolar: Also known as major depression. When 5 or more symptoms of depression are present for at least 2 weeks. These symptoms include feeling sad, hopeless, worthless, or pessimistic. [10]

Source: [1] "Glossary," U.S. Department of Energy, available at www.eere.energy.gov, 2004. [2] "Bipolar Disorder," The National Institute of Mental Health, U.S. Department of Health and Human Services, available at www.nimh.nih.gov, 2004. [3] "NWHIC Web Site Glossary," U.S. Department of Health and Human Services, Office on Women's Health, available at www.4woman.gov, 2004. [4] "Dictionary of Cancer Terms," National Cancer Institute, available at www.nci.nih.gov; cited December 2004. [5] "Women with Disabilities," U.S. Department of Health and Human Services, Office on Women's Health, available at www.4woman.gov, 2004. [6] "Glossary," Agency for Healthcare Research and Quality, U.S. Department of Health and Human Services, available at www.ahrq.gov, 2000. [7] "Diabetes Dictionary," National Institute of Diabetes and Digestive and Kidney Diseases, available at www.diabetes.niddk.nih.gov, 2003. [8] Editor. [9] "Glossary," National Institute on Alcohol Abuse and Alcoholism, U.S. Department of Health and Human Services, available at www.niaa.nih.gov, 2002. [10] "Glossary," National Center for Biotechnology Information, U.S. National Library of Medicine, National Institutes of Health, available at www.ncbi.nlm.nih.gov, cited December 2004.

At this point no one knows how many of the child's developmental diffi-culties are due to the medical consequences of an eating disorder and how many are the result of being parented by someone who is emotionally troubled and over concerned about food and weight.

This is scary stuff. I wish I had never started this stupid eating disorder. I may as well have all the bad news. What else could go wrong if I try to have a baby?

You could become depressed and frantic because of weight gain during pregnancy. You might feel so out of control of your life and body that you would try to hurt yourself or the unborn baby. You might worry and feel guilty about the damage you could be causing the baby.

You might underfeed your child to make her thin, or, you might overfeed her to show the world that you are a nurturing parent. Power struggles over food and eating often plague families where someone has an eating disorder. You could continue that pattern with your child.

Research suggests that mom's dieting and low weight can create prob-lems for the fetus, which may slow its metabolism to conserve energy. As with adults, this adjustment can lead to obesity, heart disease, and diabetes later in life. Mom's dieting can also shunt scarce nutrients to the fetal brain, short changing organs like the liver.

On the other hand, when a fetus is overnourished (mom eats too much and is overweight), it may be at risk for adult obesity and breast cancer. Elevated blood sugar can retard growth of the placenta as well. Our best advice: eat healthy, well-balanced meals and maintain a healthy normal weight for several months before you conceive and throughout the duration of your pregnancy.

This gets worse and worse, but I have a lot of love in my heart. I think I would be a good mother. The eating disorder wouldn't be that important if I had a child.

Motherhood is stressful. If you are not strong in your recovery, you will be tempted to fall back on the starving and stuffing coping behaviors that are so familiar to you. Ideally, as you begin raising a family, you will already have learned, and will have had practice using other more healthy and effective behaviors when you feel overwhelmed.

Also, eating disordered women make poor role models. Your influence could lead your daughters to their own eating disorders and your sons to believe that the most important thing about women is their weight.

I really want a baby, and I think having one would give me the motivation I need to recover. I think I would enjoy being pregnant even though handling the weight gain would be scary. What can I do to give my child and myself the best possible chance of success?

Some women with eating disorders welcome pregnancy as a vacation from weight worries. They believe they are doing something important by having a baby and are able to set aside their fear of fat in service to the health of the child. Others fall into black depression and intolerable anxiety when their bellies begin to swell. Most fall somewhere between these two extremes.

If you think you are pregnant, or if you want to become pregnant, tell your physician as soon as possible. Cooperate with prenatal care to increase the chances that your baby will be born healthy. Also, this would be a good time to check with a counselor who can help you manage your doubts, fears, and worries as you proceed through pregnancy. A couple of classes on pregnancy, childbirth, and child development after birth can give you reassuring information about what to expect. You can learn parenting skills, but role modeling comes from your sense of yourself. Acquire the former and improve the latter.

One last thought: We now have evidence that what, and how much, a mother eats during pregnancy can influence a child's physiology and metabolism after birth, perhaps setting the stage for metabolic and hormonal problems that can lead to medical and psychological problems in the child's later life. For example, undernourished pregnant moms often produce underweight, premature babies. Those infants experience a 35% higher rate of coronary death in later life and a six-fold increase in the risk of diabetes and impaired sugar metabolism than do children of mothers who received adequate nutrition while they were pregnant. Related problems include faulty insulin sensitivity, diabetes, high blood pressure, high triglyceride levels, and too little "good" cholesterol. Maternal malnutrition can also lead to impaired liver development in the child and problems with blood clotting that can lead to heart attack and stroke in adult life. (Reported by Jane Brody in the *New York Times*. October 1996)

Studies also indicate that undernourished moms give birth to children at increased risk of major affective disorders (depression, manic-depression; unipolar, bipolar disease) when they reach adolescence and adulthood. Apparently healthy fetal development of brain and nervous system requires specific nutrients, and enough of them, that may not be provided by weight loss or weight management diets.

New research indicates that pregnant women need extra energy intake (calories and nutrition) over and above their requirements when they are not pregnant. According to Nancy Butte, Ph.D., USDA Children's Nutrition Research Center, Baylor College of Medicine, "Extra dietary energy is required during pregnancy to make up for the energy deposited in maternal and fetal tissues and the rise in energy expenditure attributable to increased basal metabolism and to changes in the energy cost of physical activity." Women with eating disorders should consider this fact before they become pregnant and decide if they can handle the increased nutrition requirements of a healthy pregnancy. (Reported in the May 2004 issue of the *American Journal of Clinical Nutrition*)

Part Six

Maintaining Healthy Eating And Exercise Habits

Chapter 34

An Action Guide To Healthy Eating

Tipping The Scales In Your Favor

Have you decided to start eating healthier and become more physically active? Have you realized that healthy choices have a positive impact on not only yourself, but also those around you?

If your goal is to lose weight or maintain your current healthy weight, here are some tips to help you achieve that goal. Remember, to maintain weight, you must balance calories with the energy you burn through physical activity. If you eat more than you expend, you gain weight. If you eat less (reduce calories) than you expend, you lose weight!

Make healthy choices a habit. This leads to a healthy lifestyle! Make a commitment to eat well, move more, and get support from family and friends. Even better, start eating healthier and being active together!

Remember to be realistic about your goals. If you try to reduce the calories, fat, saturated fat, and sugar in your diet and promise to make a drastic

About This Chapter: This chapter begins with text from "Tipping the Scales in Your Favor," and "5 A Day Fruit and Vegetable Quick Tips," National Center for Chronic Disease Prevention and Health Promotion, Centers for Disease Control and Prevention, November 2004. Additional text, unless otherwise noted, is from "Action Guide for Healthy Eating," National Cancer Institute, 1995.

> ☞ **Remember!!**
> **Variety, Balance, And Moderation**
>
> There is no secret to healthy eating. Be sure to eat a variety of foods, including plenty of vegetables, fruits, and whole grain products. Also include low-fat dairy products, lean meats, poultry, fish, and legumes. Drink lots of water and go easy on the salt, sugar, and saturated fat. Good nutrition should be part of an overall healthy lifestyle that also includes regular physical activity, not smoking, and stress management.
>
> Source: "Healthy Eating Tips," National Center for Chronic Disease Prevention and Health Promotion, Centers for Disease Control and Prevention, January 2004.

change in your physical activity level, you may be setting yourself up for failure. Instead of trying to make many changes at once, set smaller, more realistic goals for yourself and add a new challenge each week.

Conduct an inventory of your meal/snack and physical activity patterns. Keep a food and activity journal. Write down not only what you ate, but where, when, and what you were feeling at the time. You will see what triggers your hunger and what satisfies your appetite. What foods do you routinely shop for? What snacks do you keep in the pantry?

Eat at least 5 servings of vegetables and fruits per day. If you're adding fruits and vegetables to your diet, try substituting them for higher calorie, less nutritious foods. Diets rich in fruits and vegetables may reduce the risk of cancer and other chronic diseases. Fruits and vegetables provide essential vitamins and minerals, fiber, and other substances that are important for good health. Most fruits and vegetables are naturally low in fat and calories and are filling.

Eat foods that are high in fiber to help you feel full. Whole grain cereals, legumes (lentils and beans), vegetables, and fruits are good sources of fiber that may help you feel full with fewer calories.

Prepare and eat meals and snacks at home. This is a great way to save money, eat healthy, and spend time with your family. When preparing meals, choose low-fat/low-calorie versions of your favorite ingredients and learn how easy it is to substitute. For example:

- Switch to 1 percent or nonfat milk and low-fat cheeses.

- Use a cooking spray instead of oil or butter to decrease the amount of fat when you cook.

- Prepare baked potatoes with low-fat blue cheese dressing or low-fat plain yogurt instead of butter or sour cream.

Use a scale and measuring cup to serve your food. Read food labels to determine serving sizes. One bowl of cereal may actually be two 3/4-cup servings. A small frozen pizza may contain up to three servings (check the nutrition information label). This could add up to more calories than you think that you're getting. Being aware of serving sizes may make it easier to avoid those extra calories.

Choose snacks that are nutritious and filling. A piece of fresh fruit, cut raw vegetables, or a container of low-fat yogurt are excellent (and portable) choices to tide you over until mealtimes. Take these snacks with you for a healthy alternative to chips, cookies, or candy.

Take your time! Eat only when you are hungry and enjoy the taste, texture, and smell of your meal as you eat it. Remember that it takes approximately 15 minutes for your stomach to signal your brain that you are full.

If you choose to eat out, remember these important suggestions: Watch your portions. Portion sizes at restaurants (including fast food) are usually more than one serving, which can result in overeating. Choose smaller portion sizes, order an appetizer and a leafy green salad with low-fat dressing, share an entree with a friend, or get a "doggy bag" and save half for another meal.

Forgive yourself. If you occasionally make mistakes, don't give up! Forgive yourself for making that choice and keep working on it. Eat an extra healthy lunch and dinner if you had a high-calorie, high-fat breakfast. Add more physical activity to your day.

Remember physical activity! Aim for at least 30 minutes of moderate-intensity physical activity five or more days of the week. If you are just starting to be physically active, remember that even small increases provide health benefits. Start with a few minutes of activity a day and gradually increase, working your way up to 30 minutes. If you already get 30 minutes of moderate-intensity physical activity a day, you can gain even more health benefits by increasing the amount of time that you are physically active or by taking part in more vigorous-intensity activities.

5 A Day Fruit And Vegetable Quick Tips

5 A Day Basics

* Fruits and vegetables look good, taste great, and contain vitamins and minerals.

* Eating 5 to 9 A Day is quick and easy. A serving is a medium-size piece of fruit; 3/4 cup (6 fl. oz.) of 100 percent fruit or vegetable juice, 1/2 cup cooked or canned vegetables or fruit, 1 cup of raw leafy vegetables, 1/2 cup cooked dry peas or beans, or 1/4 cup dried fruit.

* You can get your 5 to 9 A Day in many ways because fruits and vegetables come fresh, frozen, canned, dried, and as 100 percent fruit or vegetable juice.

♣ **It's A Fact!!**

Color Your Way To 5 A Day

There are thousands of health-promoting phytochemicals found in plants. Research is just beginning to understand how they work to improve health, so it's important to eat a wide variety of colorful orange/yellow, red, green, white, and blue/purple vegetables and fruit every day. By eating vegetables and fruit from each color group, you will benefit from the unique array of phytochemicals, as well as essential vitamins, minerals, and fiber that each color group has to offer alone and in combination.

Source: Excerpted from "5 A Day for Better Health," National Center for Chronic Disease Prevention and Health Promotion, Centers for Disease Control and Prevention, January 2005.

• Wash fresh fruits and vegetables thoroughly in water.

How Many Servings Do You Need Each Day?

It depends on your age, gender, and activity level (see Table 34.1).

Table 34.1. Recommended Daily Fruit And Vegetable Servings

	Teen Girls	Teen Boys
Calories	About 2,200	About 2,800
Vegetable Group	4 servings	5 servings
Fruit Group	3 servings	4 servings

Source: Adapted from the USDA Dietary Guidelines for Americans, 2000

Getting Started

• Not sure how to eat 5 to 9 A Day? Start the day with 100 percent fruit or vegetable juice. Slice bananas or strawberries on top of your cereal. Have a salad with lunch and an apple for an afternoon snack. Include a vegetable with dinner and you already have 5 A Day. If you need more than 5 servings per day (see chart above), try adding a piece of fruit for a snack or an extra vegetable (like carrots or green beans) at dinner.

• There are so many choices when selecting fruits and vegetables. Have you ever tried kiwifruit? How about asparagus? Try something new that helps you reach your 5 to 9 A Day.

• Keep things fresh and interesting by combining fruits and vegetables of different flavors and colors like red grapes with pineapple chunks, or cucumbers and red peppers.

• When you keep fruits and vegetables visible and easily accessible you tend to eat them more; for instance, store cut and cleaned produce at eye-level in the refrigerator, or keep a big bowl of fruit on the table.

• You can get some of your 5 to 9 A Day at restaurants too. Try some of these healthy choices.

  • Veggie pizza.

- Pasta with vegetables (but watch out for those high fat cream sauces).

- Fresh vegetable "wrap."

- Vegetable soup.

- Small salad (instead of fries).

- Plenty of fresh vegetables from the salad bar.

> ✔ **Quick Tip**
>
> What's a serving size for fruits and vegetables?
>
> - 6 ounces juice
> - ½ cup cut-up fruit or vegetable
> - 2 cups leafy vegetable
> - ¼ cup dried fruit

In A Hurry? Pack And Go For 5 To 9 A Day!

- Buy ready-to-eat packaged fresh vegetables that are already cleaned. Pre-cut vegetables and salad mixes are a terrific 5 A Day time-saver. You'll find them at your local supermarket.

- A fast food alternative? Your local supermarket may offer prepared items, including sliced melons, fresh pineapple, salad mixes, and a salad bar to satisfy your hunger.

- Fruits and vegetables are nature's original fast food. When it's snack time, grab

  - Fruit—an apple or orange, or a zip lock bag filled with sweet cherries, grapes, dried dates, figs, prunes, raisins, or apricots.

  - Vegetables—carrot sticks, broccoli, or some red, yellow, and green pepper. Try dipping your vegetables in low-fat or non-fat salad dressing.

- In a hurry for a 5 A Day treat? Pick fruits and vegetables that require little peeling or chopping, like baby carrots, cherry tomatoes, cauliflower, grapes, apples, broccoli spears, an apple, a banana, or a box of 100 percent fruit or vegetable juice.

- Here's a great way to get some of your 5 to 9 A Day. Buy low-fat yogurt, fruit juice, and fresh, canned, or frozen fruit to blend a quick fruit smoothie. Get juicy! Buy 100 percent fruit or vegetable juice to quench your thirst and satisfy one serving of your 5 to 9 A Day.

Top Your Meals The 5 A Day Way

- Try these tasty additions to add flavor to your 5 A Day salad:
  - Green or red pepper strips, broccoli florets, carrot slices, or cucumber add crunch to your pasta or potato salad.
  - Baby carrots, shredded cabbage, or spinach leaves bring color to a green salad.
  - Apple chunks, pineapples, and raisins perk up coleslaw, chicken or tuna salads.
  - Oranges, grapefruit, or nectarine slices add extra flavor to any salad.
  - Fruit juice, flavored vinegars, or herbs make low-fat salad dressings flavorful without adding fat or salt.
  - Wake up with 5 A Day! Add sliced banana, blueberries, or raisins to cereal.

- Add fresh fruit and vegetables to foods you already eat—like berries and bananas to yogurt and cereal; vegetables to pasta and pizza; and lettuce, tomato and onion to sandwiches.

- Put some punch into your party by blending 100 percent fruit juices to create a refreshing new juice. Try mixing pineapple, orange, grapefruit, or other fruit juices. Add a slice of lemon or lime as a garnish.

Cooking With 5 A Day

- Using a microwave is fast and fun. Use a microwave or pressure cooker to quickly "zap" vegetables or a potato and retain their nutrients.

- Grill fruits or vegetables. When grilling, wrap vegetables in aluminum foil, or use skewers of pineapple, yellow squash, eggplant, nectarines, zucchini, cherry tomatoes, onions, or mushrooms. Place over medium-hot coals for a fun-to-eat and flavorful BBQ treat.

- Make a quick smoothie in the blender by puréeing peaches and/or nectarines, a touch of your favorite fruit juice, crushed ice, and a light sprinkling of nutmeg.

- Make homemade salsa with tomatoes, mangoes, avocados, red onions, cilantro, and lime juice.

- Looking for a fun appetizer when you entertain? Try making spears of fruit by attaching strawberries, grapes, melon slices, or pineapple chunks onto small skewers. Use low-fat or non-fat yogurt for a dip.

> ♣ **It's A Fact!!**
> **What's a whole grain?**
>
> It's a grain that still has its outer covering, which contains the grain's fiber and many of its vitamins and minerals.

- Here's a quick fruit salad you can make in less than a minute. Open a can of juice-packed mandarin oranges and empty into a bowl. Add a sliced banana, a sliced apple, and some blueberries or raisins. There you have it—a quick way to 5 A Day.

- Cool off with a great treat! Pour 100 percent fruit or vegetable juice into an ice cube tray or popsicle mold to make juice cubes or popsicles.

- Sometimes you can eat some of your 5 to 9 A Day in its own container. Kiwifruit comes with its own serving cup and cantaloupe with its own serving bowl. Just cut them in half through the middle and scoop out each half with a spoon.

Tips On Meals And School Lunches

Most people are busy these days. They have less time than they used to for shopping and for planning what to eat. There are ways to make it easy to fit low-fat, high-fiber eating into busy schedules.

Much research in the last few years has shown that the way people eat has a lot to do with how healthy they are—and how healthy they stay. This research has also shown that eating a healthy diet, low in fat, high in fiber, with plenty of fruits and vegetables, may help to lower cancer risk.

People have heard the message. They've begun to make changes in the foods they choose and the ways these foods are cooked and served. Still, most people are eating too much fat and not enough fiber and fruits and vegetables. And people have questions about which choices to make. Do some of these questions sound familiar?

What can I eat to help stay healthy and lower cancer risk?

Experts agree that the best choice is a healthy, balanced diet that is low in fat, moderate in calories, and rich in fiber. It means:

- Eat lots of fruits and vegetables, grains, and beans.
- Include some lean meats and low-fat dairy products.
- Go easy on fats.

How can I do this easily? I want to eat right, but I don't want to give up a lot of foods that I like.

You don't have to change your whole life's eating habits. A few small actions can make a difference. Here are two examples:

- Switch to reduced- or nonfat salad dressing. Regular salad dressing has about 160 calories and 18 grams of fat in a modest 2-tablespoon serving!
- Next time you have toast, try whole wheat with jelly, fruit spread, or jam instead of white bread with butter. You'll cut back on fat, and you'll get more than twice the fiber.

✔ Quick Tip
**Try Small Amounts Of These
Low-Fat Treats**

Fig bars, vanilla wafers, ginger snaps, angel food cake, jelly beans, gum drops, hard candy, puddings made with low-fat (1 percent) or skim milk, nonfat frozen yogurt with a fruit topping, or fruit popsicles. Try pretzels or popcorn without butter or oil for an unsweetened treat.

Action Lists For Healthy Eating

The following information will show you how to make a few easy changes in the foods you choose. You will find three action lists that suggest new ways to choose and serve the foods you know and like. As you read through the lists, you may find that you already are following some of the suggestions. If so, try actions that are new for you. Start with two or three actions that you think you can do easily, and repeat them over time. They will soon become second nature, and you can add others from the lists.

Action List For Fat

Did you know there are four great reasons to eat less fat?

1. It can assist in weight loss or weight maintenance because you'll be eating fewer calories.

2. It can help reduce your risk of heart disease by reducing saturated fat, which will help lower blood cholesterol levels.

3. It may help reduce your risk of cancer.

4. Eating fewer high-fat foods means more room for fruits, vegetables, grains, and beans.

Here are some actions to get you started and keep you going.

• Use reduced-fat or nonfat salad dressings.

• Use nonfat or lower fat spreads, such as jelly or jam, fruit spread, apple butter, nonfat or reduced-calorie mayonnaise, nonfat margarine, or mustard.

✎ What's It Mean?

Phytochemicals: A chemical found in plants. Many phytochemicals are thought to reduce a person's risk of getting cancer.

Source: "Dictionary of Cancer Terms," National Cancer Institute, available at www.nci.nih.gov; cited December 2004.

- To top baked potatoes, use plain nonfat or low-fat yogurt, nonfat or reduced-fat sour cream, nonfat or low-fat cottage cheese, nonfat margarine, nonfat hard cheese, salsa, or vinegar.

- Use a little lemon juice, dried herbs, thinly sliced green onions, or a little salsa as a nonfat topping for vegetables or salads.

- Use small amounts of high-fat toppings. For example, use only 1 teaspoon butter or mayonnaise; 1 tablespoon sour cream; 1 tablespoon regular salad dressing.

- Switch to 1 percent or skim milk and other nonfat or lower fat dairy products (low-fat or nonfat yogurt, nonfat or reduced-fat sour cream).

- Cut back on cheese by using small (1 ounce) amounts on sandwiches and in cooking or use lower fat and fat-free cheeses (part-skim mozzarella, 1-percent cottage cheese, or nonfat hard cheese).

- Save french fries and other fried foods for special occasions; have a small serving; share with a friend.

- Save high-fat desserts (ice cream, pastries) for special occasions; have small amounts; share a serving with a friend.

- Choose small portions of lean meat, fish, and poultry; use low-fat cooking methods (baking, poaching, broiling); trim off all fat from meat and remove skin from poultry.

- Choose lower fat luncheon meats such as sliced turkey or chicken breast, lean ham, lean sliced beef.

Action List For Fruits And Vegetables

Did you know that there are four great reasons to eat more fruits and vegetables?

1. It is easy to do.

2. Almost all are low in calories and fat.

3. They are a good source of vitamins and minerals and provide fiber.

4. They may help reduce cancer risk.

    Here are some actions to get you started and keep you going.

    • Buy many kinds of fruits and vegetables when you shop, so you have
      plenty of choices, and you don't run out. Buy frozen, dried, and canned
      as well as fresh fruits and vegetables.

    • First use the fruits and vegetables that go bad easily (peaches, aspara-
      gus). Save hardier varieties (apples, acorn squash) or frozen and canned
      types for later in the week.

    • Use the salad bar to buy cut-up fruits/vegetables if you're in a hurry.

    • Keep a fruit bowl, small packs of applesauce, raisins, or other dried
      fruit on the kitchen counter or table.

    • Pack a piece of fruit or some cut-up vegetables in your backpack; carry
      moist Towelettes for easy cleanup.

    • Keep a bowl of cut-up vegetables on the top shelf of the refrigerator.

    • Add fruit to breakfast by drinking 6 ounces of 100 percent fruit juice
      or by having fruit on cereal.

    • Add fruits and vegetables to lunch by having them in soup, salad, or
      cut-up raw.

    • Add fruits and vegetables to dinner by microwaving or steaming veg-
      etables and having a special fruit dessert.

    • Increase portions when you serve vegetables and fruits. Season them
      the low-fat way with herbs, spices, lemon juice. If sauce is used, choose
      a nonfat or low-fat sauce.

    • Choose fruit for dessert. For a special dessert, try a fruit parfait with
      low-fat yogurt or sherbet topped with berries.

    • Add extra varieties of vegetables when you prepare soups, sauces, and
      casseroles (for example, grate carrot and zucchini into spaghetti sauce.)

- Once a week or more, try a low-fat meatless meal or main dish that features beans (tacos or burritos stuffed with pinto beans; chili with kidney beans; black beans over rice).

- Use beans as a dip for vegetables or filling for sandwiches.

- Make soup made from beans or peas—minestrone, split pea, black bean, or lentil (once a week or more).

- Try black-eyed peas or black beans as a vegetable side dish with meat or fish.

- Add beans to salads. Many salad bars feature kidney beans, three-bean salad, or chickpeas (garbanzo beans).

Action List For Whole Grains

Did you know that there are some great reasons to eat more whole grain breads and cereals?

1. They are low in fat.

2. They are good sources of fiber, vitamins, minerals, and protein.

3. They can be fixed and eaten in many ways.

✔ **Quick Tip**

What's a recommended serving size for meat? Experts suggest 3 ounces of cooked meat, which is the size of a deck of cards or a hamburger bun.

One ounce of cheese equals a 1 inch cube of hard cheese, 3 tablespoons of grated cheese, or 1/2 slices of wrapped cheese (brand differ, check label).

Here are some actions to get you started and keep you going.

- Choose whole grain varieties of bread, muffins, bagels, and rolls (whole wheat, bran, oatmeal, and multigrain).

- Choose a whole grain (oatmeal) variety when you have hot cereal, or a cold breakfast cereal that provides at least 4 grams of fiber per serving.

- Have whole-wheat varieties of pancakes or waffles.

- In recipes that call for flour, use at least half whole-wheat flour.

- For dinner at least twice a week, have whole-wheat noodles, brown rice, or bulgur (cracked wheat).

- Try higher fiber cracker varieties, such as whole rye crackers, whole grain flat bread, or multigrain crackers. Check the label to make sure you're choosing a low-fat variety.

✔ Quick Tip
Tips For Kids On Eating Well And Feeling Good About Yourself

It is no fun to worry all the time about how much you weigh, how much you eat, or whether you are thin. Here are some things you can do to be healthy and fit, have fun, and not feel bad about how you look!

- Eat when you are hungry. Stop eating when you are full.

- All foods can be part of healthy eating. There are no "good" or "bad" foods, so try to eat lots of different foods, including fruits, vegetables, and even sweets sometimes.

- When having a snack, try to eat different types. Sometimes raisins might be good; sometimes cheese, sometimes a cookie, sometimes carrot sticks or celery dipped in peanut butter.

- If you are sad or mad or have nothing to do, and you are not really hungry, find something to do other than eating. Often, talking with a friend or parent or teacher is helpful.

- Remember, kids and adults who exercise and stay active are healthier and better able to do what they want to do, no matter what they weigh or how they look.

- Try to find a sport (like basketball or soccer) or an activity (like dancing or karate) that you like and do it! Join a team, join the YMCA, and join in with a friend or practice by yourself. Just do it!

• Once a week or more, try a low-fat meatless meal or main dish that features whole grains (spinach lasagna, red beans over brown rice, brown rice and vegetable stir-fry).

• Good health, feeling good about yourself, and having fun go hand in hand. Try out different hobbies, like drawing, reading, playing music, or making things. See what you're good at and enjoy these things.

• Remind yourself that healthy bodies and happy people come in all sizes, and that no one body shape or body size is a healthy one or the right one for everybody.

• Some people believe that fat people are bad, sick, and out of control, while thin people are good, healthy, and in control. This is not true, and it is unfair and hurtful.

• Do not tease people about being too fat, too thin, too short, or too tall, and don't laugh at other people's jokes about fat (or thin) people or short (or tall) people. Teasing is unfair and it hurts.

• If you hear someone (your mom or dad, a sister or a friend) say they are too fat and need to go on a diet, tell them "Please don't, because dieting to lose weight is not healthy and no fun for kids or adults." Tell them you think they look great just the way they are. Tell them not to diet, but to eat a variety of foods and get some exercise. Tell them that being "thinner" is not the same as being healthier and happier."

• Appreciate yourself for all you are. Everyone should respect and like themselves, enjoy playing and being active, and eat a variety of healthy foods.

Chapter 35

What You Should Know About Sports Nutrition

What diet is best for athletes?

It's important that an athlete's diet provides the right amount of energy, the 50-plus nutrients the body needs, and adequate water. No single food or supplement can do this. A variety of foods are needed every day. But, just as there is more than one way to achieve a goal, there is more than one way to follow a nutritious diet.

Do the nutritional needs of athletes differ from non-athletes?

Competitive athletes, sedentary individuals, and people who exercise for health and fitness all need the same nutrients. However, because of the intensity of their sport or training program, some athletes have higher calorie and fluid requirements. Eating a variety of foods to meet increased calorie needs helps to ensure that the athlete's diet contains appropriate amounts of carbohydrate, protein, vitamins, and minerals.

About This Chapter: Text in this chapter is from "Questions Most Frequently Asked About Sports Nutrition," developed by the President's Council on Physical Fitness and Sports, a component of the U.S. Department of Health and Human Services (DHHS); available online at http://www.fitness.gov/faq.htm; cited January 2005.

♣ **It's A Fact!!**
Pre-Game FAQs

One student athlete swears he hits home runs every time he eats french fries at the pre-game meal. I thought high fat foods were not a high performance food so close to competition time. Should he continue this practice or should I encourage a different food choice?

It's true that high fat foods are not the best choice 2–3 hours before a competitive event. However, some athletes have "lucky" foods. These are foods that the athlete believes bring him or her luck before an athletic event. These foods carry with them a lot of psychological power. If you notice that the athlete does indeed perform better after consuming such a "lucky" food, then it's probably best to allow this practice to continue. A little education about what are high performance foods in general to consume together with the "lucky" food couldn't hurt.

I heard that drinking milk at the "pre-game" meal is not a good thing to do. Is this true?

Unless a particular athlete has an allergy to milk or is lactose intolerant, there is no reason to avoid 1% or skim milk. These are an excellent source of both carbohydrate and protein with very little or no fat. Having 8 ounces of skim or 1% milk or yogurt up to 2 hours before a competitive event can even help boost blood sugar (forms of carbohydrate) for the early minutes of the competition. The protein will kick in with additional fuel a little later.

We have our pre-game meal at 2:30 or 3 p.m., and the game starts at 7:00 p.m. Are we doing this right?

So far so good, but don't forget the pre-game snack about 2 hours before (around 5:00 p.m.). The snack should be about 250–350 calories, mostly carbohydrates, a little protein, and very little fat. A Power Bar, Boost, a bagel and jam, or cereal and skim milk are each good choices.

Source: Excerpted from "FAQs in Sports Nutrition." Reprinted with permission from the University of Massachusetts Amherst Center for Nutrition in Sport and Human Performance, © 2005.

Are there certain dietary guidelines athletes should follow?

Health and nutrition professionals recommend that 55–60% of the calories in our diet come from carbohydrate, no more than 30% from fat, and the remaining 10–15% from protein. While the exact percentages may vary slightly for some athletes based on their sport or training program, these guidelines will promote health and serve as the basis for a diet that will maximize performance.

How many calories do I need a day?

This depends on your age, body size, sport, and training program. For example, a 250-pound weight lifter needs more calories than a 98-pound gymnast does. Exercise or training may increase calorie needs by as much as 1,000 to 1,500 calories a day. The best way to determine if you're getting too few or too many calories is to monitor your weight. Keeping within your ideal competitive weight range means that you are getting the right amount of calories.

Which is better for replacing fluids—water or sports drinks?

Depending on how muscular you are, 55–70% of your body weight is water. Being "hydrated" means maintaining your body's fluid level. When you sweat, you lose water, which must be replaced if you want to perform your best. You need to drink fluids before, during, and after all workouts and events.

Whether you drink water or a sports drink is a matter of choice. However, if your workout or event lasts for more than 90 minutes, you may benefit from the carbohydrates provided by sports drinks. A sports drink that contains 15–18 grams of carbohydrate in every 8 ounces of fluid should be used. Drinks with a higher carbohydrate content will delay the absorption of water and may cause dehydration, cramps, nausea, or diarrhea. There are a variety of sports drinks on the market. Be sure to experiment with sports drinks during practice instead of trying them for the first time the day of an event.

What are electrolytes?

Electrolytes are nutrients that affect fluid balance in the body and are necessary for our nerves and muscles to function. Sodium and potassium are the two electrolytes most often added to sports drinks. Generally, electrolyte replacement is not needed during short bursts of exercise since sweat is approximately 99% water and less than 1% electrolytes. Water, in combination with a well-balanced diet, will restore normal fluid and electrolyte levels in the body. However, replacing electrolytes may be beneficial during continuous activity of longer than 2 hours, especially in a hot environment.

What do muscles use for energy during exercise?

Most activities use a combination of fat and carbohydrate as energy sources. How hard and how long you work out, your level of fitness, and your diet will affect the type of fuel your body uses. For short-term, high-intensity activities like sprinting, athletes rely mostly on carbohydrate for energy. During low-intensity exercises like walking, the body uses more fat for energy.

What are carbohydrates?

Carbohydrates are sugars and starches found in foods like breads, cereals, fruits, vegetables, pasta, milk, honey, syrups, and

✔ **Quick Tip**

- Tomato juice has more potassium than orange juice or a banana, and the salt in tomato juice can help keep an athlete with heavy sweat losses to stay better hydrated.

- Drinking tea and caffeinated coffee or soda within 2 hours of a meal will decrease the amount of iron the body is able to absorb from that meal.

- The first 15 minutes after strenuous activity are the most critical for replacing carbohydrates and building glycogen stores. Fruit juices rather than sports drinks pack more carbohydrate per ounce (with the exception of Gatorade, which was developed specifically for carbohydrate replacement).

- In post-competition recovery, alcohol consumption interferes with rehydration and the loading of carbohydrates in muscles (glycogen resynthesis), thus slowing recovery from strenuous activity and increasing risk of injury.

- Thick-crusted veggie pizza ordered with extra sauce, and only 1/2 the amount of cheese instead of regular pizza, provides more carbohydrate, potassium, and other nutrients for exercise recovery.

Source: Excerpted from "Quick Tips for Sports Nutrition." Reprinted with permission from the University of Massachusetts Amherst Center for Nutrition in Sport and Human Performance, © 2005.

table sugar. Carbohydrates are the preferred source of energy for your body. Regardless of origin, your body breaks down carbohydrates into glucose that your blood carries to cells to be used for energy. Carbohydrates provide 4 calories per gram, while fat provides 9 calories per gram. Your body cannot differentiate between glucose that comes from starches or sugars. Glucose from either source provides energy for working muscles.

Is it true that athletes should eat a lot of carbohydrates?

When you are training or competing, your muscles need energy to perform. One source of energy for working muscles is glycogen, which is made from carbohydrates and stored in your muscles. Every time you work out, you use some of your glycogen. If you don't consume enough carbohydrates, your glycogen stores become depleted, which can result in fatigue. Both sugars and starches are effective in replenishing glycogen stores.

When and what should I eat before I compete?

Performance depends largely on the foods consumed during the days and weeks leading up to an event. If you regularly eat a varied, carbohydrate-rich diet, you are in good standing and probably have ample glycogen stores to fuel activity. The purpose of the pre-competition meal is to prevent hunger and to provide the water and additional energy the athlete will need during competition. Most athletes eat 2 to 4 hours before their event. However, some athletes perform their best if they eat a small amount 30 minutes before competing, while others eat nothing for 6 hours beforehand. For many athletes, carbohydrate-rich foods serve as the basis of the meal. However, there is no magic pre-event diet. Simply choose foods and beverages that you enjoy and that don't bother your stomach. Experiment during the weeks before an event to see which foods work best for you.

Will eating sugary foods before an event hurt my performance?

In the past, athletes were warned that eating sugary foods before exercise could hurt performance by causing a drop in blood glucose levels. Recent studies, however, have shown that consuming sugar up to 30 minutes before an event does not diminish performance. In fact, evidence suggests that a sugar-containing pre-competition beverage or snack may improve performance during endurance workouts and events.

What is carbohydrate loading?

Carbohydrate loading is a technique used to increase the amount of glycogen in muscles. For five to seven days before an event, the athlete eats 10–12 grams of carbohydrate per kilogram body weight and gradually reduces the intensity of the workouts. (To find out how much you weigh in kilograms, simply divide your weight in pounds by 2.2.) The day before the event, the athlete rests and eats the same high-carbohydrate diet. Although carbohydrate loading may be beneficial for athletes participating in endurance sports, which require 90 minutes or more of non-stop effort, most athletes needn't worry about carbohydrate loading. Simply eating a diet that derives more than half of its calories from carbohydrates will do.

✔ **Quick Tip**
Best "Fast Food" Choices For Student Athletes

Beverages: Orange juice, low-fat/skim white or chocolate milk, lemonade.

Entrees: Pancakes, scrambled eggs, cereals, turkey, ham or roast beef sub, thick-crusted veggie pizza, char-broiled chicken sandwich, chicken fajita, baked potato, chili, soft taco (burrito) with rice and beans with either meat sauce or cheese or sour cream, plain hamburgers, pasta with tomato based sauce.

Extras: Bagel, English muffin with jelly, low-fat fruit yogurt, salad, salsa, barbecue sauce.

Omit: Butter, hashbrowns, bacon, sausage, French fries, special sauces, cheese sauces, mayonnaise, creamy dressings, tuna subs, and extra cheese on sandwiches.

Source: Excerpted from "Quick Tips for Sports Nutrition." Reprinted with permission from the University of Massachusetts Amherst Center for Nutrition in Sport and Human Performance, © 2005.

As an athlete, do I need to take extra vitamins and minerals?

Athletes need to eat about 1,800 calories a day to get the vitamins and minerals they need for good health and optimal performance. Since most athletes eat more than this amount, vitamin and mineral supplements are needed only in special situations. Athletes who follow vegetarian diets or who avoid an entire group of foods (for example, never drink milk) may need a supplement to make up for the vitamins and minerals not being supplied by food. A multivitamin-mineral pill that supplies 100% of the Recommended Dietary Allowance (RDA) will provide the nutrients needed. An athlete who frequently cuts back on calories, especially below the 1,800 calorie level, is not only at risk for inadequate vitamin and mineral intake, but also may not be getting enough carbohydrate. Since vitamins and minerals do not provide energy, they cannot replace the energy provided by carbohydrates.

Will extra protein help build muscle mass?

Many athletes, especially those on strength-training programs or who participate in power sports, are told that eating a ton of protein or taking protein supplements will help them gain muscle weight. However, the true secret to building muscle is training hard and consuming enough calories. While some extra protein is needed to build muscle, most American diets provide more than enough protein. Between 1.0 and 1.5 grams of protein per kilogram body weight per day is sufficient if your calorie intake is adequate and you're eating a variety of foods. For a 150-pound athlete, that represents 68–102 grams of protein a day.

Why is iron so important?

Hemoglobin, which contains iron, is the part of red blood cells that carries oxygen from the lungs to all parts of the body, including muscles. Since your muscles need oxygen to produce energy, if you have low iron levels in your blood, you may tire quickly. Symptoms of iron deficiency include fatigue, irritability, dizziness, headaches, and lack of appetite. Many times, however, there are no symptoms at all. A blood test is the best way to find out if your iron level is low. It is recommended that athletes have their hemoglobin levels checked once a year.

The RDA for iron is 15 milligrams a day for women and 10 milligrams a day for men. Red meat is the richest source of iron, but fish and poultry also are good sources. Fortified breakfast cereals, beans, and green leafy vegetables also contain iron. Our bodies absorb the iron found in animal products best.

Should I take an iron supplement?

Taking iron supplements will not improve performance unless an athlete is truly iron deficient. Too much iron can cause constipation, diarrhea, and nausea and may interfere with the absorption of other nutrients such as copper and zinc. Therefore, iron supplements should not be taken without proper medical supervision.

Why is calcium so important?

Calcium is needed for strong bones and proper muscle function. Dairy foods are the best source of calcium. However, studies show that many female athletes who are

---

✔ Quick Tip
Fuel Up For Fun

Whether you hit the court, the field, the track, the rink, or your back yard to get some physical activity, you'll need some fuel to keep you going! Here are some great snacks to munch on to keep your body moving and your stomach silent:

- Fresh veggies like carrots and celery sticks
- Snack-sized boxes of raisins
- Pretzels
- Low-fat yogurt
- Crackers—try graham crackers, animal crackers, or saltines
- Bagels
- Fig bars
- Fruit juice boxes (make sure you choose 100% pure fruit juice, or for an added boost, try orange juice with added calcium)
- Small packages of trail mix
- Fresh fruits such as bananas, oranges, grapes (try freezing your grapes for a new taste sensation), and berries

Source: Excerpted from "U R What U Eat," an information sheet developed by Centers for Disease Control and Prevention (CDC), a component of the U.S. Department of Health and Human Services (DHHS), April 2002; available online at http://www.bam.gov/fit4life/nofood_pr.htm.

trying to lose weight cut back on dairy products. Female athletes who don't get enough calcium may be at risk for stress fractures and, when they're older, osteoporosis. Young women between the ages of 11 and 24 need about 1,200 milligrams of calcium a day. After age 25, the recommended intake is 800 milligrams. Low-fat dairy products are a rich source of calcium and also are low in fat and calories.

Chapter 36

What's The Right Weight For My Height?

To get an accurate answer to this question, it's important to talk to a doctor who can assess you individually. Each person's body—especially if you're a growing teen—is different. Your age, your body type, your gender, where you are in your pubertal development, and a number of other factors need to be considered when evaluating your weight.

Weight alone doesn't necessarily tell you if you're overweight. People who weigh the same, for example, can have major differences in body composition (that is, the amounts of muscle, fat, and bone they have). Muscle weighs more than fat, which explains why someone with more muscles may weigh more than someone of the same size who doesn't have as much muscle. And it also helps to explain why some people lose inches when they start working out with weights but notice that the numbers on the scale either go up or stay the same.

Comparing your weight to your height is only one piece of information you can use in determining whether your body is healthy. And striving to be skinny like many actors and models often has less to do with being healthy

About This Chapter: This information was provided by TeensHealth, one of the largest resources online for medically reviewed health information written for parents, kids, and teens. For more articles like this one, visit www.TeensHealth.org, or www.KidsHealth.org. ©2004 The Nemours Center for Children's Health Media, a division of The Nemours Foundation.

than it does with feeling pressured to measure up to an unhealthy cultural ideal. Many fashion models, for example, are underweight, starving their bodies of much-needed nutrients to achieve a desired look.

How does puberty affect my height and weight?

Have you ever noticed how a friend you haven't seen in a while looks completely different after just a couple of months? Like your friend who was always the smallest guy in class but who came back from summer break looking like he was ready for the NBA!

He's not a freak of nature—in fact, his growth spurt is quite natural. During puberty, your body begins making hormones that spark physical changes, such as muscle growth in guys and weight gain in guys and girls. Once they start, the body changes of puberty will continue for several years. You can expect to grow a total of about 10 inches during puberty before you reach your full adult height.

How can I be sure I'm not overweight or underweight for my height?

If you're worried that you might be overweight or that you're not growing as fast as you should be, talk to your doctor. He or she will probably measure your height and weight over time and track the measurements on a growth chart to determine whether you're growing normally. Your doctor will also likely use these numbers to calculate your body mass index, or BMI. This measurement estimates how much body fat a person has and helps determine if that person's weight is right for his or her height.

✎ What's It Mean?

Nutrient: A chemical compound (such as protein, fat, carbohydrate, vitamins, or minerals) that make up foods. These compounds are used by the body to function and grow.

Source: "Dictionary of Cancer Terms," National Cancer Institute, available at www.nci.nih.gov; cited December 2004.

If there's a concern based on your height, weight, or BMI, your doctor may order X-rays of your bones to make sure they're maturing at the proper rate. Your doctor may also ask about your family background to find out if you've inherited traits that might make you taller, shorter, or a late bloomer (someone who develops later than your peers). The doctor can then put all this information together to decide whether you might have a weight or growth problem.

If your doctor determines that it would be healthy for you to lose weight, he or she will probably provide specific dietary and exercise recommendations based on your individual needs. Do not try to lose weight by using dangerous methods such as taking diet pills, making yourself vomit, or starving yourself. All of these things can keep you from getting the nutrients that you need to grow properly. If you try to lose weight in one of these ways, you could actually slow down your growth and sexual development.

> **☞ Remember!!**
> It's not a specific number on the scale that's important. It's having a healthy body—inside and out.

Most teens who weigh less than other teens their age are just fine. They may be going through puberty on a different schedule than some of their peers are, and their bodies may be growing and changing at a different rate. They will probably catch up in weight during their later teen years.

Chapter 37

Body Mass Index (BMI)

One of the biggest questions guys and girls have as they grow and develop is whether they're the right weight. One place to start is by learning about body mass index, or BMI, a calculation that estimates how much body fat a person has based on his or her weight and height. Although you can calculate BMI on your own, it's a good idea to ask a doctor or health professional to help you figure out what it means. BMI can be a good indicator of a person's body fat, but it doesn't always tell the full story.

What Is BMI?

The BMI formula uses height and weight measurements to come up with a number that can be plotted on a chart. The chart then tells a person whether he or she is underweight, average weight, at risk of becoming overweight, or overweight. There are different charts for males and females under the age of 20.

How Is BMI Measured?

During routine checkups, doctors typically record your height and weight. Your doctor may check your BMI as well.

About This Chapter: This information was provided by TeensHealth, one of the largest resources online for medically reviewed health information written for parents, kids, and teens. For more articles like this one, visit www.TeensHealth.org, or www.KidsHealth.org. © 2003 The Nemours Center for Children's Health Media, a division of The Nemours Foundation.

If you are calculating BMI on your own, it's important to get an accurate weight and height measurement. To calculate your BMI, follow these steps:

1. Write down your weight in pounds.

2. Divide your weight by your height in inches.

3. Divide the answer from step 2 by your height in inches.

4. Then multiply the answer from step 3 by 703.

5. The resulting answer is your BMI.

To calculate your BMI using metric measurements, follow these steps:

1. Write down your weight in kilograms.

2. Divide your weight by your height in centimeters.

3. Divide the answer from step 2 by your height in centimeters.

4. Then multiply the answer from step 3 by 10,000.

5. The resulting answer is your BMI.

With this number in hand, a doctor can determine a person's percentile on a BMI chart. A percentile is not the same as a percent; it's a means of comparing one individual to a group of people. A person's BMI percentile indicates how his or her measurements compare to other guys or girls in the same age group. Each BMI chart has eight percentile lines for 5th, 10th, 25th, 50th, 75th, 90th, and 95th percentiles. A teen whose BMI is at the 50th percentile is close to the average of the population. A teen above the 95th percentile is considered overweight because 95% of the population weighs less than he or she does. A teen below the 5th percentile is considered underweight because 95% of the population weighs more.

What Does BMI Tell Us?

In addition to using BMI to assess a person's current weight status, doctors can also use a person's BMI results, recorded over time, to track whether the person may be at risk for becoming overweight. Spotting this risk can be

helpful because the person can then make changes in diet and exercise before he or she goes on to develop a weight problem.

People don't like looking overweight, but they also should be concerned about how it can affect their health. People who are overweight
during their teen years increase their risk of developing health problems,
such as diabetes and high blood pressure. Being overweight as a teen also
makes a person more likely to be overweight as an adult. And adults who
are overweight may develop other serious health conditions, such as heart
disease.

Putting BMI In Perspective

BMI is a good indicator of body fat, but it's not perfect. For example, it's
normal for girls and guys to gain weight rapidly and show increases in BMI
during puberty. A doctor can help assess whether the weight gain is a normal
part of maturation or if it warrants concern. Also, a person can have a high
BMI because they have a large frame or a lot of muscle (like a bodybuilder)

✎ What's It Mean?

Diabetes: A disease in which the body does not properly control the amount
of sugar in the blood. As a result, the level of sugar in the blood is too high.
This disease occurs when the body does not produce enough insulin or does
not use it properly. [1]

High Blood Pressure (Hypertension): A condition present when blood flows
through the blood vessels with a force greater than normal. High blood pressure can strain the heart, damage blood vessels, and increase the risk of heart
attack, stroke, kidney problems, and death. [2]

Source: [1] "Dictionary of Cancer Terms," National Cancer Institute, available at www.nci.nih.gov; cited December 2004. [2] "Diabetes Dictionary,"
National Institute of Diabetes and Digestive and Kidney Diseases, available
at www.diabetes.niddk.nih.gov, 2003.

instead of excess fat. Likewise, a small person with a small frame may have a normal BMI, but might have too much body fat.

Heredity also plays a role in body shape and what a person weighs. People from different races, ethnic groups, and nationalities tend to have different body fat distribution and body composition. It's also true that unhealthy habits can be passed down through generations. If your family eats a lot of high-fat foods or snacks or doesn't get much exercise, there's a good chance you'll act the same. The good news is these habits can be changed for the better. Doing so can help a person reach a healthy weight and BMI. But before making any major changes, it's a good idea to talk with your doctor.

Chapter 38

How Can I Lose Weight Safely?

Weight loss is a tricky topic. Lots of people are unhappy with their present weight, but most aren't sure how to change it—and many would be better off staying where they are. You may want to weigh less or more or even look like someone else, but those goals may not be healthy or realistic for you. You may look at magazines, advertisements, and TV and wish you looked more like the models and actors do, but that's a sure way to set yourself up for disappointment. No magical diet or pill will make you look like someone you weren't meant to be. So what should you do about weight control?

Being healthy is really about being at a weight that is right for you. The best way to find out if you are at a healthy weight or if you need to lose or gain weight is to talk to a doctor or dietitian. He or she can compare your weight with healthy norms to help you set realistic goals. If it turns out that you would benefit from weight loss then you can follow a few of the simple suggestions listed below to get started.

Weight management is about long-term success. People who lose weight quickly by crash dieting or other extreme measures usually gain back all (and

About This Chapter: This information was provided by TeensHealth, one of the largest resources online for medically reviewed health information written for parents, kids, and teens. For more articles like this one, visit www.TeensHealth.org, or www.KidsHealth.org. © 2002 The Nemours Center for Children's Health Media, a division of The Nemours Foundation. Text reviewed December 2004.

often more) of the pounds they lost because they haven't permanently changed their habits. Therefore, the best weight management strategies are those that you can maintain for a lifetime. That's a long time, so we'll try to keep these suggestions as easy as possible!

Watch your drinks. It's amazing how many extra calories can be lurking in the sodas, juices, and other drinks that you take in every day. Simply cutting out a couple of cans of soda or switching to diet soda can save you 360 calories or more each day. Drink lots of water or other sugar-free drinks to quench your thirst and stay away from sugary juices and sodas. Switching from whole to nonfat or low-fat milk is also a good idea.

> ✔ **Quick Tip**
>
> **Make it a family affair.** Ask your mom or dad to lend help and support and to make dietary or lifestyle changes that might benefit the whole family, if possible. Teens who have the support of their families tend to have better results with their weight management programs. But remember, you should all work together in a friendly and helpful way—making weight loss into a competition is a recipe for disaster!

Get moving. You may find that you don't need to give up calories as much as you need to get off your behind. And don't get stuck in the rut of thinking you have to play a team sport or take an aerobics class. Try a variety of activities from hiking to cycling to rowing until you find ones you like. Not a jock? Find other ways to fit activity into your day: walk to school, jog up and down the stairs a couple of times before your morning shower, turn off the tube and help your parents in the garden, or take a stroll past your crush's house—anything that gets you moving. Your goal should be to work up to 30 to 60 minutes of aerobic exercise at least three to five times a week, but it's fine to start out by simply taking a few turns around the block before bed. This may also help you to avoid becoming a TV, video game, or Internet junkie!

Start small. Small changes are a lot easier to stick with than drastic ones. Try reducing the size of the portions you eat and giving up regular soda for a week. Once you have that down, start gradually introducing healthier foods and exercise into your life.

Stop eating when you're full. Lots of people eat when they're bored, lonely, or stressed, or keep eating long after they're full out of habit. Try to pay attention as you eat and stop when you're full. Slowing down can help because it takes about 20 minutes for your brain to recognize how much is in your stomach. Sometimes taking a break before going for seconds can keep you from eating another serving. Avoid eating when you feel upset or bored—try to find something else to do instead (a walk around the block or a trip to the gym are good alternatives). Many people find it's helpful to keep a diary of what they eat and when. Reviewing the diary later can help them identify the emotions they have when they overeat or whether they have unhealthy habits. A registered dietitian can give you pointers on how to do this.

Eat less more often. Many people find that eating a couple of small snacks throughout the day helps them to make healthy choices at meals. Stick a couple of healthy snacks (carrot sticks, a low-fat granola bar, pretzels, or a piece of fruit) in your backpack so that you can have one or two snacks during the day. Adding healthy snacks to your three squares and eating smaller portions when you sit down to dinner can help you to cut calories without feeling deprived.

Five-a-day keeps the pounds away. Ditch the junk food and dig out the fruits and veggies! Five servings of fruits and veggies aren't just a good idea to help you lose weight—they'll help keep your heart and the rest of your body healthy. Other suggestions for eating well: replace white bread with whole wheat, trade your sugary sodas for lots of water and a few cups of low-fat milk, and make sure you eat a healthy breakfast. Having low-fat cereal and milk and a piece of fruit is a much better idea than inhaling a donut as you run to the bus stop or eating no breakfast at all! A registered dietitian can give you lots of other snack and menu ideas.

Avoid fad or prepackaged diets. If we were meant to eat from cans, they'd grow on trees. It's never a good idea to trade meals for shakes or to give up a food group in the hope that you'll lose weight—we all need a variety of foods to stay healthy. Stay away from fad diets because you're still growing and need to make sure you get proper nutrients. Avoid diet pills (even the over-the-counter or herbal variety). They can be dangerous to your health; besides, there's no evidence that they help keep weight off over the long term.

Don't banish certain foods. Don't tell yourself you'll never again eat your absolutely favorite peanut butter chocolate ice cream or a bag of chips from the vending machine at school. Making these foods forbidden is sure to make you want them even more. Besides, you need to have some fat in your diet to stay healthy, so giving up all fatty foods all the time isn't a good idea anyway. The key to long-term success is making healthy choices most of the time. If you want a piece of cake at a party, go for it! But munch on the carrots rather than the chips to balance it out later in the evening.

> **☞ Remember!!**
> Try to remember that losing weight isn't going to make you a better person—and it won't magically change your life. It's a good idea to maintain a healthy weight because it's just that: healthy.

Forgive yourself. So you were going to have one cracker with spray cheese on it and the next thing you know the can's pumping air and the box is empty? Drink some water, brush your teeth, and move on. Everyone who's ever tried to lose weight has found it challenging. When you slip up, the best idea is to get right back on track and don't look back. Avoid telling yourself that you'll get back on track tomorrow or next week or after New Year's. Start now.

Chapter 39

Is A Vegetarian Diet Right For Me?

"What's for dinner?"

Have you ever noticed how some people will answer this question? They'll say, "We're having hamburgers," or "We're having fried chicken." Dinner is often meatloaf or salmon, pork chops or steak. Because meat, poultry, and fish traditionally are the focus of meals, some people think dinner just wouldn't seem right without a big chunk of protein on the table—with a vegetable and a salad filling secondary slots.

For teens like Danielle, though, that attitude toward food is a thing of the past. For more than half her life, this 17-year-old has been a vegetarian. Danielle has no intention of reverting to her former eating habits. So what made her choose this way of life, when it seems that so many people around her are chowing on Big Macs?

Vegetarian Basics

For much of the world, vegetarianism is largely a matter of economics—meat costs a lot more than, say, beans or rice. As such, meat becomes a special-occasion dish (if it's eaten at all). Even where meat is more plentiful, it's still

About This Chapter: This information was provided by TeensHealth, one of the largest resources online for medically reviewed health information written for parents, kids, and teens. For more articles like this one, visit www.TeensHealth.org, or www.KidsHealth.org. © 2003 The Nemours Center for Children's Health Media, a division of The Nemours Foundation.

used in moderation, often providing a side note to a meal rather than taking center stage.

In countries such as the United States where meat is not as expensive, other factors are usually associated with vegetarianism. Parental preferences, religious beliefs, lifestyle factors, and health issues are among the most common reasons for choosing to be a vegetarian. However, many teens like Danielle choose a vegetarian diet out of concern over animal rights or the environment. Of course, lots of people have more than one reason for their vegetarian diet.

Just as there are multiple explanations for a vegetarian diet, there is also more than one way to be a vegetarian, based on the foods a person does or doesn't eat. A semi-vegetarian, for example, eats fish and maybe a small amount of poultry along with the vegetables, fruits, grains, legumes, seeds, and nuts of a standard vegetarian diet. A pesci-vegetarian goes a step further and eats fish, but not poultry. A lacto-ovo vegetarian eats dairy products and eggs with the usual fare, but excludes meat, fish, and poultry. It follows, then, that a lacto vegetarian eats dairy products but not eggs, whereas an ovo vegetarian eats eggs but not dairy products.

> ✎ **What's It Mean?**
>
> Macrobiotic Diet: A diet made up of mostly beans and whole grains.
>
> —SAL

A more strict vegetarian diet is vegan (pronounced: vee-gun or vee-jan), or total vegetarian. Not only are eggs and dairy products excluded from this diet, but also animal by-products like honey and gelatin. Some macrobiotic diets fall into the vegan category. It is important to note, though, that a macrobiotic diet can be very restrictive and may lead to nutritional deficiencies. Teens who want to follow a macrobiotic diet need to be careful that they get enough of the nutrients their growing bodies need, particularly protein and calcium. They should begin such a diet only with the help of a registered dietitian.

Are These Diets OK For Teens?

In the past, vegetarians were sometimes viewed with suspicion. Choosing not to eat meat or other foods was considered strange and even un-American. Times and attitudes have changed dramatically, however. Vegetarians are still a minority in the United States, but a large and growing one. The American Dietetic Association (ADA) has officially endorsed vegetarianism, stating "appropriately planned vegetarian diets are healthful, are nutritionally adequate, and provide health benefits in the prevention and treatment of certain diseases."

So what does this mean for teens? If you're already a vegetarian, or are thinking of becoming one, it means that you're in good company. There are more choices in the supermarket than ever before, and an increasing number of restaurants and schools are providing vegetarian options—way beyond a basic peanut butter and jelly sandwich.

If you're choosing a vegetarian diet, the most important thing you can do is to educate yourself. That's why the ADA says that a vegetarian diet needs to be "appropriately planned." Simply dropping certain foods from your diet isn't the way to go if you're interested in maintaining good health, a high energy level, and strong muscles and bones.

Vegetarians have to be careful to include the following key nutrients because they may be lacking in a vegetarian diet: iron, calcium, protein, vitamins D and B_{12}, and zinc. If meat, fish, dairy products, and/or eggs are not going to be part of your diet, you'll need to know how to get enough of these nutrients, or you may need to take a daily multiple vitamin and mineral supplement.

Here are some suggestions:

Iron: Sea vegetables like nori, wakame, and dulse are very high in iron. Less exotic but still good options are iron-fortified breakfast cereals, legumes (chickpeas, lentils, and baked beans), soybeans and tofu, dried fruit (raisins and figs), pumpkin seeds, broccoli, and blackstrap molasses. Eating these foods with a food high in vitamin C (citrus fruits and juices, tomatoes, and broccoli) will help you to better absorb the iron. Girls need to be particularly concerned about getting adequate iron because some iron is lost during menstruation. Some girls who are vegetarians may not get adequate iron from vegetable sources and require a daily supplement. Check with your doctor about your own iron needs.

Calcium: Milk and yogurt are tops if you're eating dairy products; otherwise, tofu, fortified soy milk, calcium-fortified orange juice, green leafy vegetables, and dried figs are excellent choices. Remember that as a teen you're building up your bones for the rest of your life. Because women have a greater risk for getting osteoporosis (weak bones) as adults, it's particularly important for them to make sure they get enough calcium. Again, taking a supplement may be necessary to ensure this.

Vitamin D: Cow's milk and sunshine are tops on the list for this vitamin, which you need to get calcium into your bones. Vegans can try fortified soy milk and fortified breakfast cereals, but they may need a supplement that includes vitamin D, especially during the winter months. Everyone should have some exposure to the sun to help the body produce vitamin D.

Protein: Some people believe that vegetarians must combine incomplete plant proteins in one meal—like red beans and rice—to make the type of complete proteins found in meat. We now know that it's not that complicated. Current recommendations are that vegetarians eat a wide variety of foods during the course of a day. Eggs and dairy products are good sources of protein, but also try nuts, peanut butter, tofu, beans, seeds, soy milk, grains, cereals, and vegetables to get all the protein your body needs.

Vitamin B_{12}: B_{12} is an essential vitamin found only in animal products, including eggs and dairy. Fortified soy milk and fortified breakfast cereals also have this important vitamin. It's hard to get enough vitamin B_{12} in your diet if you are vegan, so a supplement may be needed.

Zinc: If you're not eating dairy foods, make sure fortified cereals, dried beans, nuts, and soy products like tofu and tempeh are part of your diet so you can meet your daily requirement for this important mineral.

In addition to vitamins and minerals, vegetarians need to keep an eye on their total intake of calories and fat. Vegetarian diets tend to be high in fiber and low in fat and calories. That may be good for people who need to lose weight or lower their cholesterol but it can be a problem for kids and teens who are still growing and people who are already at a healthy weight. Diets that are high in fiber tend to be more filling, and as a result strict vegetarians may feel full before they've eaten enough calories to keep their bodies healthy and strong. It's a good idea to let your doctor know that you're a vegetarian so that he or she can keep an eye on your growth and make sure you're still getting adequate amounts of calories and fat.

Getting Some Guidance

When Danielle's mom knew that she was serious about becoming a vegetarian, she made an appointment for Danielle to talk with a registered dietitian. The dietitian and Danielle went over lists of foods and recipe ideas that would give her the nutrients she needs. They discussed ways to prevent conditions such as iron-deficiency anemia that Danielle might be at an increased risk of developing. And whenever Danielle sees her family doctor, the doctor reminds her to eat many different kinds of foods each day and to get enough protein and iron.

> **☞ Remember!!**
> Remember that it's important to eat a wide variety of foods, and to try out new foods, too—regardless of whether you choose a vegetarian way of life.

Danielle also tries to remember to take a daily standard multivitamin, just in case she's missed getting enough vitamins or minerals that day.

Tips For Eating Out

Danielle admits that eating out can be difficult sometimes, but because she does eat fish, she can usually find something suitable on a restaurant menu. If not, she opts for salad and an appetizer or two. Even fast food places sometimes have vegetarian choices, such as bean tacos and burritos, veggie burgers made from soybeans, and soy cheese pizza.

Because both she and her sister are vegetarians, Danielle's family rarely eats red meat anymore. Her mom serves salmon frequently, and Danielle eats a lot of pasta, along with plenty of vegetables, grains, and fruits. Danielle is also psyched about some of the vegetarian products now available in the grocery store. The veggie burgers, hot dogs, and chicken substitutes taste very much like the real thing. She especially likes the ground soy "beef" that makes a great stand-in for ground beef in foods like tacos and spaghetti sauce.

Chapter 40

Fitness Fundamentals

Making A Commitment

The decision to carry out a physical fitness program cannot be taken lightly. It requires a lifelong commitment of time and effort. Exercise must become one of those things that you do without question, like bathing and brushing your teeth. Unless you are convinced of the benefits of fitness and the risks of unfitness, you will not succeed.

Patience is essential. Don't try to do too much too soon and don't quit before you have a chance to experience the rewards of improved fitness. You can't regain in a few days or weeks what you have lost in years of sedentary living, but you can get it back if your persevere. And the prize is worth the price.

In this chapter, you will find the basic information you need to begin and maintain a personal physical fitness program. These guidelines are intended for the average healthy teen. It tells you what your goals should be and how often, how long, and how hard you must exercise to achieve them. It also

About This Chapter: Text in this chapter is from *Fitness Fundamentals: Guidelines for Personal Exercise Programs*, developed by the President's Council on Physical Fitness and Sports, a component of the U.S. Department of Health and Human Services (DHHS); available online at http://www.fitness.gov/fitness.html; cited September 2004. Reviewed by Dr. David A. Cooke, MD, Diplomate, American Board of Internal Medicine, in 2005.

✔ Quick Tip

Every person can be active and improve physical fitness. By using the information in this chapter, you can gain fitness and improve your physical capabilities. With determination, work, and commitment, you will improve your physical abilities. You can improve your fitness, even if you are already active.

When beginning a fitness program it is important to do the correct amount of work. If you try to do too much work too soon, you might hurt or injure yourself. Getting in shape requires time and the right amount of effort. When exercising, your effort should be challenging, but not painful. If you feel too much pain or exhaustion, you should ease off. As you get in better shape, your effort will improve.

Being fit and healthy means performing exercises that will improve endurance, flexibility, and strength. There are many advantages to trying to be active in ways that improves these elements of fitness. People who are active are healthier, feel better, and perform better in school and in daily activities.

When you make exercise an important part of your day, you will begin to see the benefits. Keep a daily log of your activity. This should include time spent walking, biking, swimming, or running. Many times it is fun and rewarding to include your friends and family members in your physical activities. You can try skating, playing active games or other fun activities with friends or family members. Oftentimes you will help each other to continue to be active.

Frequently people say that they do not have enough time to be active. Try to set aside a specific time of day to be active. If you cannot do this, try to be active by watching less television, limiting your time spent on a computer, or playing fewer video games. The most important aspect is making the commitment to being active and healthy. Try your best to be active every day, and after a period of time, you will begin to see the benefits.

Source: Excerpted from *Get Fit: A Handbook For Youth Ages 6-17*, developed by the President's Council on Physical Fitness and Sports, a component of the U.S. Department of Health and Human Services (DHHS), August 2001; available online at http://www.fitness.gov/getfit.pdf.

includes information that will make your workouts easier, safer, and more satisfying. The rest is up to you.

Checking Your Health

People under 35 and in good health don't need to see a doctor before beginning an exercise program. Some conditions, however, may indicate a need for medical clearance. They are:

- High blood pressure,
- Heart trouble,
- Family history of early stroke or heart attack deaths,
- Frequent dizzy spells,
- Extreme breathlessness after mild exertion,
- Arthritis or other bone problems,
- Severe muscular, ligament or tendon problems, and
- Other known or suspected disease.

Vigorous exercise involves minimal health risks for persons in good health or those following a doctor's advice. Habitual inactivity and obesity present far greater risks.

Defining Fitness

Physical fitness is to the human body what fine-tuning is to an engine. It enables us to perform up to our potential. Fitness can be described as a condition that helps us look, feel, and do our best. More specifically, it is the ability to perform daily tasks vigorously and alertly, with energy left over for enjoying leisure-time activities and meeting emergency demands. It is the ability to endure, to bear up, to withstand stress, to carry on in circumstances where an unfit person could not continue, and is a major basis for good health and well being.

Physical fitness involves the performance of the heart and lungs, and the muscles of the body. And, since what we do with our bodies also affects what we can do with our minds, fitness influences, to some degree, qualities such as mental alertness and emotional stability.

As you undertake your fitness program, it's important to remember that fitness is an individual quality that varies from person to person. It is influenced by age, sex, heredity, personal habits, exercise and eating practices. You can't do anything about the first three factors. However, it is within your power to change and improve the others where needed.

Knowing The Basics

Physical fitness is most easily understood by examining its components, or "parts." There is widespread agreement that these four components are basic:

- **Cardiorespiratory endurance:** The ability to deliver oxygen and nutrients to tissues, and to remove wastes, over sustained periods of time. Long runs and swims are among the methods employed in measuring this component.

- **Muscular strength:** The ability of a muscle to exert force for a brief period of time. Upper-body strength, for example, can be measured by various weight-lifting exercises.

- **Muscular endurance:** The ability of a muscle, or a group of

✎ What's It Mean?

Carbohydrate: A sugar molecule. Carbohydrates can be simple, such as glucose, or complex, such as starch. [1]

Ligament: Shiny, flexible bands of fibrous tissue connecting together articular extremities of bones. [2]

Nutrient: A chemical compound (such as protein, fat, carbohydrate, vitamins, or minerals) that make up foods. These compounds are used by the body to function and grow. [1]

Protein: A molecule made up of amino acids that are needed for the body to function properly. Proteins are the basis of body structures such as skin and hair and of substances such as enzymes and antibodies. [1]

Tendons: Fibrous bands or cords of connective tissue at the ends of muscle fibers that serve to attach the muscles to bones and other structures. [2]

Source: [1] "Dictionary of Cancer Terms," National Cancer Institute, available at www.nci.nih.gov; cited December 2004. [2] "Genetics Home Reference Glossary," a service of the U.S. National Library of Medicine, available at www.ghr .nlm.nih.gov, 2004.

muscles, to sustain repeated contractions or to continue applying force against a fixed object. Pushups are often used to test endurance of arm and shoulder muscles.

- **Flexibility:** The ability to move joints and use muscles through their full range of motion.

Body composition is often considered a component of fitness. It refers to the makeup of the body in terms of lean mass (muscle, bone, vital tissue and organs) and fat mass. An optimal ratio of fat to lean mass is an indication of fitness, and the right types of exercises will help you decrease body fat and increase or maintain muscle mass.

A Workout Schedule

How often, how long, and how hard you exercise, and what kinds of exercises you do, should be determined by what you are trying to accomplish. Your goals, your present fitness level, age, health, skills, interest, and convenience are among the factors you should consider. For example, an athlete training for high-level competition would follow a different program than a person whose goals are good health and the ability to meet school, work, and recreational needs.

Your exercise program should include something from each of the four basic fitness components described previously. Each workout should begin with a warmup and end with a cooldown. As a general rule, space your workouts throughout the week and avoid consecutive days of hard exercise.

Here are the amounts of activity necessary for the average healthy person to maintain a minimum level of overall fitness. Included are some of the popular exercises for each category.

- **Warmup:** 5–10 minutes of exercise such as walking, slow jogging, knee lifts, arm circles or trunk rotations. Low intensity movements that simulate movements to be used in the activity can also be included in the warmup.

- **Muscular strength:** A minimum of two 20-minute sessions per week that include exercises for all the major muscle groups. Lifting weights is the most effective way to increase strength.

- **Muscular endurance:** At least three 30-minute sessions each week that include exercises such as calisthenics, pushups, situps, pullups, and weight training for all the major muscle groups.

- **Cardiorespiratory endurance:** At least three 20-minute bouts of continuous aerobic (activity requiring oxygen) rhythmic exercise each week. Popular aerobic conditioning activities include brisk walking, jogging, swimming, cycling, rope jumping, rowing, cross-country skiing, and some continuous action games like racquetball and handball.

- **Flexibility:** 10-12 minutes of daily stretching exercises performed slowly, without a bouncing motion. This can be included after a warmup or during a cooldown.

- **Cooldown:** A minimum of 5-10 minutes of slow walking, low-level exercise, combined with stretching.

A Matter Of Principle

The keys to selecting the right kinds of exercises for developing and maintaining each of the basic components of fitness are found in these principles:

☞ Remember!!

Physical fitness is made up of many parts. When you are physically fit you have the energy and strength to perform daily activities without getting tired. Also, you have the energy to participate in leisure and recreation activities. When you are fit you have a strong heart, lungs, and muscles. Being fit benefits your daily activities and makes it easier to meet daily demands. Fitness also improves your mental health and your ability to cope with stressful events or occurrences. Being fit will help you be successful at recreational activities, school, sports, and work. The time to begin being fit is now! Teens who are physically active and eat correctly become healthier and more active adults.

- **Specificity:** Pick the right kind of activities to affect each component. Strength training results in specific strength changes. Also, train for the specific activity you're interested in. For example, optimal swimming performance is best achieved when the muscles involved in swimming are trained for the movements required. It does not necessarily follow that a good runner is a good swimmer.

- **Overload:** Work hard enough, at levels that are vigorous and long enough to overload your body above its resting level, to bring about improvement.

- **Regularity:** You can't hoard physical fitness. At least three balanced workouts a week are necessary to maintain a desirable level of fitness.

- **Progression:** Increase the intensity, frequency, and/or duration of activity over periods of time in order to improve.

Some activities can be used to fulfill more than one of your basic exercise requirements. For example, in addition to increasing cardiorespiratory endurance, running builds muscular endurance in the legs, and swimming develops the arm, shoulder, and chest muscles. If you select the proper activities, it is possible to fit parts of your muscular endurance workout into your cardiorespiratory workout and save time.

Measuring Your Heart Rate

Heart rate is widely accepted as a good method for measuring intensity during running, swimming, cycling, and other aerobic activities. Exercise that doesn't raise your heart rate to a certain level and keep it there for 20 minutes won't contribute significantly to cardiovascular fitness.

The heart rate you should maintain is called your target heart rate. There are several ways of arriving at this figure. One of the simplest is maximum heart rate (220 - age) x 70%. Thus, the target heart rate for a 15 year-old would be 144.

Some methods for figuring the target rate take individual differences into consideration. Here is one of them:

- Subtract age from 220 to find maximum heart rate.

- Subtract resting heart rate (see below) from maximum heart rate to determine heart rate reserve.

- Take 70% of heart rate reserve to determine heart rate raise.

- Add heart rate raise to resting heart rate to find target rate.

Resting heart rate should be determined by taking your pulse after sitting quietly for five minutes. When checking heart rate during a workout, take your pulse within five seconds after interrupting exercise because it starts to go down once you stop moving. Count pulse for 10 seconds and multiply by six to get the per-minute rate.

Controlling Your Weight

The key to weight control is keeping energy intake (food) and energy output (physical activity) in balance. When you consume only as many calories as your body needs, your weight will usually remain constant. If you take in more calories than your body needs, you will put on excess fat. If you expend more energy than you take in, you will burn excess fat.

Exercise plays an important role in weight control by increasing energy output, calling on stored calories for extra fuel. Recent studies show that not only does exercise increase metabolism during a workout, but it causes your metabolism to stay increased for a period of time after exercising, allowing you to burn more calories.

How much exercise is needed to make a difference in your weight depends on the amount and type of activity, and on how much you eat. Aerobic exercise burns body fat. A medium-sized adult would have to walk more than 30 miles to burn up 3,500 calories, the equivalent of one pound of fat. Although that may seem like a lot, you don't have to walk the 30 miles all at once. Walking a mile a day for 30 days will achieve the same result, providing you don't increase your food intake to negate the effects of walking.

If you consume 100 calories a day more than your body needs, you will gain approximately 10 pounds in a year. You could take that weight off, or keep it off, by doing 30 minutes of moderate exercise daily. The combination of exercise and diet offers the most flexible and effective approach to weight control.

Since muscle tissue weighs more than fat tissue, and exercise develops muscle to a certain degree, your bathroom scale won't necessarily tell you whether or not you are fat. Well-muscled individuals, with relatively little body fat, invariably are overweight according to standard weight charts. If you are doing a regular program of strength training, your muscles will increase in weight, and possibly your overall weight will increase. Body composition is a better indicator of your condition than body weight.

Lack of physical activity causes muscles to get soft, and if food intake is not decreased, added body weight is almost always fat. Once-active people, who continue to eat as they always have after settling into sedentary lifestyles, tend to suffer from "creeping obesity."

Clothing

All exercise clothing should be loose fitting to permit freedom of movement, and should make the wearer feel comfortable and self-assured.

As a general rule, you should wear lighter clothes than temperatures might indicate. Exercise generates great amounts of body heat. Light-colored clothing that reflects the sun's rays is cooler in the summer, and dark clothes are warmer in winter. When the weather is very cold, it's better to wear several layers of light clothing than one or two heavy layers. The extra layers help trap heat, and it's easy to shed one of them if you become too warm.

In cold weather, and in hot, sunny weather, it's a good idea to wear something on your head. Wool watch or ski caps are recommended for winter wear, and some form of tennis or sailor's hat, that provides shade and can be soaked in water, is good for summer.

Never wear rubberized or plastic clothing. Such garments interfere with the evaporation of perspiration and can cause body temperature to rise to dangerous levels.

The most important item of equipment for the runner is a pair of sturdy, properly-fitting running shoes. Training shoes with heavy, cushioned soles and arch supports are preferable to flimsy sneakers and light racing flats.

✔ Quick Tip

10 Tips To Healthy Eating And Physical Activity For You

1. Start your day with breakfast. Breakfast fills your "empty tank" to get you going after a long night without food. And it can help you do better in school. Easy to prepare breakfasts include cold cereal with fruit and low-fat milk, whole wheat toast with peanut butter, yogurt with fruit, whole grain waffles, or even last night's pizza!

2. Get moving. It's easy to fit physical activities into your daily routine. Walk, bike, or jog to see friends. Take a 10-minute activity break every hour while you read, do homework, or watch TV. Climb stairs instead of taking an escalator or elevator. Try to do these things for a total of 30 minutes every day.

3. Snack smart. Snacks are a great way to refuel. Choose snacks from different food groups—a glass of low-fat milk and a few graham crackers, an apple or celery sticks with peanut butter and raisins, or some dry cereal. If you eat smart at other meals, cookies, chips, and candy are OK for occasional snacking.

4. Work up a sweat. Vigorous workouts—when you're breathing hard and sweating—help your heart pump better, give you more energy and help you look and feel best. Start with a warmup that stretches your muscles. Include 20 minutes of aerobic activity, such as running, jogging, or dancing. Follow up with activities that help make you stronger such as pushups or lifting weights. Then cool down with more stretching and deep breathing.

5. Balance your food choices—don't eat too much of any one thing. You don't have to give up foods like hamburgers, french fries, and ice cream to eat healthy. You just have to be smart about how often and how much of them you eat. Your body needs nutrients like protein, carbohydrates, fat, and many different vitamins and minerals such as vitamins C and A, iron and calcium from a variety of foods. Balancing food choices from the various food groups and checking out the Nutrition Facts Panel on food labels will help you get all these nutrients.

6. Get fit with friends or family. Being active is much more fun with friends or family. Encourage others to join you and plan one special physical activity event, like a bike ride or hiking, with a group each week.

7. Eat more grains, fruits, and vegetables. These foods give you carbohydrates for energy, plus vitamins, minerals, and fiber. Besides, they taste good! Try breads such as whole wheat, bagels, and pita. Spaghetti and oatmeal are also in the grain group. Bananas, strawberries, and melons are some great-tasting fruits. Try vegetables raw, on a sandwich or salad.

8. Join in physical activities at school. Whether you take a physical education class or do other physical activities at school, such as intramural sports, structured activities are a sure way to feel good, look good, and stay physically fit.

9. Foods aren't good or bad. A healthy eating style is like a puzzle with many parts. Each part—or food—is different. Some foods may have more fat, sugar, or salt, while others may have more vitamins or fiber. There is a place for all these foods. What makes a diet good or bad is how foods fit together. Balancing your choices is important. Fit in a higher-fat food, like pepperoni pizza, at dinner by choosing lower-fat foods at other meals. And don't forget about moderation. If two pieces of pizza fill you up, you don't need a third.

10. Make healthy eating and physical activities fun. Take advantage of physical activities you and your friends enjoy doing together and eat the foods you like. Be adventurous—try new sports, games, and other activities as well as new foods. You'll grow stronger, play longer, and look and feel better! Set realistic goals—don't try changing too much at once.

Source: "10 Tips to healthy eating and physical activity for you," developed by the President's Council on Physical Fitness and Sports, a component of the U.S. Department of Health and Human Services (DHHS), February 1998; available online at http://www.fitness.gov/10tips.html. Reviewed by Dr. David A. Cooke, MD, Diplomate, American Board of Internal Medicine, in 2005.

When To Exercise

The hour just before the evening meal is a popular time for exercise. The late afternoon workout provides a welcome change of pace at the end of the school day and helps dissolve the day's worries and tensions.

Another popular time to work out is early morning, before the school day begins. Advocates of the early start say it makes them more alert and energetic in class.

Among the factors you should consider in developing your workout schedule are personal preference, school, job, availability of exercise facilities, and weather. It's important to schedule your workouts for a time when there is little chance that you will have to cancel or interrupt them because of other demands on your time.

You should not exercise strenuously during extremely hot, humid weather or within two hours after eating. Heat and/or digestion both make heavy demands on the circulatory system, and in combination with exercise, can be an overtaxing double load.

Part Seven

If You Need More Information

Chapter 41

Additional Reading About Eating Disorders

This chapter contains a list of resources that can help you find information related to eating disorders, nutrition, fitness, and other related topics. Although some resources are intended for all audiences, many are written specifically for teens.

Internet Resources

Anorexia Nervosa
A.D.A.M., Inc.
http://www.nlm.nih.gov/medlineplus/ency/article/000362.htm

BAM! Body and Mind
Centers for Disease Control and Prevention
http://www.bam.gov

Binge Eating Disorder
Loyola University Health System
http://www.luhs.org/health/topics/mentalhealth/edbinge.htm

Eating Disorders
Medline Plus
http://www.nlm.nih.gov/medlineplus/eatingdisorders.html

Eating Disorders: Facts for Teens
American Academy of Family Physicians
http://familydoctor.org/277.xml

4 Girls Health
http://www.4girls.gov

Girl Power!
http://www.girlpower.gov

Healthfinder®
http://www.healthfinder.gov

Helpguide
http://www.helpguide.org

Nutrition.gov
http://www.nutrition.gov

Soy Unica! Soy Latina!
http://www.soyunica.org

TeensHealth.org
http://www.teenshealth.org

Books

The Athletic Woman's Survival Guide
Carol L. Otis and Roger Goldingay
Human Kinetics Publishers, Champaign, IL
August 2000
ISBN: 0736001212

Anorexia Nervosa: A Guide to Recovery
Lindsey Hall and Monika Ostroff
Gurze Books, Carlsbad, CA
October 1998
ISBN: 0936077328

Big Fat Lies: The Truth about Your Weight and Your Health
Glenn A. Gaesser and Steven N. Blair
Shelter Publications, Inc., Bolinas, CA
May 2002
ISBN: 0936077425

Bodylove: Learning to Like Our Looks and Ourselves
Rita Freedman
Shelter Publications, Inc., Bolinas, CA
June 2002
ISBN: 0936077433

Bulimia: A Guide to Recovery
Lindsey Hall and Leigh Cohn
Gurze Books, Carlsbad, CA
April 1999
ISBN: 093607731X

Bulimia Nervosa
James Mitchell
University of Minnesota Press, Minneapolis, MN
November 1989
ISBN: 0816616264

Making Weight: Healing Men's Conflicts with Food, Weight, Shape, and Appearance
Arnold Andersen, Leigh Cohn, Tom Holbrook
Gurze Books, Carlsbad, CA
April 2000
ISBN: 0936077352

Males with Eating Disorder
Arnold E. Andersen (Ed.)
Taylor & Francis, Inc.
January 1991
ISBN: 0876305567

Over It: A Teen's Guide to Getting Beyond Obsessions with Food and Weight
Carol Emery Normandi and Laurelee Roark
New World Library
March 2001
ISBN: 1577311485

Overcoming Binge Eating
Christopher G. Fairburn
Guilford Publications, Inc., New York, NY
March 1995
ISBN: 0898621798

Overcoming Night Eating Syndrome: A Step-by-Step Guide to Breaking the Cycle
Kelly C. Allison, Albert J. Stunkard, Sara L. Their
New Harbinger Publications, Oakland, CA
April 2004
ISBN: 1572243279

Surviving an Eating Disorder: New Perspectives and Strategies for Family and Friends
Judith Brisman and Margot Weinshel
HarperCollins Publishers
April 1988
ISBN: 006015859X

Transforming Body Image: Learning to Love the Body You Have
Marcia G. Hutchinson
The Crossing Press, Inc.
August 1985
ISBN: 0895941724

Articles

"Body Image: How do you see yourself? How you feel about your body has a big impact on your health. Learn to like the person you see in the mirror!" by Kathiann M. Kowalski, in *Current Health 2*, March 2003, Page 6.

"Dentists Often See First Signs of Eating Disorders," in *Nutrition Health Review*, Summer 2003, Page 5.

"Eating Disorders in Teenage Vegetarians: Cause for Concern?" by Reed Mangels, in *Vegetarian Journal*, May-June 2002, Page 25.

"Experts: Male Eating Disorders Climbing," by Michael Hill, Associated Press Writer, in *Tucson Citizen*, May 12, 2004.

"The Female Triad," by Lola Ramos and Gregory L. Welch, in *American Fitness*, May-June 2004, Page 56.

"Food for Thought," by Lisa Thaler, in *Dance Magazine*, September 2003, Page S9.

"Image Is Everything," in *American Demographics*, March 1, 2003.

"Mirror Mirror in Your Head: Your mental picture of your body can have a direct effect on your self-esteem and your behavior," by Melissa Abramovitz, in *Current Health 2*, February 2002, Page 26.

"A New Eating Disorder?" by Erik Strand, in *Psychology Today*, September-October 2004, Page 16.

"On the Teen Scene: Eating disorders require medical attention," in *FDA Consumer*, March 1992.

"Reality Check: Looking at real women's bodies will help you learn to love yours," by Geneen Roth, in *Prevention*, August 2004, Page 83.

"Stop That Treadmill: Is compulsive exercising on the rise?" by Brenda Goodman, in *Psychology Today*, May-June 2004, Page 15.

"Teenage Wasteland: Why are girls starving?" by Patti Wigington, in *Pediatrics for Parents*, March 2004, Page 4.

"TV's Big Lie: They're some of your favorite television stars, but these actresses' bodies are sending teens the wrong message about how young women are supposed to look," by Nancy Fitzgerald, in *Scholastic Choices*, April 2002, Page 6.

"Underweight People Work to Put on Pounds," by Alicia Chang, Associated Press Writer, in *Winston-Salem Journal*, September 20, 2004.

"What You Need to Know About Fad Diets: Find out the promises and pitfalls of some common fad diets," in *Current Health 2*, September 2003, Page 16.

"Young Woman with Cardiac Complications of Anorexia Nervosa," by Mori J. Krantz and Philip S. Mehler, in *Consultant*, August 2003, Page 1095.

Chapter 42

Directory Of Eating Disorder Organizations

For more information about eating disorders and other related topics, contact the following organizations.

Information About Eating Disorders

Academy for Eating Disorders (AED)
60 Revere Drive, Suite 500
Northbrook, IL 60062
Phone: 847-498-4274
Fax: 847-480-9282
Website: http://www.aedweb.org
E-Mail: info@aedweb.org

American Anorexia/Bulimia Association, Inc.
1165 West 46th Street, Suite 1108
New York, NY 10036
Phone: 212-575-6200
Website: http://www.aabainc.org

Anorexia Nervosa and Related Eating Disorders, Inc. (ANRED)
National Eating Disorder Association (NEDA)
P.O. Box 5102
Eugene, OR 97405
Toll Free: 800-931-2237
Phone: 541-344-1144
Website: http://www.anred.com

Information in this chapter was compiled from many sources deemed accurate. All contact information was verified and updated in February 2005.

Eating Disorders Coalition

611 Pennsylvania Avenue SE, #423
Washington, DC 20003-4303
Phone: 202-543-9570
Website: http://
www.eatingdisorderscoalition.org

Eating Disorder Information and Referral Center

2923 Sandy Pointe, Suite 6
Del Mar, CA 92014-2052
Toll Free: 800-843-7274
Phone: 858-792-7469
Fax: 775-261-9364
Website: http://
www.EDreferal.com
E-Mail: edreferral@aol.com

Harvard Eating Disorders Center (HEDC)

55 Fruit Street
YAW 6900
Boston, MA 02114
Phone: 617-726-8470
Website: http://www.hedc.org
E-Mail: info@hedc.org

National Association of Anorexia Nervosa and Associated Disorders

P.O. Box 7
Highland Park, IL 60035
Phone: 847-831-3438
Fax: 847-433-4632
Website: http://www.anad.org
E-Mail: anad20@aol.com

National Center for Overcoming Overeating (NCOO)

P.O. Box 1257
Old Chelsea Station
New York, NY 10113-0920
Phone: 212-875-0442
Website: http://
www.overcomingovereating.com
E-Mail: webmaster
@overcomingovereating.com

National Eating Disorders Association (NEDA)

603 Stewart St., Suite 803
Seattle, WA 98101
Referral Hotline: 800-931-2237
Phone: 206-382-3587
Website: http://
www.nationaleatingdisorders.org
E-Mail:
info@NationalEatingDisorders.org

National Eating Disorders Screening Program (NEDSP)

Screening for Mental Health, Inc.
One Washington St., Suite 304
Wellesley Hills, MA 02181
Phone: 781-239-0071
Fax: 781-431-7447
Website: http://
www.mentalhealthscreening.org/
events/nedsp
E-Mail:
smhinfo@mentalhealthscreening.org

National Women's Health Information Center

8550 Arlington Blvd., Suite 300
Fairfax, VA 22031
Toll Free: 800-994-WOMAN
(800-994-9662)
http://www.4woman.gov

National Women's Health Network

514 10th Street NW, Suite 400
Washington, DC 20004
Phone: 202-347-1140
Health Information: 202-628-7814
Fax: 202-347-1168
Website: http://
www.womenshealthnetwork.org
E-Mail: nwhn@nwhn.org

Overeaters Anonymous

P.O. Box 44020
Rio Rancho, NM 87174-4020
Phone: 505-891-2664
Fax: 505-891-4320
Website: http://
www.overeatersanonymous.org
E-Mail: info@oa.org

Renfrew Center

475 Spring Lane
Philadelphia, PA 19128
Toll Free 1-800-RENFREW
Phone: 877-367-3383
Fax: 215-482-2695
Website: http://
www.renfrewcenter.com

Information About Nutrition

American Heart Association

National Center
7272 Greenville Ave.
Dallas, TX 75231-4596
Toll-Free: 800-AHA-USA-1
Phone: 214-373-6300
Website: http://www.amhrt.org

American Dietetic Association

120 South Riverside Plaza, Suite 2000
Chicago, IL 60606-6995
Toll Free: 1-800-877-1600
Phone: 312-899-0040 x5000
Website: http://www.eatright.org

American Institute of Nutrition

American Society for Clinical
Nutrition, Inc.
9650 Rockville Pike, Suite 4500
Bethesda, MD 20814-3998
Phone: 301-530-7050
Fax: 301-634-7892
Website: http://www.asns.org
E-Mail: sec@asns.org

Center for Nutrition Policy and Promotion

3101 Park Center Drive, Room 1034
Alexandria, VA 22302-1594
Phone: 703-305-7600
Fax: 703-305-3400
Website: http://www.usda.gov/cnpp

Children's Nutrition Research Center
Public Affairs Office
1100 Bates St.
Houston, TX 77030
Phone: 713-798-6767
Fax: 713-798-7098
Website: http://www.bcm.tmc.edu/cnrc
E-Mail: cnrc@bcm.tmc.edu

Food and Nutrition Information Center
National Agricultural Library/ARS/USDA
10301 Baltimore Avenue, Room 304
Beltsville, MD 20705-2351
Phone: 301-504-5755
Fax: 301-504-6110
Website: http://nal.usda.gov/fnic

Food Marketing Institute
655 15th Street, NW
Washington, DC 20005
Phone: 202-452-8444
Fax 202-429-4519
Website: http://www.fmi.org
E-Mail: fmi@fmi.org

International Food Information Council
1100 Connecticut Avenue, NW, Suite 430
Washington, DC 20036
Phone: 202-296-6540
Fax: 202-296-6547
Website: http://www.ific.org
E-Mail: foodinfo@ific.org

Iowa State University, University Extension
Food Science and Human Nutrition Extension, 2312 Food Sciences Bldg.
Iowa State University
Phone: 515-294-3011
Fax: 515-294-8181
Ames, IA 50011-1120
Website: http://www.extension.iastate.edu/nutrition

Kellogg's Nutrition University
P.O. Box CAMB
Battle Creek, MI 49016-1986
Toll Free: 800-962-1413
Website: http://www.kelloggsnu.com

Nutrition Information Center
NY Hospital-Cornell Medical Center
Memorial Sloan-Kettering Cancer Center, 515 East 71st Street
New York, NY 10021
Toll Free: 888-675-7722
Phone: 212-639-2000
Website: http://www.mskcc.org

Nutrition Information and Resource Center
Department of Food Science
The Pennsylvania State University
8L Borland Lab
University Park, PA 16802
Phone: 814-865-9714
Website: http://nirc.cas.psu.edu/index.cfm
E-Mail: eat4health@psu.edu

U. S. Department of Agriculture (USDA)

1400 Independence Ave., SW
Washington, DC 20250
Phone: 202-720-2791
Website: http://www.usda.gov

U.S. Food and Drug Administration

Office of Consumer Affairs
Dept. of Health and Human Services
5600 Fishers Lane (HFE-88), Rm. 16-85
Rockville, MD 20857
Phone: 800-463-6332
Fax: 301-443-9767
Website: http://www.fda.gov

University of Minnesota

Department of Food Science and
Nutrition, Nutritionist's Tool Box
225 FScN, 1334 Eckles Avenue
Saint Paul, MN 55108
Phone: 612-624-1290
Fax: 612-625-5272
Website: http://www.fsci.umn.edu/
tools.htm

Weight Control Information Network

1 WIN Way
Bethesda, MD 20892-3665
Toll Free: 877-946-4627
Fax: 202-828-1028
Website: http://win.niddk.nih.gov/
index.htm
E-Mail: win@info.niddk.nih.gov

Information About Fitness

President's Council on Physical Fitness and Sports

Department W
200 Independence Ave., SW
Room 738-H
Washington, DC 20201-0004
Phone: 202-690-9000
Fax: 202-690-5211
http://www.fitness.gov

Shape Up America!

c/o WebFront Solutions
Corporation
15009 Native Dancer Road
N. Potomac, MD 20878
Phone: 240-631-6533
Fax: 240-632-1075
Website: http://www.shapeup.org
E-Mail: customer-
care@shapeup.org

Information About Mental Health

American Academy of Child and Adolescent Psychiatry

3615 Wisconsin Avenue, NW
Washington, DC 20016
Phone: 202-966-7300
Fax: 202-966-2891
Website: http://www.aacap.org

American Counseling Association

5999 Stevenson Ave.
Alexandria, VA 22304
Toll Free: 800-347-6647
TDD: 703-823-6862
Fax: 800-473-2329
Website: http://www.counseling.org

American Institute for Cognitive Therapy

136 E. 57th, Suite 1101
New York, NY 10022
Phone: 212-308-2440
Fax: 212-308-3099
Website: http://
www.cognitivetherapynyc.com

American Psychiatric Association

1000 Wilson Blvd., Suite 1825
Washington, DC 20009
Phone: 703-907-7300
Website: http://www.psych.org
E-Mail: apa@psych.org

American Psychiatric Nurses Association

1555 Wilson Blvd., Suite 602
Arlington, VA 22209
Phone: 703-243-2443
Fax: 703-243-3390
Website: http://www.apna.org
E-Mail: info@apna.org

American Psychological Association

750 First St., NE
Washington, DC 20002
Toll Free: 800-374-2721
Phone: 202-336-5500
Website: http://www.apa.org

Anxiety Disorders Association of America (ADAA)

8730 Georgia Ave., Suite 600
Silver Spring, MD 20910
Phone: 240-485-1001
Fax: 240-485-1035
Website: http://www.adaa.org
E-Mail: AnxDis@adaa.org

Association for Advancement of Behavior Therapy

305 Seventh Ave., 16th Floor
New York, NY 10001
Phone: 212-647-1890
Fax: 212-647-1865
Website: http://www.aabt.org

Body Image Program

Butler Hospital
345 Blackstone Blvd.
Providence, RI 02905
Toll Free: 888-4CARENE
Phone: 401-453-7900
Website: http://www.butler.org
E-Mail: info@butler.org

Depression and Bipolar Support Alliance
730 N. Franklin St., Suite 501
Chicago, IL 60610
Toll Free: 800-826-3632
Phone: 312-642-0049
Fax: 312-642-7243
Website: http://
wwww.dbsalliance.org

Depression and Related Disorders Association
2330 West Joppa Rd., Suite 100
Lutherville, MD 21093
Phone: 410-583-2919
Website: http://www.drada.org
E-Mail: drada@jhmi.edu

Emotions Anonymous
P.O. Box 4245
St. Paul, MN 55104-0245
Phone: 612-647-9712
Fax: 651-647-1593
Website: http://
www.emotionsanonymous.org
E-Mail:
info@EmotionsAnonymous.org

Mental Health Net
CMCH Systems
570 Metro Place North
Dublin, OH 43017
Phone: 614-764-0143
Fax: 614-764-0362
Website: http://
www.mentalhelp.net

National Foundation for Depressive Illness
American Society of
Clinical Psychopharmacology,
Inc.
P.O. Box 40395
Glen Oaks, NY 11004
Phone: 718-470-4007
Fax: 718-343-7729
Website: http://www.depression
.org

National Institute of Mental Health
6001 Executive Boulevard
Rm. 8184
MSC 9663
Rockville, MD 20892-9663
Toll Free 866-615-6464
Phone: 301-443-4513
TTY: 301-443-8431
Website: http://www.nimh.nih
.gov
E-Mail: nimhinfo@nih.gov

National Mental Health Association
2001 N. Beauregard Street
12th Floor
Alexandria, VA 22311
Toll Free: 800-969-6642
Phone: 703-684-7722
Fax: 703-684-5968
Website: http://www.nmha.org

National Mental Health Consumers' Self-Help Clearinghouse

1211 Chestnut Street
Suite 1207
Philadelphia, PA 19107
Toll Free: 800-533-4539
Phone: 215-751-1810
Fax: 215-636-6312
Website: http://
www.mhselfhelp.org
E-Mail: info@mhselfhelp.org

National Mental Health Information Center

P.O. Box 42557
Washington, DC 20015
Toll Free: 800-789-2647
Phone: 301-443-9006
TDD: 866-889-2647
Website: http://
www.mentalhealth.org

Screening for Mental Health (SMH)

One Washington Street
Suite 304
Wellesley, MA 02481-1706
Phone: 781-239-0071
Fax: 781-431-7447
Website: http://
www.mentalhealthscreening.org
E-Mail: smhinfo
@mentalhelathscreening.org

Helplines And Hotlines

Al-Anon/Alateen Hot Line

Toll Free: 800-344-2666

American Anorexia/Bulimia Association

Toll Free: 800-522-2230

Childhelp USA National Child Abuse Hot Line

Toll Free: 800-422-4453

Covenant House Nine-Line

Toll Free: 800-999-9999

Eating Disorder Awareness and Prevention

Toll Free: 800-931-2237

Hope Line Network

Toll Free: 800-SUICIDE (784-2433)

Kid Help

Toll Free: 800-543-7283

National Adolescent Suicide Hot Line

Toll Free: 800-621-4000

National Alliance For The Mentally Ill

Toll Free: 800-950-6264

National Foundation for Depressive Illness, Inc.

Toll Free: 800-239-1265

National Mental Health Association
Toll Free: 800-969-6642

National Suicide Hot Line
Toll Free: 888-248-2587

National Youth Crisis Hot Line
Toll Free: 800-HIT-HOME (448-4663)

Nationwide Crisis Hot Line
Toll Free: 800-333-4444

Rape, Abuse, And Incest National Network
Toll Free: 800-656-4673

SAFE (Self-Abuse Finally Ends)
Toll Free: 800-DONT-CUT (800-366-8288)

United Way Help Line
Toll Free: 800-233-HELP (800-233-4357)

Youth Crisis Hot Line
Toll Free: 800-448-4663

Index

Index

Page numbers that appear in *Italics* refer to illustrations. Page numbers that have a small 'n' after the page number refer to information shown as Notes at the beginning of each chapter. Page numbers that appear in **Bold** refer to information contained in boxes on that page (except Notes information at the beginning of each chapter).

A

AAFP *see* American Academy of Family Physicians
Academy for Eating Disorders (AED), contact information 313
acculturation
  American Indians 33
  Asian Americans 35–36
  Hispanics 39
action figures, described **43**
"Action Guide for Healthy Eating" (NCI) 249n
ADAA *see* Anxiety Disorders Association of America
A.D.A.M., Inc.
  eating disorders publication 15n, 57n, 85n, 103n, 193n, 207n
  Web site address 307
addictions
  described **4**
  substitutions **236–37**
AED *see* Academy for Eating Disorders
African Americans, eating disorders 29–32

age factor
  anorexia 15–16
  bulimia 15
Akron Children's Hospital, compulsive exercise publication 143n
Al-Anon/Alateen Hot Line, contact information 320
Alaska Natives
  body dissatisfaction 33
  eating disorders 32
alcohol abuse
  bulimia 105
  eating disorders 233
amenorrhea
  defined **138**
  described 49
  female athlete triad 142, 152
  see also menstruation
American Academy of Child and Adolescent Psychiatry, contact information 317
American Academy of Family Physicians (AAFP), Web site address 307
American Anorexia/Bulimia Association, Inc., contact information 313, 320

American Counseling Association, contact information 318
American Dietetic Association, contact information 315
American Heart Association, contact information 315
American Indians
  body dissatisfaction 33
  eating disorders 32
American Institute for Cognitive Therapy, contact information 318
American Institute of Nutrition, contact information 315
American Psychiatric Association, contact information 318
American Psychiatric Nurses Association, contact information 318
American Psychological Association, contact information 318
amygdala, described 50
anabolic-androgenic steroids *see* anabolic steroids
anabolic steroids
  defined **18, 138**
  eating disorders 136
  see also steroids
anemia
  anorexia 90
  defined **72, 88**
anorexia nervosa
  versus binge eating disorder 109–10
  birth problems 46–47
  bodily affects *82*
  versus bulimia 70
  causes 73–76, 79–80
  complications 85–90
  depression 23
  described 3, 6–7, 79
  diabetes 25
  diagnosis 59–60, 61, 80–81
  heredity 47
  infections 54–55
  males **74–75**
  obsessive compulsive disorder 22
  obsessive compulsive personality 20
  osteoporosis 224
  overview 69–77
  preventive measures **164**
  treatment 76–77, 199–205

Anorexia Nervosa and Related Eating Disorders, Inc. (ANRED)
  contact information 313
  publications
    laxative abuse 121n
    muscle dysmorphic disorder 143n
    night-eating syndrome 121n
"Anorexia: Signs, Symptoms, Causes, Effects, and Treatments" (Helpguide.org) 69n
ANRED *see* Anorexia Nervosa and Related Eating Disorders, Inc.
anti-anxiety agents, anorexia 204
antidepressants
  anorexia 77, 204, 216
  binge eating disorder 119
  bulimia 97, 215
  eating disorders 11
antipsychotics, anorexia 204
Anxiety Disorders Association of America (ADAA), contact information 318
asexual, defined **18**
Asian Americans
  body dissatisfaction 35
  eating disorders 34–36
  term, defined **34**
Association for Advancement of Behavior Therapy, contact information 318
asthma, defined **18**
athletes
  described **137**
  eating disorders 131–34
  eating disorders diagnosis 135–42
  excessive physical activity 24
  sports nutrition 265–73
  tips **156**
  weight control 42–43
  see also sports
"Athletes and Eating Disorders" (Powers; Johnson) 135n
avoidant personalities, eating disorders 18–20

B

BAM! Body and Mind, Web site address 307
basal, defined **240**

BED *see* binge eating disorder
behavior therapy, binge eating disorder 119
benign tumor, defined **126**
bigorexia *see* muscle dysmorphic disorder
binge eating disorder (BED)
 African Americans 29, 31, 32
 Asian Americans 36
 boys 43
 causes 112–13, 117–18
 described 3–4, 8–9
 diabetes 25
 diagnosis 113
 males **110–11**
 overview 107–15
 preventive measures **164**
 treatment 113–15, 119
binge-purge cycles, described 52–53
binge-purge syndrome *see* bulimia nervosa
bipolar disorder, defined **200, 240**
birth defects, eating disorders 241
bisexual, defined **18**
BMI *see* body mass index
body dissatisfaction, eating disorders 33, 35, 37, 136
body dysmorphic disorder
 defined **146**
 described 57
 eating disorders 23
body image
 African Americans 30
 American Indians 33
 Asian Americans 35
 boys 42
 compulsive exercise 145
 eating disorders 23
 getting help **172**
 Hispanics 37
 muscle dysmorphic disorder 146–48
 self-esteem 167–73
Body Image Program, contact information 318
body mass index (BMI)
 African Americans 30–31
 defined **31**
 overview 279–82
body size
 cultural differences 28, **28**, 38
 exercise 297
BodyWise Handbook (NWHIC) 27n, 41n

bone density test 226
bone marrow, defined **88**
borderline personalities, eating disorders 21
Bratman, Steven 121
bulimia nervosa
 versus anorexia 91–92
 versus binge eating disorder 109
 bodily affects *100*
 boys 43
 causes 101
 complications 94–96
 depression 23
 described 3, 7–8, 99
 diabetes 25
 diagnosis 57–59, 61, 92–93, 101–2
 long term health 104–5, 228
 males **94–95**
 obsessive compulsive disorder 22
 overview 91–97
 preventive measures **164**
 psychotherapy **208–9, 215**
 treatment 97, **102**, 196–98
"Bulimia: Signs and Symptoms, Effects and Treatments" (Helpguide.org) 91n
Butte, Nancy 246

C

calcium
 anorexia 7
 defined **18, 88, 200, 225, 240**
 sports nutrition 272–73
 vegetarianism 290
cancer
 binge eating disorder 119
 defined **126**
 healthy eating 257
carbohydrate loading, described 270
carbohydrates
 defined **54, 132, 296**
 described 268–69
carbs *see* carbohydrates
cardiac arrest, defined **132**
cardiac arrhythmia, defined **93**
cardiorespiratory endurance, described 296, 298

cartilage, defined **146**
Center for Nutrition Policy and
   Promotion, contact information 315
Centers for Disease Control and
   Prevention (CDC), healthy eating
   publication 249n
cerebral palsy, defined **240**
Cesarean section
   anorexia 84
   defined **81, 240**
Childhelp USA National Child Abuse
   Hot Line, contact information 320
Children's Nutrition Research Center,
   contact information 316
cholesterol, defined **88, 146, 200**
clothing, exercise 301
coaches
   eating disorders **140–41**, 142
   female athlete triad 49
cognitive behavioral therapy
   binge eating disorder 119
   bulimia 197
   eating disorders 11, 207–9
comorbidity
   defined **235**
   described **234**
"Compulsive Exercise" (Akron Children's
   Hospital) 143n
compulsive exercise, overview 143–48
compulsive overeating *see* binge eating
   disorder
constipation, defined **72, 88, 93, 126**
Cooke, David A. 293n
coronary, defined **240**
counselors
   anorexia 84
   described **210–11**
   night-eating syndrome **123**
   see also therapy
Covenant House Nine-Line, contact
   information 320
C-section *see* Cesarean section
cultural groups, eating disorders 27–39,
   43
cultural pressure
   anorexia 80
   eating disorders 47–50
cyproheptadine 203, 216

D

day hospital care, described **195**
death rates
   anorexia nervosa **71**
   eating disorders *86*
dehydration
   laxative abuse 126
   sports nutrition 267
dehydroepiandrosterone (DHEA) 86, 89, 205
dental problems
   bulimia 96, 103
   eating disorders 219–21
Department of Health and Human
   Services (DHHS) *see* US Department
   of Health and Human Services
depression
   binge eating disorder 115, 118
   body image **172**
   bulimia 8
   eating disorders 23
   Hispanics 38
   muscle dysmorphic disorder 147
   night-eating syndrome **122**
   pregnancy 244
   tryptophan 52
Depression and Bipolar Support Alliance,
   contact information 319
Depression and Related Disorders
   Association, contact information 319
DHHS *see* US Department of Health
   and Human Services
diabetes mellitus
   anorexia 90
   defined **19, 88, 112, 200, 240, 281**
   described **228**
   eating disorders 25, 227–32, **232**
   treatment 231–33
diaries, physical fitness **294**
diet and nutrition
   carbohydrates 60
   food variety **291**
   osteoporosis 50, 226
   weight loss 284
   see also healthy eating; sports nutrition
dieting
   African Americans 30
   American Indians 32
   athletes 133

dieting, continued
  binge eating disorder 109, 118
  eating disorders 161–62
  Hispanics 39
  weight loss 285
dietitians
  anorexia 77
  described **211**
  night-eating syndrome **123**
disordered eating
  described 9
  female athlete triad 152
  see also eating disorders
diuretics
  African Americans 32
  defined **18, 31, 93**
  described 7
  see also purging
dysmorphia, eating disorders 23–24, 41,
  57, **146,** 146–48

E

early detection
  anorexia 77
  boys, eating disorders 43
  eating disorders 29, 37
early puberty, eating disorders 26
Eating Disorder Awareness and
  Prevention, contact information 320
eating disorder not otherwise
  specified (EDNOS), described 9
eating disorders
  athletes 131–42
  diabetes mellitus 227–32, **232**
  diagnosis 57–62
  long term health 228
  overview 3–13
  pregnancy 239–46
  preventive measures **163–64**
  risk reduction strategies 161–65
  statistics 63–65
  substance abuse 233–37, **234**
  symptoms 9–11
  treatment 11, 193–205
  treatment overview **194–95**
"Eating Disorders" (South Carolina
  Department of Mental Health) 63n

"Eating Disorders: Anorexia and Bulimia"
  (A.D.A.M., Inc.) 15n, 57n, 85n, 103n,
  193n, 207n
Eating Disorders Coalition, contact
  information 314
"Eating Disorders: Helping a Friend"
  (University of Wisconsin - Eau Claire
  Counseling Services) 181n
Eating Disorders Information and Referral
  Center, contact information 314
eating habits
  binge eating disorder 113
  described 3
EDNOS *see* eating disorder not otherwise
  specified
electrocardiogram, defined **60**
electrolytes
  bulimia 8, 95
  defined **60, 93, 138, 200**
  described 267–68
  laxative abuse 125
emotional concerns
  anorexia 7, 71–72, 80
  binge eating disorder 109, 112, 118
  eating disorders 138
  exercise tips **169**
  night-eating syndrome **122**
emotional disorders, eating disorders 22–
  23
Emotions Anonymous, contact
  information 319
endocrine disorder, defined **72**
enema abuse, described 124–28
enzymes, defined **88**
Epstein Barr virus 55
esophagus
  bulimia 96, 104
  defined **93**
  purging 8
estrogen
  anorexia 86
  defined **88, 138, 155, 200, 225**
  female athlete triad 142
ethnic factors, eating disorders 16–17,
  32–39, **43,** 64–65, 171
excessive physical activity
  described 24
  eating disorders 49–50
  see also compulsive exercise

exercise
  anorexia 203–4, 225
  anorexia nervosa **83**
  eating disorders 136
  healthy eating 252
  overview 293–304
  physical fitness **294**
  self-esteem 178
  tips **169**
  see also compulsive exercise

F

family issues
  anorexia 80
  eating disorders 45–47, 170–71
  weight control **284**
  see also parents
family therapy
  anorexia 77, 84, 204
  eating disorders 11, 189–91, 212–13
FDA *see* US Food and Drug
  Administration
female athlete triad
  described 49–50, 149–51
  overview 139–42, 149–58
  recognition **153**
  sports participation 153–54
  symptoms 154–55
  treatment 155–57
fertility, anorexia 87–89
fetus, defined **241**
financial considerations
  therapy 188
  vegetarianism 287–88
Fitness Fundamentals: Guidelines for Per-
  sonal Exercise Programs (DHHS) 293n
fitness program, overview 293–304
"5 A Day Fruit and Vegetable Quick Tips"
  (CDC) 249n
fluoxetine 197, 215
fluvoxamine 197
Food and Drug Administration (FDA) *see*
  US Food and Drug Administration
Food and Nutrition Information Center,
  contact information 316
Food Marketing Institute, contact
  information 316

4 Girls Health, Web site address 308
"Frequently Asked Questions about
  Anorexia Nervosa" (NWHIC) 79n
"Frequently Asked Questions about
  Binge Eating Disorder" (NWHIC)
  117n
"Frequently Asked Questions about
  Bulimia Nervosa" (NWHIC) 99n
"Frequently Asked Questions about
  Eating Disorders" (NWHIC) 3n
friends
  binge eaters **114**
  body image 165
  bulimia 96–97, **184**
  eating disorders 12–13, 181–85, **182–83**
  female athlete triad 157–58

G

gastrointestinal problems
  anorexia 90
  laxative abuse 125–27
gender factor
  anorexia nervosa **71**
  athletes 133, 135–36
  bulimia **92**
  eating disorders 5, 16
  excessive physical activity 24
  muscle dysmorphic disorder 147
  puberty 168–69
  vegetarianism 24–25
geriatric, defined **225**
gestational diabetes, described **230**
Girl Power!, Web site address 308
glucocorticoid, defined **225**
glucose, defined **200**
group therapy, eating disorders 11
guided imagery, bulimia 198

H

Harvard Eating Disorders Center
  (HEDC), contact information 314
health care providers
  described **210–11**
  eating disorders 187–91
  questions **189, 190**

Healthfinder, Web site address 308
healthy eating
    food colors 252
    overview 249–63
    sports nutrition 266, 268, 272
    student athletes 270
    tips 250, 257, 262–63, 302–3
    weight control 286
    see also diet and nutrition; sports
        nutrition
heart arrhythmia, defined 72
heart disease
    anorexia 87
    binge eating disorder 119
    bulimia 95
HEDC see Harvard Eating Disorders
    Center
Helpguide, Web site address 308
Helpguide.org, publications
    anorexia 69n
    bulimia 91n
heredity
    addictions 46
    anorexia 80
    binge eating disorders 112
    body mass index 282
    eating disorders 6, 47
    obesity 46
high blood pressure see hypertension
Hispanics
    body dissatisfaction 37
    eating disorders 32, 36–39
    term, defined 37
histrionic personality, defined 18
homosexuality
    defined 18
    self-esteem 42
Hope Line Network, contact information
    320
hormones
    anorexia 85–86
    defined 54, 81, 146, 155, 225, 241
    eating disorders 50–52
    stress 50–51
    see also anabolic steroids
hospitalizations
    bulimia 197
    eating disorders 191
    family therapy 212

HPA see hypothalamic-pituitary-adrenal
    axis
hypertension (high blood pressure)
    binge eating disorder 119
    defined 112, 241, 281
hypnosis, bulimia 198
hypochondria, defined 18
hypochondriasis, defined 18
hypoglycemia, anorexia 90
hypomania, defined 139
hypothalamic-pituitary-adrenal axis (HPA)
    50–51
hypothalamus
    binge eating disorders 112
    described 50

I

ideal body weight, eating habits 3
Indian Adolescent Health Study 33, 34
infections, anorexia 54–55
infertility, defined 88
initial assessment, described 194
injuries, proper care 145
inositol 198
inpatient treatment, described 195
insulin, defined 241
insurance coverage, therapy 188
intelligence quotient (IQ)
    defined 19, 241
    eating disorders 19
International Food Information Council,
    contact information 316
interpersonal therapy, eating disorders
    210–11
intravenous feeding, anorexia 203
Iowa State University, contact information
    316
ipecac 106
IQ see intelligence quotient
iron
    sports nutrition 271–72
    vegetarianism 289–90

J

Johnson, Craig 135n

K

Kater, Kathy 161n
Kellogg's Nutrition University, contact
    information 316
Kid Help, contact information 320

L

lacto-ovo vegetarian, described 288
Latinas
    eating disorders 36–39
    term, defined 37
    see also Hispanics
laxative abuse, described 124–28
laxatives
    African Americans 32
    defined 12, 31, 93, 112, 132, 155
    see also purging
"Laxatives and Enemas: Not the Way
    to Go" (Anorexia Nervosa and Related
    Eating Disorders, Inc.) 121n
leptin, described 52
ligaments, defined 146, 296
light therapy, bulimia 198
low blood pressure, defined 72, 200
Loyola University Health System, Web site
    address 307
Luvox (fluvoxamine) 197

M

macrobiotic diet, defined 288
males
    anorexia nervosa 74–75
    binge eating disorder (BED) 110–11
    bulimia nervosa 94–95
    eating disorders 41–43
    see also gender factor
malnutrition, defined 54, 200, 225, 241
manic depression, defined 242
McCoy, Tom 150
media messages
    African Americans 30
    critical viewing 176–77
    eating disorders 5, 133, 162–65, 170

media messages, continued
    Hispanics 37
    obesity 48
medical practitioners, described 211
medications
    anorexia 77, 204–5
    anorexia nervosa 216
    binge eating disorder 119
    bulimia 106, 197–98
    eating disorders 11, 196, 215–16
    osteoporosis 226
Medline Plus, Web site address 307
menopause, defined 225
menstrual, defined 60, 81
menstruation, bulimia 104
    see also amenorrhea
Mental Health Net, contact information
    319
mental illnesses, bulimia 8
Meridia (sibutramine) 198
metabolic disorder, defined 72
metabolism
    African Americans 30–31
    defined 31, 54, 112, 132, 201, 242
military personnel, excessive physical
    activity 24
miscarriage
    defined 12, 81, 242
    eating disorders 240
mononucleosis, defined 54
muscle atrophy, anorexia nervosa 83
muscle dysmorphic disorder
    boys 41
    overview 146–48
    wrestlers 24
"Muscle Dysmorphic Disorder (Bigorexia)"
    (Anorexia Nervosa and Related Eating
    Disorders, Inc.) 143n
muscular endurance, described 296–97, 298
muscular strength, described 296, 297

N

narcissism
    defined 19
    eating disorders 21
National Adolescent Suicide Hot Line,
    contact information 320

National Alliance for The Mentally Ill, contact information 320
National Association of Anorexia Nervosa and Associated Disorders, contact information 314
National Ballet School Program **154**
National Cancer Institute (NCI), healthy eating publication 249n
National Center for Overcoming Overeating (NCOO), contact information 314
National Eating Disorders Association (NEDA), contact information 314
National Eating Disorders Screening Program (NEDSP), contact information 314
National Foundation for Depressive Illness, contact information 319, 320
National Institute of Mental Health (NIMH), contact information 319
National Institutes of Health (NIH), osteoporosis publication 223n
National Mental Health Association (NMHA), contact information 319, 321
National Mental Health Consumers' Self-Help Clearinghouse, contact information 320
National Mental Health Information Center, contact information 320
National Suicide Hot Line, contact information 321
National Women's Health Information Center (NWHIC)
contact information 315
publications
anorexia nervosa 79n
binge eating disorder 117n
body handbook 27n, 41n
bulimia nervosa 99n
eating disorders 3n
National Women's Health Network, contact information 315
National Youth Crisis Hot Line, contact information 321
Nationwide Crisis Hot Line, contact information 321
Native Americans *see* Alaska Natives; American Indians

NCOO *see* National Center for Overcoming Overeating
NEDA *see* National Eating Disorders Association
NEDSP *see* National Eating Disorders Screening Program
neurological, defined **242**
neurological problems, anorexia 89–90
neurotransmitters, eating disorders 51–52
"Night-Eating Syndrome" (Anorexia Nervosa and Related Eating Disorders, Inc.) 121n
night-eating syndrome, described 122–24
NIH *see* National Institutes of Health
NIMH *see* National Institute of Mental Health
NMHA *see* National Mental Health Association
nutrients, defined **72, 112, 155, 201, 242, 276, 296**
nutrition counseling
anorexia 199, 202–3, 225
bulimia 197
eating disorders 11
Nutrition.gov, Web site address 308
Nutrition Information and Resource Center, contact information 316
Nutrition Information Center, contact information 316
NWHIC *see* National Women's Health Information Center

O

obesity
African Americans 30–31
American Indians 33
Asian Americans 36
binge eating disorder 119
cultural pressures 47–48
heredity 46
Hispanics 38–39
obsessive compulsive disorder, bulimia 8
obsessive compulsive personality, eating disorders 20
olanzapine 204, 216
ondansetron 198
organ failure, anorexia 90

"Orthorexia Nervosa" (Palo Alto Medical Foundation) 121n
orthorexia nervosa, described 121–22
osteopenia 89
osteoporosis
  anorexia 7, 89
  defined **42, 139, 146**
  described 49
  eating disorders 223–26
  female athlete triad 139, 152–53
  males 42
outpatient treatment, described **194–95**
Overeaters Anonymous, contact information 315
overeating, stress **48**
  see also binge eating disorder
overweight
  African Americans 30–31, 32
  American Indians 33
  binge eating disorder 8
  body mass index 280–81
  boys 43
  described **21**
  see also obesity
ovulate, defined **81**

P

Pacific Islanders
  eating disorders 34, 36
  term, defined **34**
Palo Alto Medical Foundation, orthorexia nervosa publication 121n
pancytopenia 90
PANDAS *see* pediatric autoimmune neuropsychiatric disorders associated with streptococcus
panic disorder, eating disorders 22
parents
  anorexia 45–46
  eating disorder diagnosis 60–61
  eating disorders **212–13**, 244–45
  see also family issues
pediatric, defined **225**
pediatric autoimmune neuropsychiatric disorders associated with streptococcus (PANDAS) 55
percentile, described 280

perfectionism
  anorexia 85
  Asian Americans 35
  eating disorders 138
  self-esteem 179
Periactin (cyproheptadine) 203
pernicious anemia, anorexia 90
personality disorders, eating disorders 17–21
pesci-vegetarian, described 288
phobias, eating disorders 22
physical activity
  excessive 24
  healthy eating 252
  overview 293–304
physical fitness
  described **298**
  tips **302–3**
phytochemicals, defined **258**
pituitary gland, described 50
postmenopausal, defined **201, 225**
postpartum depression, defined **242**
post-traumatic stress disorder (PTSD), eating disorders 22–23
potassium
  bulimia **92**, 103
  defined **104, 201**
  purging 8
Powers, Pauline S. 135n
pregnancy
  anorexia 84
  bulimia 102, 105
  eating disorders 12, 239–46
prenatal, defined **242**
President's Council on Physical Fitness and Sports
  contact information 317
  sports nutrition publication 265n
progestin, defined **201**
prostate, defined **201**
protein
  defined **60, 296**
  sports nutrition 271
  vegetarianism 290
Prozac (fluoxetine) 197, 215
psychiatrists
  described **210**
  eating disorders 187–88
psychological effects, anorexia 86–87
psychologists, described **210**

psychotherapy
  binge eating disorder 119
  bulimia 215, **215**
  eating disorders 11, 196, 207–13
PTSD *see* post-traumatic stress disorder
puberty
  defined **54, 170**
  eating disorders 26
  self-esteem 168–69
  weight gain 276
purging
  African Americans 29
  depression 52–53
  described 7
  Hispanics 39

Q

"Questions Most Frequently Asked About
  Sports Nutrition" (DHHS) 265n

R

racial factor, eating disorders 27–32, 64–65,
  171
Rape, Abuse, And Incest National Network, contact information 321
Renfrew Center, contact information 315
reproductive hormones
  anorexia 86
  eating disorders 52
residential care, described **195**
retinopathy, anorexia 90
Rigby, Cathy **150–51**
Risperdal (risperidone) 216
risperidone 216

S

SAFE (Self-Abuse Finally Ends), contact
  information 321
saving face, described 35
schizophrenia, defined **201**
SCOFF questionnaire, described **58**
Screening for Mental Health (SMH),
  contact information 320

selective serotonin reuptake inhibitors
  (SSRI)
  anorexia 204
  bulimia 197
  eating disorders 11
self-esteem
  body image 167–73
  boys 41
  compulsive exercise 145
  described **179**
  eating disorders 6, 20
  getting help **172**
  Hispanics 38
  improvement 175–79
semi-vegetarian, described 288
serotonin 6, 52, 112
sertraline 197, 204
serving sizes, described **254, 261**
sexual abuse, eating disorders 46
Shape Up America!, contact information 317
sibutramine 198
SMH *see* Screening for Mental Health
social environment, eating disorders 6
social factors, eating disorders **51**
social workers, described **211**
socioeconomic factors, eating disorders 17,
  30, 37
South Carolina Department of Mental
  Health, eating disorders publication 63n
Soy Unica! Soy Latina!, Web site address 308
sports, eating disorders 6, 131–34, 135
  see also athletes
sports nutrition, overview 265–73
SSRI *see* selective serotonin reuptake
  inhibitors
starvation, anorexia 77
statistics
  anorexia 85
  anorexia nervosa **71**
  athletes, eating disorders 131–32
  binge eating disorder 111–12
  bulimia 103
  eating disorders 63–65, 135–36, 219
  night-eating syndrome 123
steroids
  boys 41
  defined **42, 139, 147**
  see also anabolic steroids; hormones
streptococcal infections, anorexia 54–55

stress
  anorexia 80
  binge eating disorder 108
  eating **48**
  eating disorders 6
  hormonal problems 50
substance abuse
  American Indians 34
  bulimia 8, 105–6
  eating disorders 233–37, **234**
suicide, anorexia 86–87
supplements
  anorexia 205
  sports nutrition 271–72
  vegetarianism 289–90
support groups
  anorexia 77, 84
  binge eating disorder 119
  bulimia **184**, 196

T

talk therapy *see* psychotherapy
TeensHealth.org, Web site address 308
tendons, defined **147**, **296**
testosterone
  anorexia 89
  defined **88**, **225**
  steroids **42**
tests
  bone density 226
  eating disorders **58**, 62
  intelligence quotient **19**, **241**
therapy
  body image **172**
  compulsive exercise 145
  eating disorders 187–91, 207–13
  laxative abuse 128
  unrealistic expectations 196
"Things to Think About Regarding
  Treatment" (University of Minnesota)
  187n
thyroid, defined **54**, **88**, **139**, **201**
"Tipping the Scales in Your Favor" (CDC)
  249n
"Tips for Developing a Healthy Body
  Image" (Kater) 161n
tobacco use, eating disorders 233–37

topiramate 119
treatment teams
  anorexia 202
  eating disorders 11, **140–41**
triglycerides, defined **243**
tryptophan 52
tubal feeding, anorexia 203
type 1 diabetes mellitus
  anorexia 90
  defined **19**, **88**
  described **230**
type 2 diabetes mellitus
  binge eating disorder 119
  defined **19**
  described **230**

U

unipolar, defined **243**
United Way Help Line, contact
  information 321
University of Minnesota
  contact information 317
  eating disorders treatment publication
    187n
University of Wisconsin, helping friends
  with eating disorders publication 181n
USDA *see* US Department of Agriculture
US Department of Agriculture (USDA),
  contact information 317
US Department of Health and Human
  Services (DHHS), publications
  fitness guidelines 293n
  sports nutrition 265n
US Food and Drug Administration (FDA),
  contact information 317

V

vegan, described 288
vegetarianism
  eating disorders 24–25
  overview 287–92
vitamin B12
  anorexia 90
  vegetarianism 290
vitamin D, vegetarianism 290

vomiting
  African Americans 32
  treatment 198
  see also purging

W

walking, laxative abuse 127–28
water pills *see* diuretics
Weight Control Information Network,
  contact information 317
weight gain
  anorexia 202–3
  binge eating disorder 108
  exercise 300–301
  overview 275–77
weight loss
  binge eating disorder **119**
  bulimia **92**
  exercise 300–301
  laxative abuse 125
  safety concerns 283–86
  wrestlers 131, 133–34

weight obsession, described **10**
"What People with Anorexia Nervosa
  Need to Know About Osteoporosis"
  (NIH) 223n
whole grain, described **256**
workout schedule, described 297–98
wrestlers
  muscle dysphoria 24
  weight loss 131, 133–34

Y

Youth Crisis Hot Line, contact
  information 321

Z

zinc
  anorexia 203
  vegetarianism 290
Zoloft (sertraline) **102**, 197, 204
Zyprexa (olanzapine) 204, 216